THE INTREPID NEW YORKER

THE INTREPID NEW YORKER

A Guide to
Turning New York
into a Manageable
Small Town

KATHY MAYER BRADDOCK
& TORY BAKER MASTERS

VILLARD BOOKS

NEW YORK

1 9 9 2

Library of Congress Cataloging-in-Publication Data
Braddock, Kathy Mayer.
    The intrepid New Yorker: how to turn New York City into a manageable small town/ Kathy Mayer Braddock and Tory Baker Masters.
—1st ed.
      p.   cm.
    Includes index.
    ISBN 0-679-73758-8
    1. New York (N.Y.)—Handbooks, manuals, etc.   I. Masters, Tory Baker.   II. Title.
F128.18.B7   1992
974.7′1—dc20   91-42463

Manufactured in the United States of America

9   8   7   6   5   4   3   2

First Edition

Design by Robert Bull Design

DEDICATION

To Philip, Charlie, and Sam

ACKNOWLEDGMENTS

Thanks go first to the many New Yorkers who work hard to make this city a better place to live and who opened their doors wide to us to help us with our research; thanks to a very dedicated group of professionals at Villard Books without whom, we discovered, a book could not be born. Thanks especially to Peter Gethers, who believed in this book, to our editor, Stephanie Long, and to organizational wiz Gail Bradney, who worked tirelessly to make a mountain of information as user-friendly as possible. Thanks to our husbands who put up with a lot in the name of the "creative process": Howie Masters, who, very early in the mornings, would get handed a cup of coffee and pages of the book to edit while commuting on the train; and John Braddock, for ten years of financial planning and hands-on support in the development of The Intrepid New Yorker Company.

CONTENTS

INTRODUCTION

CAN YOU TELL the difference between the City's "real" deals and the "raw" deals? Has New York City become more threatening than challenging? Is a *good* public school in New York City a contradiction in terms? Ten years ago, The Intrepid New Yorker Company was launched in response to what we perceived to be an ever-growing frustration on the part of even the most tenacious New Yorkers to cope with big city life. We are the number one personal service business in New York City. We save our clients money, time, and sanity. As project expeditors and problem solvers, we help our clients unsnag disputes with services with whom they are unhappy; link them up with top-notch services they can count on; supervise complex jobs such as home renovations; sleuth out New York's best buys; unravel bureaucratic red tape; offer practical advice and resources on everything from affordable, quality child care to skilled realtors ... and much more.

By helping our clients, we developed "tricks" to thriving in this city ... such as ways to do food-staples shopping once a month at half the price; ways to double one's apartment storage space; ways to deal swiftly with city bureaucracies, from finding good public schools to protesting a parking ticket; ways to get consistently good attentive service from local merchants; ways for consumers to spot the "real" deals; ways to sell an apartment in a soft market; ways to work with a community to make streets safer and service people more responsive.

We were surprised to find that even our most "jaded" (by their own admission) New York clients thought we possessed some secret. We would hear: "I've lived here for eighteen years and never knew that," "How come no one knows about that?" and "How do you do what you do?" What we had that our clients didn't have—until now

---

—was ten years of experience and piles of research on thousands of services, laborers, government agencies, public institutions, and stores all in one place, at our fingertips. We have also developed over the years a tried-and-true methodology that gets results every time. For the first time we are sharing our evaluations, recommendations, and survival philosophy in book form in order to help elevate the quality of every New Yorker's life. No one knows better than we that sooner or later we can all use some help from someone who knows the ins and outs of the city. And in these days of economic insecurity, that help has never been more necessary.

This is not a traditional resource or guide book on New York. *The Intrepid New Yorker* is more like an owner's instruction manual to the City. What we present is not only a reference book full of tested resources, tips, and inside information, but also a proactive, street-smart *approach* to living in New York City. Follow our step-by-step methodology and incorporate the Intrepid New Yorker philosophy, and we believe you will be able to create your own small, manageble town within this extraordinary but challenging city.

HOW TO USE THIS BOOK

In order to effectively communicate our approach, we have divided the book into two parts. Part I includes two chapters that explain our philosophy and offer general instruction and resources to help every New Yorker with day-to-day life in this city. Chapter One, The Intrepid New Yorker Day-to-Day Coping Manual, teaches you basic living skills from getting good service from local merchants to cutting your errand time in half. Chapter Two, The Intrepid New Yorker Assertiveness Training Manual, instructs New Yorkers on how to become knowledgeable consumers and how to assert ourselves to get what we want out of this city as a matter of course.

Part II includes seven chapters on very specific subjects offering resources and instruction that New Yorkers will need at different times in their lives, such as how to play the real estate game, taking the despair out of home renovation, making community streets safer, how to find a quality child care program, and much more.

THE INTREPID NEW YORKER SEAL OF APPROVAL

The services, stores, and individuals in this book have been discovered by the Intrepid New Yorker Company over the years or recommended to us by satisfied customers or professionals whom we trust. All of these services, stores, and individuals have been researched by The Intrepid New Yorker, and most have been tested personally through our service business. We feel confident that all of the services, stores, and individuals mentioned in this guide are deserving of our "Intrepid New Yorker Seal of Approval."

A word of caution: Over time, businesses do change hands and the quality of goods and services can improve or decline dramatically. We will continue to update this list of approved services, stores, and individuals as we update our guide on a yearly basis. New names will appear; some names will disappear. In the final analysis, however, you have to be your own best judge of quality. In addition, our facts have been checked and rechecked—services offered, hours of operation, location, telephone numbers, etc.—but it's always a good idea to make a phone call before visiting a particular business to make sure their status has not changed.

PART ONE

INTREPID APPROACH

O·N·E
THE INTREPID NEW YORKER DAY-TO-DAY COPING MANUAL

Day-to-day coping in New York City can be frustrating, exasperating, sometimes even infuriating. Just try to find a taxi in the pouring rain; get a license renewed without spending a day at the motor vehicle bureau; account for how one hundred dollars got spent in a day; find a plumber who brings the right tools the first time and doesn't leave a mess; encounter a salesperson who says hello and thank you and actually believes the customer is right . . .

THE INTREPID PHILOSOPHY

The Intrepid New Yorker is here to tell you that you can take control of these situations and change the outcome; that you can get what you want out of this city, the way you want it. That you can do *better* than cope here, you can thrive. It starts with our tested four-part philosophy that, if adopted, will change the way you experience your life here:

❚NTREPID PHILOSOPHY

ATTITUDE I *will* get what I want out of this city exactly the way I want it.

APPROACH I will do the work it requires to become an active, not passive, city dweller and consumer because the benefits are real; step by step, I will turn New York City into a manageable, small town.

KNOWLEDGE Information is the key to the city. Once I have it and know how to use it, I will improve the quality of my life here.

ECONOMICS Sometimes it's better to pay more, sometimes it's worth the search to pay less; but I should always get a fair deal for the money I spend.

Got the basic philosophy? We're going to infuse it into your daily life!

TURNING YOUR NEIGHBORHOOD INTO A MANAGEABLE SMALL TOWN

Does New York ever feel like a small town to you? Ask yourself the following questions:

☞ When was the last time you talked to your neighbor instead of staring at the floor numbers in the elevator?

☞ Do you often feel that your extra money and free time get spent on necessities and errands?

☞ How often have you had to waste an entire day waiting for an installation or a delivery?

☞ Can you name your own neighborhood's block association or do you even know if you have one?

☞ When was the last time you felt as if you actually got what you paid for?

☞ When was the last time you felt as if you really got "small town" attention and service in this city?

We know how most of you answered these questions. But you

don't have to leave town. The Intrepid New Yorker is going to show you that you can:

- ✔ turn your neighborhood into a manageable, small town
- ✔ establish a sense of belonging and community
- ✔ get exceptional, personalized attention from your local service people
- ✔ cut your errand time by at least half
- ✔ find reliable labor
- ✔ get your essential needs met efficiently and at much lower prices

❗ INTREPID APPROACH

Plot your own ten-block radius. Find out who lives and works in your immediate vicinity and begin some long-term relationships. You must get past the idea of seeing New York City as one huge, overwhelming, unmanageable city and begin to see it for what it also is—a series of small, neighboring towns that are approachable and knowable, and much more in your control. You can find "Main Street" in each one, complete with friendly merchants who know your needs, the town minister, a librarian who will call you when your favorite book comes in, the local public school, a community affairs police officer who works with you to make your streets safer, a community board that helps you resolve your neighborhood's problems, an active block association eager for new members, and a community newspaper dedicated to reporting what's going on where you live. Just take a look. Within the ten-block radius of where you live, in *your* neighborhood, you can find all this. But it requires work on your part. What you have to do is decide to make a real commitment to your community and make the connections with the people in it. We guarantee the quality of your life will improve and your own small town will emerge.

GETTING EXCELLENT, PERSONALIZED SERVICE IN THIS TOWN

Inadequate service is rampant throughout New York. The City's a big place and anyone can throw up a shingle. But excellent service is available too; just don't wait to stumble across it—go after it.

People who live in the country talk affectionately about how they know everyone in town, how loyal and helpful small-town service folk are to their customers, that it's like one big family. This city is too big for that kind of an atmosphere to exist without effort, and unfortunately New Yorkers are notorious for not extending themselves. If you are willing to change your ways, you can bring a little bit of "Main Street" to your community.

INTREPID APPROACH
Cultivate good relationships with your local service people.

Doing this will have a direct impact on the quality of life you will experience here. If you think about it, they *are* like an extended family—you depend on them to take care of your day-to-day needs. If you work at getting to know them, treat them well, and make them care about you as a customer and as a human being, they really won't let your ice cream melt, they really will deliver after hours for you, they really will lend you emergency taxi money, and that's not all:

Your mailman will:

☒ look out for special packages and letters
☒ bring you stamps
☒ mail letters for you

Your doorman and superintendent—even if you don't live in a doorman building, you can expect the same from other buildings' doormen and superintendents if you make a point of getting to know them —will:

◗ receive packages for you
◗ spot parking spaces or watch your car
◗ let you use the phone in the lobby
◗ tell you about apartment availabilities
◗ help you with chores on their day off
◗ share with you their list of reliable handymen

Your garage manager will:

🚗 take much better care of your car
🚗 help with small maintenance problems

- 🚗 drive your car for you to be fixed when you can't
- 🚗 bargain with you for lower rates if you don't use your car often
- 🚗 help you get city resident parking tax rebates

Your supermarket manager/butcher/store cashiers will:

- 🛒 tell you when the fresh food is in
- 🛒 offer you special cuts of beef
- 🛒 let you in on special sales
- 🛒 give you quarters for laundry
- 🛒 cash checks
- 🛒 let you set up charge accounts

Your other neighborhood services—e.g., liquor store, cleaners, hardware store, green grocer, pharmacy, photo store, tailor, florist, shoe repair—will:

- ✳ stretch their policies for you
- ✳ deliver after hours
- ✳ let you pay later
- ✳ give your request priority handling
- ✳ special-order items for you
- ✳ always give you the best of what they offer
- ✳ give you their list of service people and laborers they like (They are an excellent source for this—your local hardware store might find you a great electrician; your Korean market, a great baby-sitter. Service people are obviously well connected to other service people.)
- ✳ provide a safe haven if you ever need help
- ✳ possibly even barter with you (We have bartered our Intrepid skills for discounted or free produce. We organized our florist's closets in return for free flowers.)

The Intrepid New Yorker has found ways to get small-town service from our local bank. When opening a new account never walk in off the street to the first bank officer you see. He'll barely give you the time of day. If you want a bank officer to take you seriously right from the beginning, call to make an appointment. If you can get a referral from a friend or a business associate, all the better. You can turn it into a business meeting that will set the tone for an ongoing personal yet professional relationship with your banker. That means he will pay particular attention to your needs and will sometimes bend the rules. It's not unheard of to be able to negotiate for better rates on such things as auto loans, banking fees, and CDs.

One Intrepid New Yorker is terrible at arranging flowers and it takes her twice as long as it does most people. If you're like her, your arranging days are now over. Take your vase to your florist, pick out the flowers you want, and he will arrange them in the vase for you.

INTREPID APPROACH

You can turn average service from a local merchant into a higher-quality service. You may not be thrilled in general with the service you get from your local dry cleaner, electronic repair, or shoeshine shop, but don't make the assumption that good service only exists for people who have the money to pay for it. You can do a lot to make local merchants give you much better service than you are receiving right now:

☛ **Educate yourself.** You have to become more knowledgeable about the quality of service you should be receiving so that you know what to ask for. You can become knowledgeable by calling the better-known, top services in New York, and/or the Department of Consumer Affairs and ask them what you should expect from a particular service. (For different phone numbers and more information about what the Department of Consumer Affairs offers in terms of consumer information see page 73.)

> The very top dry cleaners clean only twenty shirts an hour. They do the collars and the cuffs by hand. Then they put the shirts in plastic containers overnight so that they are perfectly moist for pressing. This type of service will run you $7 a shirt. By contrast, your average local dry cleaner will use huge commercial machines that clean one hundred shirts per hour, and huge pressing machines that have a tendency to pinch collars and cuffs. This service will run you $1.50 a shirt. The Intrepid New Yorker suggests an in-between alternative for getting shirts cleaned to your satisfaction: Hire a laundress to come to your home at $10 an hour who can clean three shirts per hour for a total of $3.50 a shirt.

For example, The Intrepid New Yorker called up one of the top dry cleaning services in the city and asked them directly what we should know about and should ask of our own local dry cleaners. These are some of the tips they gave us:

✳ The number one procedure that ages clothing is pressing, because it wears down the fibers and creates a sheen. Ask your dry cleaner if they can steam your clothes instead.

✳ Your clothes are dry-cleaned with solvents. Ask your cleaners how often they distill their solvents. The more often the solvents are distilled the brighter and cleaner your clothes will look. The top dry cleaners distill their solvents three times a week.

✳ Fluorocarbon solvents should be used on delicate fabrics such as silk and sequins. Tell your cleaners you want them cleaned that way.

✳ Starch cuts a shirt's life in half. The average shirt lasts about two years. Have your cleaners use light starch.

✳ Ask your dry cleaner to cover or remove very delicate buttons before cleaning. Ask them to remove shoulder pads. Ask them to cover belt buckles and clean belts separately from the garment. Always show them any specific concerns you have about a piece of clothing before handing it over to be cleaned.

☞ **Take charge.** You are paying your local merchants to do work for you. As the "employer" you can do more to "manage" your local service people by telling them how you would like to have the job done.

☞ **Be personable.** It is human nature for people to want to work harder for people they know and like. And get to know the manager or the owner of the store in addition to the person behind the counter; the person in charge is the one in the strongest position to bend the rules and go out of her way for you, and she will if you make an effort.

☞ **Try a service out first.** Give your local shoe repair, dry cleaner, etc. a "test subject" to repair so you can see what kind of work they actually do. Don't prep them or tell them how you want the job to turn out; see how thorough they are on their own.

☞ **Comparison shop.** And get at least three estimates on the cost of a job, especially a large job, before deciding which service to use. The only way to find out what labor really costs and to be sure that you are not getting ripped off is to compare prices.

If, even after you have followed all the above steps to getting better service in your neighborhood, you are still not happy, consult page 351 for our picks of exceptional essential services in town.

❡ INTREPID APPROACH
You can get most services to de-liver and usually for free. Your cleaners will pick up *and* deliver; your green grocer, liquor store, hardware store, pharmacy, and supermarket all deliver. You will find that many stores beyond your local neighborhood ser-vices will, too; before you make an un-necessary trip, ask. Many restaurants deliver now. (See page 34 to get your restaurant delivery guide to Manhat-tan.) And don't forget, if you've worked at setting up those relation-ships, you'll get odd-hour deliveries or you'll have neighbors willing to receive deliveries in your absence.

•

Zip-Clips is a free newspaper filled with coupons to clip out and take to your local restaurants, stores, and service shops for dis-counts. The Intrepid New Yorker knows it covers most of the Upper West Side and East Side, but it might cover other areas by now. Call (212) 580-1988 to find out if it now covers yours. If so, you will be sent this "thrifty" publication.

•

THE INTREPID PAGES
OF
EXCEPTIONAL ESSENTIAL SERVICES

You won't be able to find all the essential services you need within a ten-block radius; therefore, we are including our list of services that have been given the Intrepid New Yorker "Seal of Approval."

$ = inexpensive $$ = moderate $$$ = expensive
P = pickup   D = delivery

We suggest:

BOOKSTORES

BARNES & NOBLE ★ Locations Throughout NYC ★ $
All the best-sellers mentioned on *The New York Times* list are discounted. They also have tables of other discounted books such as art, literature, cooking, etc. This chain is noted for carrying a large selection of textbooks at their store at 18th Street and Fifth Avenue, and they take back secondhand books for credit.

BURLINGTON BOOK SHOP ★ 1082 Madison Avenue (81st and 82nd Streets) ★ (212) 288-7420 ★ $$ ★ D
For serious personal attention. They will look up anything, order anything, deliver anything. They will be happy to open a charge account for you, which makes phoning in orders a breeze. Jane Trichter and her staff have a wonderful knack for choosing just the right book.

GOTHAM BOOK MART ★ 41 West 47th Street ★ (212) 719-4448 ★ $
"Wise men fish here" reads the sign over the entrance. Good selection of literature with very helpful salespeople.

THE STRAND ★ 828 Broadway (at 12th Street) ★ (212) 473-1452
★ 159 John Street (near South Street Seaport) ★ (212) 809-0875 ★ $
A great source for buying secondhand books. It is also a wonderful place in which to browse.

DRUGSTORES

It is a good idea to get to know your local drugstore. You want to establish a relationship for those rush deliveries and special concerns. Try to open a house charge account and give them a little business each month. They tend to be on the pricy side so you don't want to do your everyday and bulk shopping there.

DUANE READE DRUGSTORES ★ Locations Throughout the City ★ $

PATHMARK DRUGS ★ Locations Throughout the City ★ $

RAEMART DRUGS ★ 630 Third Avenue (at 41st Street) ★ (212) 682-3191 ★ 1221 Avenue of the Americas (48th and 49th Streets) ★ (212) 575-0027 ★ $

RICKY PHARMACY ★ 718 Broadway (Waverly Place and Washington Place) ★ (212) 979-5232 ★ $ ★ limited delivery
They have an excellent selection of family-sized items. They discount Tiffany perfume and they often have discontinued lines of products that you'd given up looking for.

DRY CLEANERS

There must be as many dry cleaners in New York as there are Chinese restaurants. How do you find a good one? A lot of people complain about their local cleaner, but truthfully, if you are diligent about what you tell your dry cleaner or laundry to do, you should get good service. (See page 8 for dry-cleaning tips; see also sidebar below.)

JEEVES ★ 39 East 65th Street ★ (212) 570-9130 ★ $$$ ★ P/D
Whites tend to stay white. Shirts can be laundered, tears repaired, and stains almost always come out.

JOHN HARRISON ★ 1475 Second Avenue (at 77th Street) ★ (212) 744-6155 ★ $$ ★ P/D
Very good. Monthly billing and winter storage available.

WINDSOR ★ 294-2400 ★ $$$ ★ P/D only
You can usually call for a same day pickup. They do an excellent job on whites and hard-to-clean delicate fabrics.

New York School of Dry Cleaners ★ 116 East 27th Street ★ (212) 684-0945 ★ $$
The New York School of Dry Cleaners is an association of dry cleaners as well as a school. They do most of their work for museums or restoration projects. If your garment has an impossible stain, call Mr. Eisen. He will have his people do an analysis of the stain and try to get it out. This does not come cheap. But depending on the cost of the garment it might be worth it. If they can't get it out, no one can.

EXTERMINATOR

Acme Exterminating ★ 460 Ninth Avenue (35th and 36th Streets) (212) 594-9230 ★ $$

Unfortunately New York is full of rodents and bugs and you must take necessary precautions. We have found Acme to be responsible and timely. There is no magic secret; just constant upkeep.

FLORISTS

The type of flower arrangement you like is as personal as the type of art that appeals to you. Don't get bullied into going to "name" florists. Others can do just as well given some input from you.

THE FLOWER DISTRICT ★ Sixth Avenue from 26th Street to 29th Street ★ $ ★ Some D

We suggest you walk the area looking and pricing. The entire area specializes in plants and flowers, both real and dried. What the stores lack in personal service you get back in serious discounts.

PARKSIDE FLORIST ★ 100 East 96th Street ★ (212) 534-6304 ★ $$ ★ D

The owners, Andy and John, are creative yet have an ability to supply clients with exactly what they really ask for. Call your order in the day before. They are as good at making a $25 arrangement as they are at landscaping your terrace.

ROSES, ROSES, ROSES ★ Locations Throughout the City ★ $ ★ D

This chain certainly took the mystique out of roses. A dozen cost as little as $6. Many deliver.

SPRING STREET GARDEN ★ 186½ Spring Street ★ (212) 966-2015 ★ $$ ★ D

They are quite accommodating and have a good eye for what will last.

GOURMET FOOD STORES

Everyone knows about the following food stores, and for good reason: They are the best.

BALDUCCI'S ★ 424 Sixth Avenue (at 9th Street) ★ (212) 673-2600 ★ $$$ ★ D

Fresh produce, cheese, cold cuts, and prepared foods.

BARNEY GREENGRASS ★ 541 Amsterdam Avenue (86th and 87th Streets) ★ (212) 724-4707 ★ $$$ ★ D

All kinds of smoked fish.

DEAN & DELUCA ★ 560 Broadway (at Prince Street) ★ (212) 431-1691 ★ $$$ ★ D

Incredible choice of exotic fruits and vegetables, cheeses, breads, pasta, and much, much more.

FAIRWAY ★ 2127 Broadway (74th and 75th Streets) ★ (212) 595-1888 ★ $

Prices are as low as we have seen for high-quality cheese, cold cuts, salads, smoked fish, and produce.

WHOLE FOODS IN SOHO ★ 117 Prince Street ★ (212) 673-5388 ★ $$
The largest health food store in the city; includes the widest selection of organic produce.

ZABAR'S ★ 2245 Broadway (82nd and 83rd Streets) ★ (212) 787-2000 ★ $$
This place makes New York great.

HARDWARE STORES

You can repair more than you think on your own and spend less money in the process if you know where to buy the right parts and tools. These two stores will guide you so that making a mistake is nearly impossible. They are also a great source for everything from halogen bulbs to odd-shaped sponges.

GRACIOUS HOMES ★ 1220 Third Avenue (70th and 71st Streets) ★ (212) 517-6300 ★ $$ ★ D
Overall the best, most helpful well-stocked hardware/supply store in Manhattan. If they don't carry the item, they will try and get it for you. And the best part is, if you have a major credit card, you can just phone in your order. You don't even have to go.

RELIABLE HARDWARE ★ 303 Canal Street (Broadway and Mercer) ★ (212) 966-4166 ★ $ ★ D
A large store well stocked with most items that you would need. Their location enables them to have more than reasonable prices.

LAUNDRIES

Depending upon how concerned you are with perfection, your local laundry should be able to satisfy most of your needs. For those antique linens and fine sheets, expect to pay more for no-worry cleaning.

LAUNDRY OF MISS EVANS ★ 75 East 138th Street ★ (212) 234-2334 ★ $$$ ★ P/D
Simply the best laundry in town.

LINENS LIMITED LAUNDRY ★ By Mail: 240 North Milwaukee Street, Milwaukee, Wisconsin 53202 ★ (800) 637-6334 ★ $$
We know many people who ship their fine linens to be cleaned here. They pay attention to all the details.

SERGIO ★ (212) 562-4788 ★ $
Sergio is a find. He can arrange to come to your home one day a week and do all your laundry, including your shirts.

TIECRAFTERS ★ 116 East 27th Street ★ (212) 867-7676 ★ $$ ★ P/D
Cleans and repairs all ties. Can alter any tie to match the styles of the day. A real find, especially with what ties cost these days.

LIQUOR STORES

Shop around for liquor. Prices and services vary a great deal all over the City. If you know exactly what you want, and don't need a lot of information and attention, there are great discount places to take advantage of.

ASTOR WINES & SPIRITS ★ 12 Astor Place (near Broadway) ★ (212) 674-7500 ★ $$ ★ D
A true emporium taking up a wide corner swath in Greenwich Village. A well-run operation with a knowledgeable staff and very good sales that motivate customers to use the ubiquitous shopping carts. They are good at judging how many bottles you will need for a party and they are usually willing to take back unopened bottles.

GARNET WINES & LIQUORS ★ 929 Lexington Avenue (68th and 69th Streets) ★ (212) 772-3211 ★ $ ★ D
Their very reasonable prices make up for a slight lack of personal service. If you know what you want, and you don't want to spend much, this is the place.

K & D WINES & SPIRITS ★ 1366 Madison Avenue (95th and 96th Streets) ★ (212) 289-1818 ★ $ ★ D
This family-owned and -operated business is the largest wine shop on Madison Avenue. They have an extensive selection of both national and international wines. Phone orders are handled with the same concern and knowledge as in-person purchases.

SHERRY-LEHMANN ★ 679 Madison Avenue (61st and 62nd Streets) ★ (212) 838-7500 ★ $$ ★ D
Getting a bottle from Sherry-Lehmann is like getting a gift from Tiffany. The name is sure to impress.

NEWSSTANDS

New York has it all when it comes to news and information in any language.

DEPENDABLE NEWS SERVICE ★ 360 West 52nd Street ★ (212) 586-5552 ★ $
The only store where you can find back issues of your favorite American dailies and weeklies.

HOTALINGS ★ 142 West 42nd Street ★ (212) 840-1868 ★ $$
The indispensable store to locate almost every out-of-town domestic

and foreign-language newspaper and periodical—for a markup. Be sure to phone ahead as supplies are limited and deliveries lag by a day or more of publication date. For a small fee, they will reserve for you.

PAN AM BUILDING ★ 200 Park Avenue (at 45th Street) ★ $
The largest and most comprehensive newsstand in the city is located here. If they don't have it, you can bet they can get it, providing it's current.

NOTIONS STORES

Remember life before fancy specialty stores when a hanger was just a hanger and not a piece of art? Believe it or not, you can still buy a plain old hanger.

GREENBERG & HAMMER ★ 24 West 57th Street ★ (212) 586-6270 ★ $
A small Midtown store. Great for all your basic sewing supplies. High rents have forced most of these notions stores out of business. Thank goodness this one still exists.

TENDER BUTTONS ★ 143 East 62nd Street ★ (212) 758-7004 ★ $
Imagine a store that spends twenty minutes helping you pick out a 60-cent button. It has the most extensive selection of buttons in the city, not to mention their wonderful collection of cuff links.

WOOLWORTH ★ Locations Throughout the City ★ $
Great stuff at real people's prices. Wonderful for thread, candy, mops, brooms, knitting needles, hangers, stockings, plastic containers, etc. They also have special value sections each week and senior citizen discounts. They recently acquired all the Lamston stores.

PHOTO SHOPS

One-hour photo developing is the greatest for instant gratification, but you do pay more for it, and you won't necessarily have the best pictures. New York has some of the most experienced film labs in the world. For important pictures it can be worth it to use them. And you won't always pay more.

If you want to get a leg up on everyone else who is looking for apartments, you can get a copy of **The New York Times** Sunday real estate section on Saturday morning. Just call your local newspaper delivery service. If you don't get the paper delivered, look in the yellow pages under newspaper delivery. Most places will be happy to sell you a copy and most are usually open from 5:00 A.M. to 10:00 A.M. Also **The Village Voice,** which has a good real estate section, arrives hot off the press first at the Sheridan Square newsstand in the West Village on Wednesday mornings at 6 A.M.

MODERN AGE ★ 210 East 58th Street ★ (212) 752-3993 ★ $$

Specializes in contact sheets and enlargements. They develop on the premises and expertly reproduce old photographs. Bring any photo that requires special attention here.

MYSTIC COLOR LAB ★ By Mail: P.O. Box 144 Mason's Island Road, Mystic, Connecticut 06355 ★ (800) 367-6061 ★ $ ★ D

A mail-order photo house. They send you the prepaid postage security mail pouch and all you do is slip your film in the bag with a check. It takes about a week to get your photos back. A great service, especially for those of us who never get around to taking the film in in the first place. And it doesn't cost extra for the luxury.

SEAMSTRESS/TAILOR

Always a challenge to find someone you like but always a necessity. Any of these people can help you maintain your wardrobe and do good alterations. For additional names and numbers of people who make and repair clothes, see page 142.

Robert E. Lee ★ (212) 349-5065 Bobby is a leather fixer extraordinaire. He runs a one-man rotating corporate shoe-shine and light-repair business. Call him around 5 P.M. to arrange a time when he can come to your office.

CLAUDIA BRUCE ★ 140 East 28th Street ★ (212) 685-2810 ★ $$

Specializes in difficult alterations as well as the everyday hems and loose buttons. By appointment only.

EUROPA ★ 328 East 66th Street ★ (212) 249-8716 ★ $$

Aaron is one of the nicest, most attentive shopkeepers in the city. He is an expert in both men's and women's alterations.

MITA ★ 344 East 63rd Street ★ (212) 207-8600 ★ $$

A pleasant seamstress who has a good eye. If she can't do it, she will tell you.

SOPHIA ★ 1200 Lexington Avenue (81st and 82nd Streets) ★ (212) 744-8239 ★ $

She has a good feeling for how a garment should fit, and if she has the time, she is great at making duvet covers, skirts for your bed, etc.

SHOE REPAIR SHOPS

New York is a walking city so shoes tend to wear down fast. When you have spent megabucks for new shoes, you want to repair your favorites rather than replace them. A good cobbler can make them last years longer. It is worth it to pay a little more.

EVELYN & SAM ★ 400 East 83rd Street ★ (212) 628-7618 ★ $$

The best in the city for dying shoes and bags. They also do expert work on cleaning bags and briefcases.

JAMES SHOE REPAIR ★ 1426 Lexington Avenue (93rd and 94th Streets) ★ (212) 722-0041 ★ $$

Nick Pecchia never forgets a pair of shoes or the person who brought them in. He does give you a ticket but that is only for your peace of mind. He repairs all shoes, belts, and bags. An artisan from way back, he can restore nearly any pair of shoes to its original condition. And the turnaround time is fast.

JIM'S SHOE REPAIR ★ 50 East 59th Street ★ (212) 355-8259 ★ $$

A great repair place that is centrally located. A wonderful shop to get a shine while you watch the parade of people go in and out.

T. O. DEY ★ 9 East 38th Street ★ (212) 683-6300 ★ $$

Custom shoe making as well as all types of repair work.

VIDEO RENTALS

What's great about these three stores is that they pick up and deliver, a wonderful luxury if you're sick in bed or if you just don't want to face the sleet and cold.

VIDEO CONNECTION ★ 2240 Broadway (at 80th Street) ★ (212) 724-2727 ★ $$ ★ P/D

Depending on the type of membership you have they do deliver from 70th to 90th Streets, Central Park West to the Hudson River.

VIDEO ROOM ★ 1487 Third Avenue (at 84th Street) ★ (212) 879-5333 ★ $$ ★ P/D

If you take out a $75 yearly membership you will receive their free pickup and delivery service as well as one free video a month. Locations covered: from 59th to 96th Streets, East Side to West Side.

VIDEO STOP INC. ★ 367 Third Avenue (between 26th and 27th Streets) ★ (212) 685-6199 ★ $$ ★ P/D

If you prepay your first twenty videos at $2.50 apiece, you become a member and receive free pickup and delivery. Locations covered: from Houston to 49th Streets, East River to Eighth Avenue.

THE IMPORTANCE OF GETTING TO KNOW YOUR NEIGHBOR

Four inches of wall separate us from our next-door neighbors, but they might as well live in China. It takes a natural disaster to get New Yorkers to talk to each other and get helpful. And we chat for weeks after about what a wonderful experience we had during that snow-storm or blackout because we were an interactive, small-town community for a moment. We obviously like the way it feels, but, ironically, we don't pursue it as a matter of course. We revert back to being cynical and aloof. It's time to drop that act. If you have chosen New York City as your hometown, why do it halfheartedly?

INTREPID APPROACH
Make a point of getting to know some of the people in your building. Introduce yourself and make an effort when you see them. Pick an evening and invite them over for a drink. That one gesture alone will give you a solid basis for an ongoing relationship. You will be surprised how good it feels to know who's on the other side of that wall and be comfortable enough to ask each other for favors and assistance when needed.

INTREPID APPROACH
Join your block association. Almost every block in New York City has one. If you want to really feel like you belong, this is the organization to become a part of. Block associations work as a united organization to get appropriate needs met for *your* neighborhood. You will meet caring, involved people who are looking for the same small-town spirit as you are. You can find out about your block association by reading bulletin boards at your local stores, asking neighbors, or by calling your local community board (see page 87) or police precinct (see page 306). For excellent tips about neighborhood organizing and for related informative guides, see the list of free neighborhood self-help publications, page 301.

We at the Intrepid New Yorker have children. Our next-door neighbor works out of his home. He baby-sits all the time for us on no notice. Many times when we've gotten stuck at the office, we have called him and asked him to take over for the baby-sitter who had to get home. If the baby is asleep, he can take the baby monitor into his own apartment and listen from there. It alleviates all our anxiety attacks about trying to get home on time. In return, we accept packages for him, water his plants, and feed his dog when he's away.

Having made this effort, here's what you can expect:

Next-door neighbors will:

* let you borrow a cup of sugar—literally!
* help baby-sit
* be there for you in an emergency
* exchange keys

* water your plants, pick up mail, and watch your apartment when you're away
* accept packages and deliveries for you
* share parking spaces
* give access to service people when you are out

Block associations will:

❏ help you fight for changes you think are necessary to make the neighborhood better

❏ be a great source for finding baby-sitters, laborers, playmates for your children, etc.

❏ help you in an emergency

❏ exchange favors

❏ make you feel that you are not just investing in an apartment, but an entire community for you and your family

❏ make your block a lot safer

CUTTING YOUR ERRAND TIME IN HALF

New Yorkers don't have the luxury of jumping in their car and going to the town mall to do one-stop shopping. We simply cannot logistically get our errands for the week done in a couple of hours. We spend, on an average five hours a week, 260 hours a year doing errands. That's a ten-day vacation lost to chores! The Intrepid New Yorker can cut that by at least half.

❱ INTREPID APPROACH
Take advantage of personal care services that make house calls. Add up the amount of time and money you waste getting from appointment to appointment. You can spend only half of your Saturday getting all those appointments out of the way without ever leaving home. The tailor, seamstress, laundress, manicurist, masseuse, exercise instructor, haircutter—they'll all come to you. Depending on who you choose, you might pay a little more, but you might also pay a little less; you don't have to go high end to get good service. The Intrepid New Yorker has found all sorts of people willing to come to our home to make extra free-lance and moonlighting dollars. If you do spend slightly more, it's a quality of life issue. You are relaxed, you can make phone calls, write letters, watch TV, be with your family.
Here's how you find them:

- by word of mouth through friends
- by asking service people you already patronize if they will come to your home after hours or if they know anyone who will
- by thinking logically about the kinds of places that hire the people you are looking for (For example, Paul Stuart must have a fitter; Pierre Michel has haircutters, Jack La Lanne has fitness instructors, etc.)

THE INTREPID PAGES
OF
HOUSE-CALL PERSONAL CARE SERVICES

You'll be surprised by how many different types of professionals will make house calls beyond the ones we've listed below.

$ = inexpensive $$ = moderate $$$ = expensive

COOKS

Wouldn't it be nice to come home to a home-cooked meal? These less-prosperous times will find us spending less money in restaurants and entertaining more often at home. You can find a cook who will come to your home for no more or less than it would cost to eat out. One way to do it inexpensively is to contact professional cooking schools (see page 45), or call:

BORN TO FEAST ★ (212) 787-9698 ★ $
Darcy McCulloch is a trained chef and can easily prepare a home-cooked meal for you and your friends. She can arrange for any additional help you may need as well as choose the appropriate wines.

BRIDIE ★ (718) 271-7821 ★ $
A pleasant Irish woman who has been cooking for years. She is great for an intimate dinner for two or a party of five hundred.

DONNA MARIA MINISSALE ★ (212) 777-7041 ★ $
She prepares gourmet vegetarian meals. She will prepare fish and chicken but no meat dishes.

JANIE FEINSTEIN ★ (212) 759-5029 ★ $
Janie can either cater a big party, drop off dinner, or come to your home to prepare a well-rounded delicious meal.

EXERCISE

If you don't exercise because you can't ever seem to make it to the gym, then make them come to you, at home or at the office. It does cost more, but it can be a worthwhile extra expense in terms of time saved and really getting committed to being in shape once and for all.

BODY ART ★ (212) 593-5771 ★ $$
Body Art can arrange private, at-home instruction. They offer various techniques: Alexander, stretch, weight training, Nautilus, calisthenics, and aerobics. It will cost approximately $60 an hour.

ENERGETICS UNLIMITED ★ (212) 879-1566 ★ $$
Bonita owns this very personalized exercise-placement company. She has the unique ability to match your needs with exactly the right instructor. Her rates are $55 per one-hour session.

LIVINGSTON MILLER ★ (212) 662-4814 ★ $$–$$$
He has been helping people to feel better with a steady regime of exercise for over fifteen years. He can teach aerobics, stretching, weights, as well as therapeutic techniques.

> If you want to seriously cut down on the cost of home fitness, try calling a local gym or exercise class and see if any instructors might be willing to moonlight.

LOLA STANTON ★ (212) 662-3571 ★ $
Very accommodating. Specializes in aerobics, calisthenics, and stretching. Costs approximately $40 an hour.

TERRY KING ★ (718) 788-0437 ★ $$$
Terry designs home gym systems and acts as a personal trainer as well.

FIREWOOD DELIVERY

SAM THE FIREWOOD MAN ★ (212) 772-5979 ★ $$
You don't have to go out in the cold. Sam delivers to your door.

MAKEUP ARTISTS AND HAIRDRESSERS

It is just as easy to get someone to come to your home to cut your hair or apply your makeup as it is to go to a salon. Ask at your own favorite places or consider ours.

BARBARA CAMP ★ (212) 877-0201 ★ $$
Barbara will come to your home and make you look like royalty. She will teach you how to apply your own makeup. A onetime visit from her could change your look forever.

JIM INDERATO ★ (212) 675-2566 ★ $ $$

Jim is an agent for some of the top hair and makeup people in New York. All you need to do is call Jim and tell him what you need and how much you want to spend. He is great at matching your needs with his list of professionals.

LORI KLEIN ★ (212) 996-9390 ★ $$

You can arrange for a onetime makeup lesson, special occasion makcup applications, or even get a group of friends together for a class.

TINA ★ (212) 369-9102 ★ $$

Tina has worked for some of the most prestigious hair salons in New York. She enjoys doing haircuts for people in their homes.

MANICURE, PEDICURE, AND MASSAGE

Once you get to know the owners of your local manicure and massage shops, they should be able to arrange for someone to come to your home. Or call:

JEANETTE ★ (212) 627-5971 ★ $

Jeanette has training in physical rehabilitation as well as massage technique. She is bright, reliable, and quite strong. You absolutely cannot go wrong.

JUTTA OF HANOVER ★ 160 East 56th Street ★ (212) 832-1887 ★ $$

Jutta offers a wide range of services in her shop, but if you want to stay put in your office she offers an "office chair massage." For a two-hour commitment and $120, she will give six people each a twenty-minute massage in her special chair—that's $20 apiece. This massage restores energy to your mind and body.

LARRY WEINBERG ★ (516) 829-3643 ★ $$

Larry will even come to your hotel room. He is an expert in both Swedish and Amma massage. And if he still feels tension, he doesn't stop when the hour is up.

LISA CORWIN ★ (212) 727-2576 ★ $$

Lisa specializes in reflexology. Her other talent is in providing you with nutritional guidance.

MARGIE MANDELBURGER ★ (212) 366-9374 ★ $$

Margie is a pleasant, reliable, and professional masseuse.

MARGOT NAVIA ★ (212) 472-0677 ★ $$
Margot is meticulous. She brings exactly what is needed for the perfect manicure and pedicure. A manicure costs $20. A manicure and pedicure cost $55.

THE SWEDISH MASSAGE SCHOOL ★ (212) 924-5900 ★ $$
If you call Dolores on Tuesday, Wednesday, or Thursday, she will arrange for a licensed massage therapist to come to your home or office. She will match your needs with the right therapist. It costs $50 to $75 an hour.

PLANT CARE
PLANT SPECIALISTS ★ (212) 839-9414 ★ $$
These indoor and outdoor plant experts will take good care of your greenery.

SEAMSTRESS
ANNE KYNANZI ★ (201) 843-6544 ★ $$
Anne is the ultimate in men's and women's alterations. She can work with any type of fabric.

VISUAL AND AUDIO SPECIALIST
ED MEENAN ★ (212) 260-6074 ★ $$$
He will come to your home to consult with you and then purchase the appropriate home entertainment system for your needs and your budget.

WINE INSTRUCTORS
CHUCK & JULIE WEINBERG ★ (718) 886-6521 ★ $$
By day, public school teachers; by night, two of the most knowledgeable wine experts. In-home wine classes with a group of your friends can be easily arranged.

● INTREPID APPROACH

Do your mailing from home! How often do you let important packages and letters that you have to mail collect dust at home because you hate having to wrap them and lug them to the post office? There are so many competitive services wanting nothing more than to come to your home and take packages off your hands that there are fewer and fewer reasons today to make that pilgrimage. And these companies do everything! Besides offering pickup and delivery at your door, they will even bring the packing materials you need—all this at the cost of a few extra dollars.

This is what you can avail yourself of:

- scores of same-day and overnight delivery companies with competitive rates that are not outrageous
- the old-fashioned surface carriers like UPS, which don't take any longer to deliver a package than the post office
- messengers who can deliver something across town for you at a cheaper price than the round-trip taxi you would have paid for
- couriers that will fly your valuable package to its destination and hand-deliver it
- your friendly mailman who will bring you stamps and mail your letters if you are nice to him

If you don't have a doorman, take your package to the doorman or neighbor you made friends with down the street. If you develop a relationship with the company driver, he might be willing to make you his first or last appointment.

Be aware that the post office is your only choice for certain airmail special deliveries, registered or return-receipt mail, or when sending to a P.O. box number.

> •
> You can order a complete description of what all the overnight delivery services offer and cost by calling the Better Business Bureau at (212) 533-7500 and asking for the BBB advisory on choosing an overnight delivery service.
> •

> •
> If you have something that must get to an executive floor of a company ASAP, a messenger will never get past the mail room. The Intrepid New Yorker suggests you send someone like a well-dressed college student who won't get stopped in the lobby.
> •

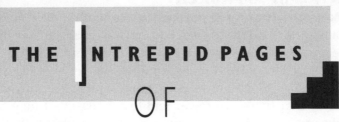

THE INTREPID PAGES
OF
DOING YOUR MAILING FROM HOME

$ = inexpensive $$ = moderate $$$ = expensive

OVERNIGHT, SECOND-DAY, AND REGULAR MAIL SERVICES

FEDERAL EXPRESS ★ (212) 777-6500 ★ $$$ ★ 8:00 A.M.–8:30 P.M.
Fed Ex will pick up within one hour of calling and provide you with some packing materials. Pickups only in the afternoon till 8:30 P.M.

UNITED PARCEL SERVICE ★ (212) 695-7500 ★ $$ ★ 7:30 A.M.–6:30 P.M.
UPS has a second-day delivery service that is less expensive than the next-day delivery offered by other companies.

UNITED STATES POSTAL SERVICE ★ (212) 330-2542 ★ $ ★ 8:30 A.M.–6:00 P.M.
Express mail on demand pick-up service is available for up to seventy-pound packages. Their last pickup is at 7:00 P.M. and you must call at least one hour before.

OTHER MAILING SERVICES

MAIL BOXES ETC. ★ Locations Throughout the City ★ $$$
They can take care of most of your mailing and packing needs but there is no pickup and delivery. It is the alternative to going to the post office to mail a package.

RSA SHIPPING ★ (800) 221-9370 ★ $$
Most overnight companies and even the post office have weight limitations. RSA can ship very large packages. All items must be pre-packed but they do pick up and deliver.

MOBIL MESSENGER ★ (212) 751-7765 ★ $$
If you need to get a letter or package messengered around the City, Mobil is the company to call. They will pick up and deliver C.O.D. if you do not have an account.

INTREPID APPROACH

Shop once a month and at half price for all your essential home and food supplies. Wouldn't it feel liberating not to have to run to the store every five minutes? The fact is, we have more space to store items than we realize (see Chapter Six for ways to increase storage space in small apartments) and if we bought our essentials once a month, we'd save not only time, but money—lots of it.

There are specialty stores in New York that will sell to the consumer at wholesale prices if you buy in bulk such items as:

- beverages from beer to seltzer
- food from dairy products to farm-fresh produce to meat
- stationery supplies

☞ **Here's how you find them:** You can find wholesalers who will sell to the consumer by looking through the Business to Business Yellow Pages. (We'll tell you where to get one later in this chapter.) You look under "meat" or "stationery," for example, and call and ask whether they will sell to you, how much you have to buy to make it worth their while, and whether they deliver. If their minimum is too high for you, go in on it with a friend.

☞ **Here's how to pick up your orders:** Plan one day a month to do all your bulk shopping. Place all your orders in advance so they're ready when you get there. If you have a car in the City, go with a friend who can sit in the car while you run in to pick up your orders. If you don't have a car, it pays to hire a car service for $15 an hour. The money and hours saved by not shopping piecemeal makes it well worth it.

The Intrepid New Yorker buys meat wholesale. Every month we buy about ten pounds of chicken, twelve lamb chops, ten pounds of chopped meat, twelve steaks. We call our wholesale man on the phone, tell him what we want and how we want it cut; he wraps the meat in freezer paper in the portions we request and then delivers it to our door the next day. **The bill is less than half** what we would pay in any supermarket and it is freezer-ready! It doesn't take up that much space in the freezer and we're done with our meat shopping for the month.

We tell our clients that when they can't get to the wholesale stores, the very least they can do is to do once-a-month shopping at their own supermarket; they don't sell wholesale but you can buy their cheaper, generic labels in bulk. The quality is often indistinguishable from the brand labels. And we tell them they should always take advantage of special sales: The Intrepid New Yorker once bought six bottles of detergent when they were marked down from $6 to $3.50—that was a $15 savings. And most supermarkets deliver. It's the next best way to go.

THE INTREPID PAGES
OF
WHERE TO FIND
WHOLESALE STAPLES

$ = inexpensive $$ = moderate $$$ = expensive
D = deliver

Buying food in New York is a treat because you can truly find any herb, spice, noodle, etc. that you desire; however, you often pay the price for such specialty items. We attempt to cut your staples bill in half so that you have more left over for those fun foods that make shopping and cooking so exciting.

BEVERAGE WHOLESALERS
Why pay top dollars for sodas, beer, and mixers when you don't have to? And many places deliver.

B & E QUALITY BEVERAGE ★ 511 West 23rd Street ★ (212) 243-6812 ★ $ ★ D

GIMME SELTZER ★ (718) 297-9560 ★ $ ★ D (only delivery)

GRILL BEVERAGE ★ 261 Delancey Street (corner of Columbia) ★ (212) 475-7171 ★ $ ★ D

GREENMARKETS
On the facing page is a list of locations and yearly schedules of the greenmarkets throughout the City. There is no cheaper or fresher way to buy your produce, baked goods, cheeses, flowers, lobsters, and many other wonderful foodstuffs. All items are sold directly to you with no middleman, so no markup. You can't be sure exactly which items are being sold that day, so be flexible with your grocery list.

MEAT WHOLESALERS
Your freezer can hold much more than you think so don't be frightened by the minimum requirements.

CITY WHOLESALERS ★ 305 East 85th Street ★ (212) 879-4241 ★ $
Just phone in your order the day before and indicate how you want it

GREENMARKET SCHEDULE

MARKET	DAYS	DATES
MANHATTAN		
City Hall	Tuesdays	Year-round
(Park Row)	Fridays	Year-round
World Trade Center	Tuesdays	June–December
Church and Fulton Streets	Thursdays	Year-round
Federal Plaza	Fridays	Year-round
(Broadway and Thomas Street)		
Washington Market Park	Wednesdays	Year-round
(Greenwich and Reade Streets)	Saturdays	Year-round
St. Mark's Church	Tuesdays	June–November
(10th Street and Second Avenue)		
West Village	Saturdays	June–November
(Gansevoort and Hudson Streets)		
Union Square	Wednesdays	Year-round
(17th Street and Broadway)	Fridays	Year-round
	Saturdays	Year-round
Roosevelt Island	Saturdays	Year-round
(Bridge Plaza)		
Sheffield Plaza	Wednesdays	Year-round
(57th Street and Ninth Avenue)	Saturdays	Year-round
IS 44	Sundays	Year-round
(77th Street and Columbus Avenue)		
West 102nd Street	Fridays	June–November
(102nd Street and Amsterdam Avenue)		
West 125th Street	Tuesdays	July–November
(Adam Clayton Powell Boulevard)		
West 175th Street	Thursdays	June–December
(Broadway)		
BRONX		
Poe Park	Tuesdays	June–November
(Grand Concourse and East 192nd Street)		
BROOKLYN		
Cadman Plaza West	Tuesdays	Year-round
(Montague Street)	Saturdays	Year-round
Grand Army Plaza	Saturdays	July–November
Albee Square	Wednesdays	July–November
(Fulton Street and Dekalb Avenue)		

to be freeze-wrapped and in what quantities. Delivery is available within a certain distance. Great meat at great prices.

14TH STREET FOOD DEPOT ★ 416 West 14th Street ★ (212) 366-6668 ★ $
You can get most of your wholesale meat here, but they also sell eggs, cheeses in bulk, vats of olive oil, nuts, butter, and other staples. You purchase in large quantities and save bundles.

PASTRIES
LET THEM EAT CAKE ★ 287 Hudson Street (at Spring Street) ★ (212) 989-4970 ★ $ ★ D
They bake for many of the gourmet food stores throughout the City and they will also sell to you at wholesale prices.

STATIONERY SUPPLIES
STAPLES ★ 1075 Avenue of the Americas (40th and 41st Streets) ★ (212) 944-6744 ★ $
★ (800) 333-3330 for delivery in NYC
Every item you could possibly want for the home or office. There's a $15 delivery charge.

TRASH BAGS, LIGHT BULBS, PAPER TOWELS
AMERICAN WHOLESALE LIGHTING COMPANY ★ By Mail: (718) 372-6000 ★
(516) 669-4860 ★ $
This is strictly a phone-order operation and you can save a bundle.

Cutting Down on Service-and-Installation Waiting Time

There are ways to cut down on the time you wait for delivery, installation, and servicing at home. Almost all delivery, repair, and installation dispatchers in New York City will tell you that they can't give you a specific time of arrival, that someone will show up in your home either between the hours of 8:00 A.M. to 1:00 P.M. or the afternoon hours of 1:00 to 6:00—take it or leave it. So you wait and wait, and invariably they don't even show up within those hours. There goes the day.

❦ INTREPID APPROACH
You can get the first appointment of the day. As an example, here's how it would work with the cable or phone company. (Be aware that it will take perseverance and about a half hour of your time. But a half hour is better than five wasted hours.) First, ask to speak to the dispatcher's supervisor; dispatch-

ers don't have the authority to bend the rules. If she tells you her supervisor is not in, insist on speaking to someone in authority, even if that means going all the way up the ladder to the president's office. We have found that assistants to the presidents can be very helpful. When you get someone in authority on the phone, tell him politely that your profession does not allow you to take the better part of a day off and that you are willing to wait a week or two for a first appointment of the day.

Rule #1: Don't give up. You will get that first appointment.

Rule #2: Always be diplomatic and nice. Appeal to people's human side. Be firm and definitive, never angry or rude.

Rule # 3: Make sure you have names. Keep a list of all the people you have talked to along the chain of command so you don't get bounced back to people you've already spoken to. Also, people in telephone relations tend to be more cooperative when they know that you have their names.

❚ INTREPID APPROACH
There are other ways to avoid waiting at home for servicing, delivery, and installation. For instance, here's how it works with home appliance repair and furniture deliveries: The dispatchers might not set their servicing and delivery schedules until the night before, so you can't call up and demand a first appointment for a few weeks from now. However, most delivery people carry beepers or have car phones these days. So just ask them to call you at work when they are one or two stops away from your home. You can jump into a taxi and be there to greet them. When you talk to the dispatcher, don't let him tell you there is no way to reach these guys—it's just not true. You could probably also handle your cable and phone servicing this way; it depends on your flexibility.

❚ INTREPID APPROACH
There are ways to get the right service and delivery the first time. Here's how it works, for example, with the cable and phone companies: Be as specific as you can about the type of installation or repair required. Don't expect the dispatchers to ask you the right questions. *Spell it out for them.* The cable and telephone companies dispatch different units depending on what the need is, and you want to make sure you don't get the wrong man with the wrong equipment.

Important point to remember: If you live in a doorman building, make sure your building allows workers in at 8:00 A.M. Doorman buildings have policies they have to adhere to.

Here are some names and phone numbers you may need to keep in your back pocket if you aren't getting any satisfaction from your basic home services:

Manhattan Cable
President—Mr. Victor Lobasso.
Assistant to the President—Mr. Robert Riedinger
(212) 598-7200

Paragon Cable
President—Mr. John Rigsby
Secretary—Mrs. M. Downey
(212) 304-3100

Con Edison
President—Mr. Eugene McGrath
Secretary—Melba Hernandez
(212) 460-4982

New York Telephone
President—Mr. Richard Jalkut
Area Operations Manager—Mr. Roy Jackson
(212) 395-2552

US Sprint
President—Mr. Ron Lemay
Assistant to the President—Ms. Adele Blinn
(913) 624-6926

MCI
President—Mr. Bert Roberts
Assistant to the President—Ms. Melanie Heatley
(202) 887-2171

Essential References for Day-to-Day Coping

● INTREPID APPROACH
There is essential reference information you should have at your fingertips. New Yorkers would spend far less time completing tasks if they had access to important information and services right at home.

The Yellow Pages

It isn't just an excellent guide for finding services and products. It also includes information on everything from activities for children and Lincoln Center seating charts to airport terminal maps, public transportation maps, and listings of museums and libraries.

The White Pages

It also contains an emergency care guide, the blue pages of government listings, and zip codes.

Business to Business Yellow Pages

This is a very important publication to be aware of. It is a special yellow pages for finding products and services used by businesses. It gives New Yorkers much greater access to a wide range of products and services at lower prices. The Business to Business Yellow Pages lists all the wholesalers and manufacturers, not the retail stores. New York City is the East Coast mecca for all wholesalers and importers for everything from clothing to food to toys. Not all sources will sell to the consumer, but many will, so it is worth the search. As we said earlier, the catch is that you will have to buy in bulk—but often the minimum-required order isn't as big as you might think.

Here's how to get it: By calling your local telephone business office, which is listed on your monthly bill. They will ship it to you free of charge.

> You can buy the hottest fad items for kids at Sona Co., 104 West 27th Street, in the toy wholesale district. Bubble Necklaces are $9 a dozen, snap bracelets, $6 a dozen.

800 Directories

Most people aren't aware these directories exist. They have a consumer version and a business-to-business version. *This is what they offer:*

☆ countrywide 800 numbers
☆ "800" catalogs and gift ideas
☆ mileage charts to and from every major city
☆ calorie charts
☆ weights and measures chart
☆ interest rate and discount tables

> The Intrepid New Yorker needed bath towels. We looked up "towels" in the business-to-business yellow pages and called several manufacturers and suppliers and asked what brands they sell. We found one that made the monograms for Ralph Lauren bath towels. They had a four-set minimum on regular bathsheets but none on the monogrammed ones. We went to their showroom and paid cash for one monogrammed bathsheet; it cost $40 as opposed to $69 at Ralph Lauren.

Here's how to get it: Call (800) 426-8686. You can request the consumer 800 directory for $9.95 and the business-to-business 800 directory for $14.95. American Express, Visa, MasterCard, and AT&T cards are accepted.

Official Airline Guide

This is a must if you travel a lot. This publication puts you in control of how you get to your destination and how much it is going to cost. You will no longer be at the mercy of one ticket agent or one airline.

The pocket version is a monthly and offers you every possible connection of flights on every airline in and out of every major airport in the country. It costs $72 for a one-year subscription.

The desktop version offers you every possible connection of flights in and out of all major airports including the smaller airports. You can get one that also includes all airline fares, and you can subscribe on a monthly or bimonthly basis. The price starts at $208.

Here's how to get it: Call (800) 323-3537.

Zagat Restaurant Guide

This is simply the best restaurant guide to New York. You can get it at almost any bookstore.

"We Deliver"

This is a neighborhood guide to restaurants that deliver, and comes complete with menus. This guide covers the East Side, Upper East Side, Upper West Side, and soon, the lower sections of Manhattan.

Here's how to get it: Call (212) 288-4745.

The New York Convention and Visitor's Bureau Guide

It's not just for the tourist. It will tell you everything you need to know about what is happening year-round in this city, including:

- seasonal calendars of all activities and events occurring in New York
- New York hotel guide with room prices
- sports activity information
- shopping information

Here's how to get it: Call The New York Convention and Visitor's Bureau, Inc. at (212) 397-8222, or go in person to 2 Columbus Circle (59th Street and Broadway).

Michelin Guide

This is one of the best overall guides to New York City for veteran and newcomer. It includes:

- a restaurant locator
- a hotel locator

- a cultural attractions locator
- an overall sports and recreation locator
- all necessary maps
- seating charts of arenas and theaters

New York **Magazine;** *The New Yorker,* **and** *The Village Voice*
These are excellent sources for:

- points of interest about New York
- extensive up-to-date lists of recreational and cultural activities

Corky Pollan's *Shopping Manhattan*
This is an excellent, overall guide to shopping in New York City. You can buy *Shopping Manhattan* (Penguin 1989) in most major bookstores.

The Green Book
This is a book put out by the City of New York on all government agencies and services, and lists whom to call depending on what particular assistance you need. You can find anything in this book from places to apply for a permit or license, a list of all foreign consulates, and municipal parking lots, to school boards, golf courses, and real estate information sources—you name it.

Here's how you get it: Call City Books at (212) 669-8245 or go to City Books at 61 Chambers Street in Manhattan.

THE INTREPID PAGES

OF

HOTLINES

(212) 777-FILM ★ movie locator

(212) 888-FOOD ★ New York restaurant switchboard: Call and enter the first four letters of the restaurant you want to go to. You will be automatically switched there. If you don't know where to eat, this number also gives descriptions and locations.

(212) 315-2705 ★ extended weather forecast: If you wait until the end of the recording you can get specific questions answered.

(212) 976-1313 ★ sportsphone for up-to-the-minute information

(212) 976-4141 ★ stock market information ★ Dow-Jones report

(212) 340-0849 ★ New York public library branch locator

(212) 967-8585 ★ general post office information

(212) 220-8681 ★ plant and flower hotline: You can find out what's wrong with yours.

(212) 556-0990 ★ farmer's market locator and schedule

(212) 566-4121 ★ alternate side of the street parking regulations

(212) 566-3406 ★ highway emergencies: Cave-ins, potholes, e.g.

(212) 477-4430 ★ Parking violations help hotline

(212) 362-7000 ★ car lockouts locksmith

(212) 487-4398 ★ consumer complaints at Consumer Affairs Department

(212) 533-6200 ★ public inquiry and complaints at Better Business Bureau

(212) 566-5700 ★ Mayor's Action Center: Receives calls about your problems and complaints.

(212) 577-0800 ★ one-stop information on activities, employment, benefits, home services, etc. for the elderly

(212) 960-4800 ★ housing complaints

(212) 966-7500 ★ noise and smell complaints

(212) 219-8090 ★ trash complaints

(212) 566-2525 ★ to report broken streetlamps and traffic lights

(212) 374-5000 ★ police headquarters for precinct referrals

(212) 683-0862 ★ electrical emergencies, gas and steam leaks

611 ★ New York Telephone twenty-four-hour repair

(800) 526-2000 ★ AT&T equipment service and complaints

(800) 722-2300 ★ New York Telephone wiring service and complaints

(212) 764-7667 ★ twenty-four-hour poison control center

THE INTREPID PAGES

OF
SERVICES OPEN
TWENTY-FOUR HOURS A DAY
(Or Close to It)

BOOKSTORES

DOUBLEDAY ★ 724 Fifth Avenue (at 57th Street) ★ (212) 397-0550
Monday through Saturday until midnight.

ST. MARKS ★ 12 St. Mark's Place (8th Street between Second and Third Avenues)
★ (212) 260-7853
Until 11:30 P.M., seven days a week.

CLEANERS

MIDNIGHT EXPRESS ★ Long Island City ★ (212) 921-0111
They pick up and deliver in Manhattan up until 11:00 P.M. Turnaround
time is two business days. Next-day service is available for more
money.

DRUGSTORE (WITH PHARMACY)

KAUFMAN ★ Lexington at 50th Street ★ (212) 755-2266
This is the only one that can dispense prescriptions twenty-four hours.

DRUGSTORE (WITHOUT PHARMACY)

LOVE DISCOUNT ★ 2030 Broadway (at 69th Street) ★ (212) 877-4141
Open till 2:00 A.M.

ELECTRICIAN

MICHAEL ALTMAN ★ (212) 681-2900
Twenty-four hours a day, seven days a week. Emergency service costs
$95 per hour after 4:00 P.M.

FLORIST

RIALTO FLORIST ★ 707 Lexington Avenue (57th and 58th Streets) ★ (212) 688-3234
Open until 11:00 P.M.

GAS STATION

CAPITOL ★ 640 First Avenue (at 36th Street) ★ (212) 679-7585
Open twenty-four hours.

GASETERIA ★ 800 Lafayette Street (at Houston Street) ★ (212) 226-9530 ★ 2 West End Avenue
(at 59th Street) ★ (212) 245-9830
Open twenty-four hours.

AA ALON ★ 542 West 53rd Street ★ (212) 265-8270
Car repairs only, open twenty-four hours.

MESSENGER

AIR COURIERS ★ 20 West 22nd Street ★ (212) 242-1160
Twenty-four-hour service.

NEWSSTANDS

GEM SPA ★ 131 Second Avenue (at St. Mark's Place) ★ (212) 529-1146
Open twenty-four hours.

PLUMBING

FARRUGIA PLUMBING AND HEATING ★ 225 W. 34th Street ★ (212) 873-8626
Twenty-four-hour emergency service.

RAPID ROOTER ★ (212) 675-4171
Emergency service twenty-four hours.

POST OFFICE

33rd Street and 8th Avenue ★ (212) 967-8585
8:30 A.M.–7:45 P.M.
All services except registered mail and limited services for packages.
(212) 330-4000. Twenty-four-hour Touch-Tone answer line.

RESTAURANTS

AROUND THE CLOCK CAFE ★ 8 Stuyvesant Street (Third Avenue and 9th Street)
★ (212) 598-0402
The name says it.

BRASSERIE ★ 100 East 53rd Street ★ (212) 751-4840
Open twenty-four hours.

EMPIRE DINER ★ 210 Tenth Avenue (at 22nd Street) ★ (212) 243-2736
Twenty-four-hour Americana.

FLORENT ★ 69 Gansevoort Street (two blocks south of 14th Street at Ninth Avenue) ★ (212) 989-5779

Open twenty-four hours.

SUPERMARKETS

FOOD EMPORIUMS ★ Locations Throughout the City

Open twenty-four hours.

TRANSLATOR

ALL-LANGUAGE SERVICES INC. ★ 545 Fifth Avenue (at 45th Street) ★ (212) 986-1688

Round-the-clock translations.

FINDING A HANDYMAN YOU CAN TRUST

New Yorkers, like everyone else, have to depend on handymen to keep their homes in day-to-day working order. The problem here, however, is that there is no small-town accountability to weed out bad seeds in the labor force. Therefore, it's up to you to make the right hire.

❧ INTREPID APPROACH
The first step to finding a good handyman is to change your approach to hiring. Think of people such as your plumber, your electrician, your rug and curtain cleaners as employees you will trust completely to take care of you and your home for life. If you look for a handyman with that relationship in mind, you will be much more critical in your final decision. After you have found him through word of mouth or the yellow pages, ask him the following questions before you hire:

1. How long have you been in the business?
2. What kind of work do you specialize in?
3. Will you always be doing the repairs yourself or be sending in subordinates? If you send subordinates, will you supervise their work?
4. What do you charge?
5. How do you require payment?
6. May I have three references? (If it is a big job, ask to go and actually see his work.)
7. What is the time frame in which you will complete the job?
8. Is the work guaranteed? Do you stand behind your work?
9. Are you bonded and insured? (See below.)

Bonded means that the company has posted a bond with their insurance company as a protection against theft; theoretically, that means that if a worker steals something from your home you the client have some protection. The problem is, you have to prove that an item was stolen.

Insured means that the company's insurance company protects you the client against property damage. Once again, the burden of proof falls on you; however, if you have hired a reputable and honest company there won't be an issue of having to prove who's in the wrong. If an honest worker broke something, he would call his company right away to say so.

THE INTREPID PAGES

OF

"DOWN HOME" HANDYMEN

$ = inexpensive $$ = moderate $$$ = expensive

CARPET AND FURNITURE CLEANING

New York is a haven for dirt and soot. Don't think that your apartment is the only one in constant need of a good cleaning. White rugs—what a horror! Your carpets and upholstered furniture will last a lot longer if you take care of them.

DELMONT CARPET CLEANING ★ (718) 531-4700 ★ $$

Reliable and accommodating. They do their best to give you the exact time they will arrive and if you are not satisfied with the job they will keep coming back at no extra charge until you are.

CHIMNEY SWEEP

D. W. KOLVENBACH ★ (212) 879-3035 ★ $$

Ask for Doug, a very nice person who does great work. If you want to make some changes to your fireplace, he will work with an installer.

SOOTENDERS ★ (212) 410-7431 ★ $

They try to be as accommodating as possible and will work on Saturdays and Sundays.

> We tell all our clients to always put in writing exactly what the job entails, what it is going to cost, and the time frame in which it will be completed and have both parties sign it.

DRAPERIES, BLINDS, UPHOLSTERED WALL CLEANING

CLEAN TEX ★ (212) 283-1200 ★ $$

They are the people to call to clean your drapes and curtains. The only company that truly knows how to deal with custom curtains and blinds. They do the removal and the installation. Also great for upholstered walls, wall-to-wall carpeting, and area rugs.

NAPTHA ★ (212) 686-6240 ★ $$

If you have very simple curtains (on pins) they do good work. Also available to clean rugs, carpets, and upholstered furniture.

ELECTRICIAN

We suggest you ask your building super to recommend an electrician. Your local hardware store might refer someone to you for a small job. *But,* you do not want a bargain-basement technician when it comes to doing dangerous work.

SPIELER & RICCA ★ (718) 392-4100 ★ $$

Ask for Frank or Ron and call between 7:00 A.M. and 8:00 A.M. They are a very large company and do mostly big jobs, although they do have two trucks that work the City doing jobs for individuals. Many of the top decorators use them.

HANDYMAN

It is not easy to find someone to help you fix all those annoying repairs. We suggest you ask your local hardware store, super, or:

FERNANDO DUQUE ★ (718) 965-4656 ★ $

No insurance or bonding. A bright, reliable, hardworking man. His day is fairly busy but if you need a hand he is a good guy to know. He also has a van that he uses for light moving jobs. He is extremely careful and diligent.

HOUSEHOLD HELP

There are several ways to find help: Ask any of the household help and employees in your building; ask your office cleaners; share your friend's.

DIRT BUSTERS ★ (212) 721-HELP ★ $$

David runs this very efficient and pleasant cleaning service. He is very flexible when it comes to trying to fill a request. He arranges for home and office cleaning, day or night. They specialize in crisis cleaning. All they need is two hours' notice.

MAIDS UNLIMITED ★ (212) 369-9100 ★ $$$

Mr. Van and Mr. Cohen are smart businessmen. They saw the need for someone to pool and supervise a crew of rotating cleaners. They can arrange to have someone come to you on a regular or onetime basis. For an extra fee, they can bring all the equipment too.

SERGIO ★ (212) 562-4788 ★ $

A real find in this city of grime. He is a fantastic cleaner who pays attention to all the details.

PLUMBER

To find a plumber, ask your building manager or call:

KRAUSS ★ (212) 860-5300 ★ $$$

A very competent group of plumbers. Their only drawback is that it can take a long time for them to schedule an appointment for smaller jobs.

ROTO-ROOTER ★ (718) 849-2842 ★ $$

Excellent for stopped-up or clogged drains.

WINDOWS WASHED

EAST END WINDOW CLEANERS ★ (212) 879-5590 ★ $$

Mr. Kay has run this company for years. If you are persistent, he will narrow down the time that you will have to wait for your window washer.

FLAT IRON ★ (212) 876-1000 ★ $$

Another good choice. They clean windows from 55 Hudson Street to 105th Street.

☛ **One last suggestion:** If you are hiring a company for a big job, call the Better Business Bureau to find out if there are any complaints or liens against them. For public inquiries and complaints, their number is (212) 533-6200. (For extensive information about this bureau and how it operates see page 75).

TAPPING NYC'S PROFESSIONAL SCHOOLS FOR EXPERT HELP

From time to time we really need to hire a professional for a special assignment. Photographers, musicians, caterers, decorators, secretarial assistants, dressmakers. If you really want to, you can go with the big names like Glorious Foods, Bachrach Photographers, Peter Duchin. The Intrepid New Yorker advises that unless you can afford big names, hire the talent before their names get big.

INTREPID APPROACH
Hire your help from the dozens of professional schools and universities in New York. New York City attracts the most talented young professionals from all over the country, not only because of the opportunities here but because it offers the widest selection of fine schools in which to perfect their craft. There is more available talent for the asking here than anywhere else in the world. These kids go on to become the Craig Claibornes, the Donna Karans, and the Itzhak Perlmans of tomorrow.
   Here's how you tap in:

- The schools expect you to call and request temporary employment for their students and they are set up to handle your request professionally. Call and ask for their temporary employment office. Expect two to four weeks to fulfill your request.
- In order to get precisely what you want you must be explicit about what your needs are and make sure the school feels they can be met. At that point, interview the student(s) and check their portfolio and references. If you insist on having their most prized, senior student, it may cost you extra, but it will never cost you as much as going to an established professional. Sometimes you will negotiate the price with the student; sometimes the school sets it.
- If you don't need to tap into a particular talent, but you just need a part-time helper to baby-sit, to run errands, to give you a lesson on your computer, help chaperon a birthday party, all the large schools like NYU, Barnard, Columbia, even the Screen Actors Guild are happy to post the information on the bulletin board in their temporary-employment department. And don't forget—you can use the schools to get any kind of lesson taught or question answered from how to make a soufflé to how to translate a French proverb.

THE INTREPID PAGES
OF
PROFESSIONAL SCHOOLS

The yellow pages has a section of schools arranged by subject. It's an excellent way to start looking for hired help, or call:

AAA BARTENDERS INTERNATIONAL SCHOOL ★ Placement Office: (212) 868-3303
You can hire the instructors themselves; the students are a little cheaper. All are fully competent to help with liquor selection and setting up and will wear the standard uniform. The school will make sure you get the right person. Average cost is $12 to $15 an hour.

BARNARD COLLEGE ★ Career Services Office: (212) 854-2033
Mail your job description to 3009 Broadway, NY, NY 10027-6598, or fax it to 854-7491. It will be posted and the fee is set between you and the student.

COLUMBIA UNIVERSITY ★ Student Employment Office: (212) 854-2391
They will post the job description on their board. There is no set fee. You will negotiate that with the student you hire.

JUILLIARD ★ Placement Office: (212) 799-5000
The director and associate director will find the right people for the job. The fee is set by the school. A three-piece band is $75 per person, per hour, with a one-hour minimum.

KATHERINE GIBBS SECRETARIAL SCHOOL ★ Placement Office: (212) 867-9307
Ask for Terry. She will post the job. The fee is set by you and the student.

NEW YORK RESTAURANT SCHOOL ★ (212) 947-7097
Your request gets posted on the board. But Rebecca checks the student out to make sure he's the right one for you. You will hear from undergrads and postgrads. The average is $15 an hour. It is negotiable.

NEW YORK SCHOOL OF INTERIOR DESIGN ★ (212) 753-5365
Talk to Ms. Chapin about the scope of the job. She can find you someone to do anything from choosing paint colors to renovating an

apartment. Most of the students you get will be graduates. The fee is set between you and the student.

NEW YORK UNIVERSITY ★ Student Employment Office: (212) 998-4433

They will post the job description on their bulletin board. An interested student will call you. The price is set between the two of you. The minimum is $5 an hour. You will primarily attract undergraduates. NYU wants you to call them when you have found someone so they can take it off the board.

PARSONS SCHOOL OF DESIGN ★ (212) 229-8940

The school will check the student's portfolio to make sure they are good enough for the job. You can tap into fashion designers, photographers, and interior decorators. The fee is set between you and the student.

PETER KUMP'S COOKING SCHOOL ★ (212) 410-4601

Tell the school exactly what you are looking for. The description is posted on the board, and postgrads and undergrads consult the board. You will set the fee with the student but the price averages about $15 to $20 an hour.

SCHOOL OF VISUAL ARTS ★ (212) 679-7350

The job description will go up on the board. You will have access to photographers, video experts, calligraphers, graphic designers. The fee is negotiable. Could be as high as $100 an hour.

SCREEN ACTORS GUILD ★ (212) 827-1524

Talk to Merna. The job will be posted. It will cost you approximately $12 an hour.

THE INTREPID PAGES

OF
PROFESSIONAL FREE-LANCE
OFFICE SERVICES

ADVERTISING

SUSAN KIRBAN ★ (203) 454-8720

Susan spent twenty years working for some of the largest advertising firms in the world. She now works on a free-lance basis. You can hire her as either an art director or copywriter or both.

SWING DIXON ★ (212) 645-0626

Here you will find two very talented people willing to help you create an interesting campaign or brochure.

ARTWORK/ILLUSTRATION

JIMMY PALMIOTTI ★ (212) 725-2744

Jimmy is one of the most talented illustrators and photo retouchers in this city.

COMPUTER HELP

PC BASICS ★ (718) 856-5686

Debra Kane owns this very helpful computer company. She works with IBM and IBM-compatible machines and offers customized training for individuals or companies. For those who are working on a computer at the office and feel that they could use some more explanation, you can hire her to come to your office at lunchtime and she will very discreetly show you what you need to know.

MORT TANNER ★ (212) 362-1245

Mort is a computer programmer by day and a free-lance computer troubleshooter by night. He has the capability to set up computers, do minor household computer repairs, unbug detection devices, hook up modems, and much more.

INFORMATION RETRIEVAL

ON LINE NIGHTLINE ★ (212) 601-2959

This is an information retrieval service specializing in computer data base searches supported by library research. Their hours are 7:30 P.M. TO 11:30 P.M. If you do not have time to find something out, they do.

INTERPRETERS/TRANSLATORS

THE INTERNATIONAL WORD, INC. ★ (212) 980-4534

Can accommodate all language-translations in a quick and accurate manner.

PUBLIC RELATIONS

PANDA COMMUNICATIONS ★ (212) 860-8720

This firm is run by Linda Miller, an expert in the field of public relations. The wonderful thing about her company is that you can hire her on a daily basis or by the month.

WORD PROCESSING

WORDPRO ★ (718) 769-6682

Maureen Perry is intelligent, precise, quick, and reliable—everything you want in a word processor. Call her after 6:00 P.M.

COPING WITH YOUR CITY PET

Having a dog in New York has its pluses. For example, walking one's dog in this city is without a doubt one of the best ways we have ever found to meet otherwise unapproachable people. One of our clients found herself chatting every morning on the street corner with Henry Kissinger! But, the daily care and maintenance of any animal, especially a dog, in this city is not easy, particularly if you are a working person.

You might want to consider the following:

- ❧ You can't let your dog out the back door, so you should think about living next to a park where your dog can run.
- ❧ You will need to find professional dog-walkers to walk your dog when you are at work during the day.
- ❧ Your dog is going to be in close quarters with a lot of other people and their dogs. If he's got behavior problems, you may need an obedience school.
- ❧ If you are invited away for a weekend or you have been called away on a business trip, you can't just leave your dog in your studio apartment. And you will be hard pressed to find a neighbor who will take him. In the best of worlds you will want to be able to leave your dog in a comfortable, home environment.

Well, predictably, there are services in this city that will do everything from walk your dog to provide day care.

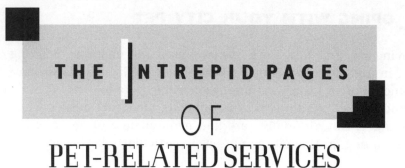

THE INTREPID PAGES
OF
PET-RELATED SERVICES

$ = inexpensive $$ = moderate $$$ = expensive

ADOPT A PET

ASPCA ★ 441 East 92nd Street ★ (212) 876-7711
It will cost you $55 to adopt a dog and $45 to adopt a cat, but these fees include various shots, spaying and neutering costs, carrying cases, and literature.

BIDE-A-WEE HOME ASSOCIATION ★ 410 East 38th Street ★ (212) 532-4455
It will cost you $30 to adopt a dog or cat over six months old and $55 to adopt a dog or cat under six months, which includes spaying/neutering fees.

FRIENDS OF ANIMALS ★ 11 West 60th Street ★ (212) 247-8120
They can advise you where to buy a pet.

HUMANE SOCIETY ★ 306 East 59th Street ★ (212) 752-4840
Dogs cost $50 to $100; Cats cost $50 or $75. The Humane Society will contribute $10 toward spaying or neutering.

EMERGENCY NUMBERS

ANIMAL POISON CONTROL ★ (212) 340-4494 or (800) 548-2433

TWENTY-FOUR-HOUR EMERGENCY ANIMAL MEDICAL CENTER ★ 510 East 52nd Street ★ (212) 838-8100

GROOMING CARE

JIM SUMMER ★ (212) 861-2836 ★ $$$
For those who want their dogs groomed at home.

PET SUPERETTE ★ 187 East 93rd Street ★ (212) 534-1732 ★ $$
Call in advance because they do book up. They have a van that can pick up your dog or cat and bring him home.

YUPPIE PUPPY PET CARE ★ 274 West 86th Street ★ (212) 877-2747 ★ $$

They not only groom dogs but cats as well. There is no pickup or delivery.

PET SUPPLIES
R. C. STEELE CATALOGUE ★ By Mail: (800) 872-3773 ★ $
A wholesale supply catalogue (no food). They deliver right to your door for half the price of New York stores.

TRAINING
BASHA DIBRA ★ (212) 796-4541 ★ $$$
Trainer to the stars.

CITY DOG OBEDIENCE SCHOOL ★ 158 West 23rd Street ★ (212) 255-3618 ★ $$
Here your dog can train in group classes.

YUPPIE PUPPY PET CARE ★ 274 West 86th Street ★ (212) 877-2747 ★ $$
All of their training occurs in their town house designed for dogs.

WALKING/BOARDING
JIM BUCK ★ (212) 860-8680 ★ $$$
This is "the" dog-walking company on the Upper East Side. They will walk dogs in packs from 59th Street to 96th Street. They also provide boarding services in a home environment.

AMY CUMMINGS ★ (212) 242-5087 ★ $$
If you are thinking of leaving town for a weekend call Amy and see if she will take your dog. Your dog will have to be screened first to be sure that he gets along with any other animals that might be there at the time.

PET PATROL ★ (212) 924-6319 ★ $$
Here you will find someone willing to walk your dog solo. They also arrange boarding in a home environment.

REBECCA SNOW ★ (212) 477-6253 ★ $$
She mostly walks dogs in the East Murray Hill area. She walks between two to four dogs at one time.

YUPPIE PUPPY PET CARE ★ 274 West 86th Street ★ (212) 877-2747 ★ $$
Aside from doing the typical dog-walking, the Yuppie Puppy has day care for dogs. You can drop your dog at 8:00 A.M. and pick him up again at 9:00 P.M. During that time your dog will be fed, played with, and walked. What more could you want for your dog?

GETTING IN AND OUT AND AROUND NYC

Unless you are one of the elite, and can chopper, limo, or yacht your way around New York, getting from one end of the city to the other is a daily problem that most people share. The Intrepid New Yorker is going to try to make it as painless as possible.

MANHATTAN ADDRESS LOCATOR

To find the location of a number on the following avenues of Manhattan, cancel the last figure of the number, divide the remainder by 2, and add or subtract the given key number.

Thus: *Where is 934 Third Avenue?*
Divide 93 by 2 = 46, plus 10 = 56th Street

To find addresses on numbered cross streets, remember that numbers increase east or west from Fifth Avenue, which runs north–south.

Avenue A	add 3	8th Avenue	add	9
Avenue B	add 3	9th Avenue	add	13
Avenue C	add 3	10th Avenue	add	13
Avenue D	add 3	11th Avenue	add	15
1st Avenue	add 4	Amsterdam Avenue	add	59
2nd Avenue	add 3	Audubon Avenue	add	165
3rd Avenue	add 10	Columbus Avenue	add	60
Park Avenue South	add 8	Convent Avenue	add	127
5th Avenue		Edgecombe Avenue	add	134
Up to 200	add 13	Ft. Washington. Avenue	add	158
Up to 400	add 16	Lenox Avenue	add	110
Up to 600	add 18	Lexington Avenue	add	22
Up to 775	add 20	Madison Avenue	add	27
From 775 to 1286–see below:		Manhattan Avenue	add	100
Up to 1500	add 45	Park Avenue	add	34
Above 2000	add 24	Pleasant Avenue	add	101
Avenue of the Americas	sub. 12	St. Nicholas Avenue	add	110
Broadway–see below:		Wadsworth Avenue	add	173
7th Avenue	add 12	West End Avenue	add	59
Above 1800	add 20	York Avenue	add	4

EXCEPTIONS

Broadway   Up to 754, below East 8th Street: no key due to the many named streets.
   Above 754, apply above rule, but deduct following key number:
   From 754 to 858 deduct 29.
   From 859 to 958 deduct 25.
   Above 1000 deduct 31.
Riverside Drive   Below 567, drop last figure, add 73 to remainder.
Central Park West   Drop last figure, add 60 to remainder.
5th Avenue   From 775 to 1286, drop last figure and deduct 18 from remainder.

Taxis

❗ INTREPID APPROACH

You can greatly increase your odds of finding a cab when you need one the most. You claim you can't find one in the pouring rain, during rush hour, on a critical shopping day. Yes you can. Think Intrepidly.

During rush hour:

- If it is early morning, the taxis will be dropping workers off on Wall Street and Midtown. Logically, they will be coming back uptown empty, so look for them on avenues that run uptown.
- During rush hour at night you would look for them on avenues that run downtown. When everyone is looking for cabs, walk to the outer avenues away from all the other taxi seekers.

Think also about the neighborhood you are in. Decide where taxis would logically be picking up and dropping off. For example:

- ☞ If you live on the Upper East Side, taxis will be dropping people off at early morning doctor's appointments on Park Avenue and at schools.
- ☞ If you live downtown, early morning taxis will be coming back uptown from dropping people off in the Wall Street area. So look for them on the avenues that run uptown.
- ☞ If you live in the east 50s and 60s, cabbies change shifts in Queens and come back over the 59th Street bridge empty.
- ☞ If you live or work near train and bus stations, you will find plenty of cabs, especially during rush hours.

> Don't stand in clusters if you are in a hurry to get a cab; that's like waiting on line. If you walk aggressively in the direction you see most of the cabs coming from, you will be one of the first, not the last, people to get a cab.

- ☞ If you are anywhere near the theater district near curtain time, you know you will be able to find plenty of cabs there. If you have just gotten out of the theater, walk west and a few blocks south away from the crowds; cabs will be coming back up from dropping people off at the train and bus stations.

Other ways to get a cab:

- ☞ Hotels are the most luxurious places to get cabs. And you don't have to stay in a hotel in order for a doorman to find you one; a goodwill fee should take care of any guilt you may feel.
- ☞ Don't forget the small-town approach. You don't always have to fight for a cab, you can share one. Turn to the person waiting next to you and ask her if she would like to share the cab she just found. In New York it doesn't cost any extra to make two stops.

Car Services

INTREPID APPROACH
You can end your anxiety about getting there on time and in one piece. It is amazing how few New Yorkers take advantage of car services unless their companies pay for it. A car service does not always mean a stretch limo with a chauffeur in white gloves. There are many variations to that, including a comfortable town car or a taxi that you can reserve. The extra cost is worth it when it takes the anxiety out of getting to that critical meeting or school recital when it's pouring rain or rush hour. Presto! It's waiting for you at your door.

Here's what you need to know:

Car services can be amazingly inexpensive when hiring them by the hour—as little as $15 an hour with a two-hour minimum within Manhattan. If you have the occasional big shopping day coming up, hire a car for a couple of hours; they will take you door-to-door, wait for you, and you have the added luxury of leaving all your packages and coats in the car. To cut the cost even more, go in on it with a friend. Spending a little more for certain reasons can make a huge difference in the quality of your life. Factor in the emotional and physical price you would have paid trying to get around the City at Christmas time, fighting the crowds, the subways, trying to find taxis, and schlepping packages and coats.

- Shop around for a reliable service that shows up on time.
- Find them through friends, your office, ask yellow cabbies, or consult the yellow pages.
- Many services will let you reserve in advance without having an account.
- These services charge a flat rate and will cost you a few dollars more than a regular taxi. If you were stuck in rush hour in a yellow cab with the meter running, however, it would probably cost about the same.

Garages

INTREPID APPROACH
You don't have to sell your car; there are inexpensive parking garages. Parking garages are notoriously expensive in Manhattan; we've seen spaces go for $400 a month. Many New Yorkers will actually sell their most treasured form of transportation to avoid paying the monthly bill.

We have alternatives:

- If you use your car infrequently or just on weekends and want to continue keeping it near your home, try bargaining with your garage for lower rates.

The rationale for this is that the garage won't have to attend to your car nearly as much and can store it away.

- In addition to the 8¼ percent parking tax collected by garages and parking lots in New York City, there is a 10 percent surcharge; if you spend $400 a month on your garage, that's an additional $40 a month or an additional $480 a year! However, Manhattan residents who have their cars registered to their Manhattan address and park their cars on a monthly basis may apply for an exemption from that surcharge. To obtain it, you must apply to the New York City Department of Finance for an exemption certificate and present it to the garage. For information you can call (212) 306-5707 or write to that department c/o Parking Tax Exemption Section, 151 West Broadway, Room 200, NY, NY 10013.

- As a rule of thumb, the farther you get to the outskirts of Manhattan, the cheaper the rates are; look near or along the waterfront areas if you can afford not to have your car just around the block. You can pay as little as $125 a month for a covered garage. What you have to factor in is the cost of transportation to and from. The least expensive of all the garages are the open garages; if you have a cover for your car, you may not mind.

- If you want to go the fantastically cheap route—under $100 a month—you should consider across the river. Family residences in Queens and New Jersey often have signs in their windows advertising their garage space. You can also look in the *Jersey Journal* and the Sunday *New York Times* in the classified automobile listings. Some garages just across the Hudson in New Jersey run about $70 a month. If you use your car infrequently, it is well worth the twenty-minute subway ride.

- The Intrepid New Yorker saved money by sharing their car with a friend. Neither one of us had to have access to a car all the time. We shared the cost of the insurance and the garage. We put the terms in writing. It worked well.

An important note: Most parking lots and garages are required to be licensed by the New York City Department of Consumer Affairs, and a sign with the department's complaint telephone number should be conspicuously posted.

Drivers

🦶 **INTREPID APPROACH**
Hire a chauffeur to drive your car. If you have a car of your own in the City, you can hire a chauffeur to take you around on that big shopping day or to that important meeting. The Intrepid New Yorker knows a place that only charges $12 an hour (see Intrepid pages, page 56).

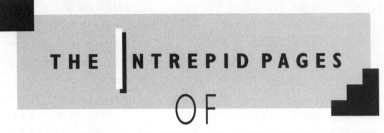

THE INTREPID PAGES
OF
GETTING AROUND NEW YORK

CAR SERVICE

Note: A yellow cab from 96th Street and Park Avenue to Wall Street can cost up to $16 with tip, and much more in a traffic jam. There are many times when hiring a car can be more economical, convenient, and comfortable. Here's how they compare:

BELL TAXI ★ (212) 206-1700

Open twenty-four hours, seven days a week, they accept credit cards and cash. Their cars are very nice—always a Lincoln or Mercury Town Car—and drivers wear suits. Some cars have mobile phones. To hire a car for an extended period, there is a two-hour minimum, at $30 per hour, and each stop is $4. To go to just one destination—from 96th Street and Park Avenue to Wall Street—is $19. Gratuities are expected. This company is reliable and reservations are accepted.

TEL AVIV ★ (212) 777-7777 ★ (212) 505-0555

They are open twenty-four hours, seven days a week and accept both credit cards and cash. Their cars are plain four-door family cars and the drivers wear street clothes. To hire a car for an extended period of time, there is a two-hour minimum in Manhattan, with no charge for stops. The rate is $15 an hour. To go to just one destination—from 96th Street and Park Avenue to Wall Street—is $14. Gratuities are expected. A reliable company that accepts reservations.

CHAUFFEURS

If you have your own car, why not?

CHAUFFEURS UNLIMITED ★ (212) 362-5354

They are open twenty-four hours, seven days a week, and usually need a day's notice. Their chauffeurs cannot begin a job after 8:00 P.M. The charge is $12 per hour, three hours minimum, with a 15 percent gratuity expected. The chauffeur drives under your insurance claim and wears a full uniform. Cash only.

PARKING GARAGES

For the least expensive within Manhattan, always look on the outer avenues, near and along the rivers, and the extreme north and south ends of the island.

CITY MUNICIPAL PARKING ★ (718) 786-6621

The city lots offer short-term parking only. There are six municipal lots in Manhattan, the largest is 54th Street and Eighth Avenue; the rate there is $2.40 per hour, the night rate from 7:00 P.M. to 9:00 A.M. is $8.40. It's a good deal!

EDISON PARK ★ Locations Throughout the City ★ (212) 267-4050

They offer long-term parking and are open twenty-four hours, seven days a week. The rate is under $250 per month, with some indoor locations.

GGMC PARKING ★ 503–519 39th Street
★ (212) 564-1139

They offer long-term parking and are open twenty-four hours, seven days a week. Their rates are $125 per month for valet parking, plus tax; $200 per month for park and lock, plus tax. This is an indoor, heated garage with about a 1,000-car capacity. GGMC might begin a shuttle service at night.

> You can place your own ad that says you are looking for a parking space in the classified automobile sections of **The New York Times** or the local community papers in New Jersey and the boroughs.

> The Exotic Car Emporium at 438 West 19th Street does repairs and body work on mostly foreign cars, but they won't snub you if yours is domestic. Their mechanics are intelligent, articulate, and well dressed. And if that isn't enough, they pick up and deliver. Call (212) 807-0899.

CAR RENTALS

INTREPID APPROACH

There are ways to get deals and reliable service out of car rental companies. Every New Yorker has a story: "After all the extra costs, I might as well have rented a helicopter." "I waited on line for two hours with a guaranteed reservation to discover they had no cars left." "I was over the Triborough Bridge before realizing the gas gauge was on empty." "I am a law-abiding, honest adult who was refused a car because I only owned one credit card, not two." Okay. You're mad as hell but you really don't have to take this anymore.

Here's what you need to know:

☞ Rates vary widely and constantly for daily, weekly, or weekend rentals, so it is critical to call at least three different places to compare rates. There are also widespread discrepancies between rate information provided by individual branches of nationally operating firms and rate information for those same branches provided by the firms' national toll-free telephone numbers. Make sure you check the branch's cost against the national toll-free number cost and get the better rate.

☛ Often, calling way in advance will get you a discount; find out what discount packages are being offered and when.

☛ Special rates will apply for certain time periods. When you talk to the agents on the phone make sure you make them tell you the cheapest way to go. For example, a six-day rate may be more expensive than the seven-day package they are offering at that time.

☛ There are hidden charges such as insurance fees, gasoline charges, younger driver surcharges, and drop-off fees usually in fine print at the bottom of the ad. *Read them.*

☛ Renting a car in the boroughs or somewhere else in the tristate area can be so much cheaper that it is worth the trip out there to pick up the car, especially if you are renting for a week or more.

There is a lot to be said for going with some of the cheaper, lesser-known rental agencies in Manhattan.

☛ You can get some real deals. But there are pitfalls you must pay attention to. The first "must" is to call the Better Business Bureau and find out if any complaints have been filed against the company (see page 75).

☛ Then make sure when you talk to these places that they guarantee your reservation, and *always* take down the name of the person you talked to.

☛ Find out if they have emergency road service.

☛ Make them tell you what their policy is and if there are any hidden costs.

☛ Make sure before you drive the car out of their lot that there is a full tank of gas, and water and oil in the car. Inspect the car completely to make sure it's clean and everything is working. As long as you take the time to check, you should be all right.

> The Intrepid New Yorker rents cars from National Rent-A-Car at the Gateway Hotel in Newark, New Jersey. It is almost half the price of a rental in Manhattan. We just take the twenty-minute Path train to the Newark train station and National is right across the street. If you want to save some serious dollars, call their 800 number at (800) 227-7368.

☛ The one plus with going with big-name companies like Hertz and Avis is that you know what you are getting. The bottom line is you must demand good service and accept nothing less from lesser-known companies.

You do have rights!

☛ New York General Business Law Section 391-i prohibits rental car agencies from requiring a credit card. Don't let rental car companies tell you you have to have one or two credit cards to rent a car. You can pay by cash, up front, and leave a deposit. When you call to reserve a car you will get transferred to their "cash" department. They will do a background check on you before approval, which takes a few extra days. If any rental car company refuses to let you pay cash, file a complaint with the Better Business Bureau (see page 75).

☛ New York City Consumer Protection Regulation 501 requires that rental car firms that take reservations make available either the car reserved or a similar car *within one half hour* of the reserved time, either at the reserved location or at another location to which the consumer is transported without charge. If you run into this situation, make sure you demand to talk to a supervisor or manager immediately, let them know you know the law, and demand immediate satisfaction.

The Intrepid New Yorker highly recommends that you join an automobile club like AAA if you drive often. For a nominal yearly fee of $40, you can get all sorts of benefits such as free, guaranteed emergency road service, free towing to an AAA service station, discount car rentals, trip planning, etc. Membership would afford you the protection you might not be guaranteed from a lesser-known car rental company. The telephone number of AAA is (212) 757-2000.

☛ New York General Business Law Section 391-g provides that rental car firms may not refuse to rent a car to anyone eighteen years of age or older if insurance is available.

STREET PARKING

INTREPID APPROACH
You can find a parking space in Manhattan if you change your approach. How many New Yorkers have considered murder in order to secure a parking space? The Intrepid New Yorker says common sense will do.

Here are some tips:

♦ Circling the same ground continually makes no sense. There is no reason why anyone will be more apt to pull out of a space on one block over another, and you spend most of your time waiting for the light to turn green. If you pick a lookout spot and stay there, you can watch the pedestrians who might be heading toward their cars and it establishes you as the next in line. And you save gas.

♦ If you park in the same area every day, pay attention to typical parking patterns and try to time your arrival with someone else's departure. Make an effort to get to know the other parkers because you could form a "parking association" and share each other's spaces. Try leaving a note on their windshield as an introduction. And don't forget to get to know the doormen in the area. Offer a "goodwill fee"; they might be willing to spot spaces for you.

1992 PARKING CALENDAR

January

sun	mon	tues	wed	thurs	fri	sat
			1	2	3	4
5	6	7	8	9	10	11
12	13	14	15	16	17	18
19	20	21	22	23	24	25
26	27	28	29	30	31	

February

sun	mon	tues	wed	thurs	fri	sat
						1
2	3	4	5	6	7	8
9	10	11	12	13	14	15
16	17	18	19	20	21	22
23	24	25	26	27	28	29

March

sun	mon	tues	wed	thurs	fri	sat
1	2	3	4	5	6	7
8	9	10	11	12	13	14
15	16	17	18	19	20	21
22	23	24	25	26	27	28
29	30	31				

April

sun	mon	tues	wed	thurs	fri	sat
			1	2	3	4
5	6	7	8	9	10	11
12	13	14	15	16	17	18
19	20	21	22	23	24	25
26	27	28	29	30		

May

sun	mon	tues	wed	thurs	fri	sat
					1	2
3	4	5	6	7	8	9
10	11	12	13	14	15	16
17	18	19	20	21	22	23
24	25	26	27	28	29	30

June

sun	mon	tues	wed	thurs	fri	sat
	1	2	3	4	5	6
7	8	9	10	11	12	13
14	15	16	17	18	19	20
21	22	23	24	25	26	27
28	29	30				

July

sun	mon	tues	wed	thurs	fri	sat
			1	2	3	4
5	6	7	8	9	10	11
12	13	14	15	16	17	18
19	20	21	22	23	24	25
26	27	28	29	30	31	

August

sun	mon	tues	wed	thurs	fri	sat
						1
2	3	4	5	6	7	8
9	10	11	12	13	14	15
16	17	18	19	20	21	22
23	24	25	26	27	28	29
30	31					

September

sun	mon	tues	wed	thurs	fri	sat
		1	2	3	4	5
6	7	8	9	10	11	12
13	14	15	16	17	18	19
20	21	22	23	24	25	26
27	28	29	30			

October

sun	mon	tues	wed	thurs	fri	sat
				1	2	3
4	5	6	7	8	9	10
11	12	13	14	15	16	17
18	19	20	21	22	23	24
25	26	27	28	29	30	31

November

sun	mon	tues	wed	thurs	fri	sat
1	2	3	4	5	6	7
8	9	10	11	12	13	14
15	16	17	18	19	20	21
22	23	24	25	26	27	28
29	30	31				

December

sun	mon	tues	wed	thurs	fri	sat
		1	2	3	4	5
6	7	8	9	01	11	12
13	14	15	16	17	18	19
20	21	22	23	24	25	26
27	28	29	30	31		

A ALTERNATE SIDE PARKING RULES SUSPENDED

Restrictions in effect for street sweeping will be suspended, including:

- The 8 A.M. to 11 A.M. or 11 A.M. to 2 P.M. "No Parking" Sanitation Rules.
- Signs Reading: "No Parking 8 A.M. to 6 P.M.," which are in effect on alternate days, on opposite sides of the street (e.g., "No Parking 8 A.M. to 6 P.M. on Tuesday and Thursday" on one side, and "No Parking on Monday and Friday" on the other side).
- The 2 A.M. to 6 A.M. Sanitation regulations in the Manhattan Garment District.
- The 12 Midnight to 8 A.M. sanitation regulations.
- On legal holidays (see below), signs reading: "No Parking 8 A.M. to 9 A.M.," which are located in parking meter zones.

All other regulations, including parking meters, remain in effect. Motorists are advised to check signs carefully before parking.

S SUNDAY RULES IN EFFECT

When "Sunday" parking rules are in effect, parking will be permitted wherever signs indicate that parking is legal on Sundays. Parking meter regulations will apply only at meters where they are in effect on Sundays. Motorists are advised that "No Standing Anytime" and similar rules are not affected by "Sunday" regulations.

HOLIDAY	DATE	DAY	RULES
New Year's Day*	1/01	Wed	Sunday
Martin Luther King, Jr.'s Birthday*	1/20	Mon	ASP Suspended
Lincoln's Birthday	2/12	Wed	ASP Suspended
Washington's Birthday	2/17	Mon	ASP Suspended
Holy Thursday	4/16	Thu	ASP Suspended
Good Friday	4/17	Fri	ASP Suspended
Passover: First Day	4/18	Sat	ASP Suspended
Passover: Second Day	4/19	Sun	Sunday
Holy Thursday (Orthodox)	4/23	Thu	ASP Suspended
Good Friday (Orthodox)	4/24	Fri	ASP Suspended
Passover: Seventh Day	4/24	Fri	ASP Suspended
Passover: Eighth Day	4/25	Sat	ASP Suspended
Memorial Day*	5/25	Mon	Sunday
Solemnity of Ascension	5/28	Thu	ASP Suspended
Shavuot: First Day	6/07	Sun	Sunday
Shavuot: Second Day	6/08	Mon	ASP Suspended
Independence Day*	7/04	Sat	Sunday
Assumption of the Blessed Virgin	8/15	Sat	ASP Suspended
Labor Day*	9/07	Mon	Sunday
Rosh Hashannah: First Day	9/28	Mon	ASP Suspended
Rosh Hashannah: Second Day	9/29	Tue	ASP Suspended
Yom Kippur	10/07	Wed	ASP Suspended
Columbus Day Observed*	10/12	Mon	ASP Suspended
Succoth: First Day	10/12	Mon	ASP Suspended
Succoth: Second Day	10/13	Tue	ASP Suspended
Shemini Atzereth	10/19	Mon	ASP Suspended
Simchas Torah	10/20	Tue	ASP Suspended
All Saint's Day	11/01	Sun	Sunday
Election Day*	11/03	Tue	ASP Suspended
Veteran's Day	11/11	Wed	ASP Suspended
Thanksgiving Day*	11/26	Thu	Sunday
Immaculate Conception	12/08	Tue	ASP Suspended
Christmas Day*	12/25	Fri	Sunday

*Legal Holiday

Note: Parking regulations for street sweepiong are suspended on Wednesdays and Saturdays due to the cancellation of street cleaning on those days.

THE INTREPID PAGES

OF
PUBLIC TRANSPORTATION
INFORMATION

*We can't change New York's public transportation system but we
can give you the telephone numbers you need so you at least know
how to get there from here.*

TRAINS

AMTRAK—(800) 872-7245
Long Island Railroad—(718) 217-5477
Metro North—(212) 532-4900
Metroliner—(800) 523-8720
New Jersey Transit—(201) 460-8444
Path trains—(212) 466-7649
Staten Island Rapid Transit—(718) 447-8601

SUBWAYS/BUSES

City subway and bus information—(718) 858-7272
Subway schedules—(718) 330-1234
Port Authority Bus Terminal Information
  —(212) 564-8484
Greyhound/Trailways bus lines
  —(212) 971-6363
Subway lost and found—(718) 330-4484
Bus lost and found—(718) 625-6200
Carey Bus (airport bus)—(718) 632-0500

TAXIS

Complaints—(212) 221-8294
Lost and found—(212) 840-4734

AIRPORTS

John F. Kennedy—(718) 656-4444
LaGuardia—(718) 476-5000
Newark—(201) 961-2000

> Newark Airport can be much easier to negotiate than the other two. If you live on the west side of Manhattan, it can take you much less time to get there. We have also found that the airport itself can be much less congested and more manageable in general. You will find that they have many of the same flights you need to and from the major cities.

COPING WITH GOVERNMENT BUREAUCRACY

Red tape exists. We can't escape it. From social security to passports to driver's licenses to jury duty we have to deal with it. The one thing we can do is cut through it for you.

❗ INTREPID APPROACH:
You can get better service from government bureaucrats by following three rules of thumb:

Rule # 1: There is only one reasonable time to go to any of these places if you don't want to wait on line all day—fifteen minutes to a half hour before their doors open in the morning.

Rule # 2: If you need to talk to these agencies, call them first thing in the morning before they get inundated with calls; you won't be put endlessly on hold, and you'll get a cheerier representative at that hour.

Rule # 3: It is easy to get upset dealing with government employees. But they have a tough job themselves dealing with customers who are always angry and frustrated. Our advice to you is that you only attract bees with honey: the nicer you are and the more you appeal to their human side, the more cooperative they will be with you, and the more likely to bend the rules.

Jury Duty

Most people have to serve on jury duty eventually. The rule is you can get three official deferments sent in by mail or handled in person before you have to serve. If you have a job that you feel you just can't afford to leave you can push the system a little and keep writing letters until they absolutely insist you appear.

When you do go, the address is 60 Centre Street, Room 139. They are open from 9 A.M. to 4:30 P.M.

The only people who are exempt are people with disabilities, catastrophic illnesses, attorneys, nurses, doctors, psychologists, judges, law enforcers, politicians, felons, people over seventy years old, mothers who stay at home with their children, and self-employed individuals. *For further information call:* (212) 374-3810.

> We tell our clients that if you can't get through to a government representative on the phone, call the equivalent offices in Washington, D.C. We have found those offices to be more accessible. We also recommend taking advantage of earlier time zones around the country. If it's 5:30 P.M. in New York, and you still don't have the information you need, call the equivalent government agencies out west.

Birth Certificate

You can obtain a birth certificate for you or your child by showing up in person at the Health Department, 125 Worth Street, Room 133, between 8:00 A.M. and 4:30 P.M. You need a driver's license or another photo I.D. from your job. You can walk out the door with your certificate. It will cost you $15.

If you have no I.D. with you, you can get it mailed out to you or your parents the same day. The information they will need is the full name on the birth certificate, date of birth, mother's maiden name, father's name, hospital or borough where birth occurred, and the reason for the request.

If anyone other than yourself or your child is obtaining the certificate for you, that person has to bring a signed authorization and his own proof of I.D.

If you want to do it all by mail, send the same information, and a check for $15, to the Department of Health, Vital Records, 125 Worth Street, New York, New York 10013 in a self-addressed, stamped envelope. It takes six weeks.

If you are calling long distance and want to put it on a Visa or MasterCard, call (212) 566-6404. It will cost an additional $5. *For further information call:* (212) 619-4530.

Motor Vehicle Bureau

For registration, plates, and license, you must appear in person at 141–155 Worth Street between 7:30 A.M. and 4:30 P.M.

To renew a license bring your current license, a proof of signature (such as a credit card), plus proof of your current address with a utility or credit card bill. You will pay a fee of $17.50. You will need to fill out a MV44 form there.

If you are getting a car registration and plates for the first time, you have to fill out form MV82. You have to have one proof of ownership and proof of New York State Insurance, and sales tax clearance. You also need your birth certificate and proof of signature. There will be fees such as $5 for the title, $5 for the plates, and a $15 surcharge. On top of that there will be a fee on the weight of your car.

If you are simply renewing your registration, you need a proof of signature along with your renewal reminder.

New residents have thirty days to apply for a license and register their cars. You can pick up or get sent a license application, driver's manual, and auto registration form. A valid out-of-state license exempts you from a road test but you have to pass the vision, road sign, and written test. You can't make an appointment by phone. You have to write to the Preliminary Test Office at the same building. The written tests are given from 8:00 A.M. to 2:00 P.M. and cost $17.50. You will walk away with your temporary license.

If your license has lapsed, or you are applying for your first, you have to take the written test and then receive your learner's permit. You then must take a three-hour course at a licensed driving school. Finally, you take the road test. Sometimes it is hard to get an appointment in the city. It might be easier to take your road test out of town. *For further information call:* (212) 645-5550.

Traffic Tickets and Towing

Traffic tickets will cost you $30 if the meter has expired; $40 if you're parked on the wrong side of the street in an alternate side of the street parking zone; $45 for parking within fifteen feet of a hydrant or for double parking, or for parking in a no parking or no standing zone. Fines increase by $5 if you don't pay up within eight days and by $10 after thirty days. They will charge you interest on those charges as well.

If you come across a traffic cop in the process of writing you out a ticket, there is no point in trying to talk your way out of it; he can get suspended for an incomplete ticket.

If you think your car has been towed call (212) 924-0636 to make sure. If it has you have to go direct to the pound with the car's registration and insurance card and your driver's license. If your name is on the registration *and* your check, you can pay by check. Otherwise it's cash, certified check, or traveler's checks. It will cost you $125 plus $5 a day for storage.

> •
>
> If you entrepreneurs with commercial vehicles are sick of either paying or contesting one more parking ticket, call The Ticket Fighters. For a small fee they will do it for you. (212) 666-6514.
> Even if your vehicle isn't commercial, they might be willing to offer a little advice on how to handle your particular problem.
>
> •

Marriage License

With the proper documents you can get your marriage certificate instantly. Both future husband and wife have to show up in person to get a marriage license. The marriage license bureau in Manhattan is at 1 Centre Street. There are bureaus in every borough. The hours are 9:00 A.M. to 4:00 P.M.

You must marry within sixty days of obtaining your marriage license and it is only usable in New York State.

You will need proof of age and identification—either a passport, driver's license, birth certificate, military I.D., or school or work I.D.

You do not need to get a blood test or physical exam. The fee is $30, payable in cash. Also, any prior marriages must be listed in terms of termination date, where the marriage was ended and who the defendant was in the divorce.

If you just need a marriage record you can call (212) 791-7378. *For all other information call:* (212) 269-2900.

Social Security Card

If you lose your social security card, you can call (800) 772-1213 and request a new one. They will tell you where to send for it by mail or which location to get it in person. In either case you have to either bring with you or send originals of two forms of I.D.; it can be a library card, a health insurance card, a club card—it doesn't have to be important I.D.

If you need to apply for a new social security card for your child you can do it by mail or in person. Either way it takes two to three weeks.

By mail you need to send originals of the child's birth certificate, another record of his birth like his footprints, his hospital bracelet, a pediatrician's bill, a document with your child's name and address on it, and some I.D. of your own like a canceled check, utility bill, or voter's card. There is no fee for this and they will return your documents.

If you go in person, call the 800 number above and find out which office is closest to where you live. There are many locations in the city. We suggest you do not go to the one at Federal Plaza downtown; all government buildings seem to attract lines of people. The uptown offices are much less crowded.

Passport

You can get a new passport at 630 Fifth Avenue, Room 270 between 7:30 A.M. and 4:00 P.M. If you are getting a passport for the first time, you must go in person, bring with you proof of U.S. citizenship, your certified birth certificate, and one photo I.D. like a driver's license, employment card, school I.D., military card, plus two passport photos that you have had taken at any number of passport photo places around the city. The fee is $65. If you are renewing your passport, someone else can do it for you and all they need to bring are two passport photos and your old passport. The fee is $55. You can do it by mail if you have had your passport for at least 12 years and were 16 or older at the time of issuance.

If you have an emergency and must get your passport right away, you must bring your airline tickets in as proof.

During holiday seasons the line starts to form an hour before the doors open at the passport office. If you can, avoid that office at all costs during those peak times.

❗INTREPID APPROACH
You can also apply for your first passport at several post offices around the city. You simply take the same information with you. The reason to go to a post office? Fewer lines, less time. It takes longer to get the passport—about three weeks— because they have to send the information on to the passport office. But if you are not in a hurry it's a wonderful tip to know. You can also pick up a passport renewal form #DSP-82 from any of the places below and mail it to the New York Passport Agency accompanied by your two passport photos, a check for $42, and your old passport.

Here are all your options:

If you don't feel like dealing with getting a passport at all—period —you don't have to. Just call Passport Plus at (800) 367-1818 if you are calling from out of town or (212) 759-5540 from Manhattan. Someone else will do the whole thing for you. It will cost you $50 if you need your passport within a week; $65 within forty-eight hours; $100 within twenty-four hours; $150 the same day. If you are getting your first passport, you will have to go yourself, but Passport Plus guarantees you won't wait more than twenty minutes.

Passport Agency
630 Fifth Avenue (between 50th and 51st Streets), Mezzanine
New York, New York 10111, (212) 541-7700

Post Offices *
General Post Office, 8th Avenue and 33rd Street, (212) 967-8585
Ansonia Station, 1980–90 Broadway (between 67th and 68th Streets)
Church Street Station, 90 Church Street (corner of Vesey St.)
Cooper Station, 93 Fourth Avenue (corner of 11th St.)
Franklin D. Roosevelt Station, 909 Third Avenue (between 54th and 55th Streets)
Manhattanville Station, 365 West 125th Street
* Ask the General Post Office for post offices in the boroughs.

Clerks of the State Supreme Court
Court House, 60 Centre Street, NYC 10007

New Supreme Court
60 Adams Street, Brooklyn,
New York 11201

County Building
851 Grand Concourse
Bronx, New York 10451

WHERE TO FIND OASES IN NYC

The Intrepid New Yorker wanted to end this chapter on coping by encouraging New Yorkers to take better advantage of the many oases available in New York City to drift into during a hectic day. New Yorkers, more than almost any other species of urban dweller, need to have a place to stop, catch our breath, regroup, and recharge. And oases exist all over Manhattan. If more of us took advantage of them, even for five or ten minutes at a stretch, we would probably be a lot calmer and New York would appear a bit sunnier. Try it just once, and see if we're right.

> Many of the urban oases can be used as places to conduct business meetings for those of us who work out of our homes. Not only are they quiet, tranquil, and free, many have chairs and tables and food service.

INDOOR OASES

AT&T ★ 550 Madison Avenue (at 56th Street)
Chemcourt ★ 277 Park Avenue (44th and 45th Streets)
Citicorp Center ★ Lexington Avenue (53rd and 54th Streets)
Equitable Center ★ 787 Seventh Avenue (52nd and 53rd Streets)
Ford Foundation ★ 320 East 43rd Street
The Frick Museum reflecting pool ★ 1 East 70th Street
The Galleria ★ 115 East 57th Street
IBM ★ 590 Madison Avenue (at 57th Street)
Olympic Tower ★ 641 Fifth Avenue (51st and 52nd Streets)
Park Avenue Plaza ★ 55 East 52nd Street
Trump Tower ★ 725 Fifth Avenue (57th Street)
World Financial Center ★ West Street

OUTDOOR OASES

Cloisters ★ Fort Tryon Park
The Conservatory Gardens ★ Fifth Avenue at 105th Street
Greenacre Park ★ 51st Street between Second and Third Avenues
Jefferson Library Rose Garden ★ 425 Sixth Avenue (at 10th Street)
The McGraw-Hill Waterfalls ★ 48th Street between Sixth and Seventh Avenues
Paley Park ★ 53rd Street between Fifth and Park Avenues
Rockfeller Center ★ Fifth Avenue at 50th Street

THE INTREPID NEW YORKER ASSERTIVENESS TRAINING MANUAL

Often, when New Yorkers go out of town, they rediscover with shock that the minute they leave New York people are easygoing, courteous, and more than willing to be helpful. Getting some perspective on what the rest of the world is like makes it tough to come back to what we have all become accustomed to—bad attitudes and lousy service.

And contrary to popular belief, many New Yorkers have become too complacent; we tolerate being victims of inadequate service rather than standing up for our rights and demanding the kind of service paying customers deserve. Yes, there are oases of hospitable and helpful people here, but we doubt there is a soul in New York who doesn't have a horror story to tell.

❗ INTREPID APPROACH
Keep this in mind: If it weren't for the consumer, no services would exist. It is time to stop being victims, realize the power and protection we have as consumers, and start demanding nothing less than excellent service in this city. You may feel like David up against Goliath, but with the right approach, you can do a lot to turn New York City service people into hospitable, helpful folk again. This city has every conceivable service and product, but it's up to you to find it and then make sure you get it *precisely the way you want it.*

Here are some of the problems our clients came to us with:

---

1. The deal that was not a deal "I got a call from a bank that was promising two $100 bonus certificates on any airline if I would join their city travel club for $49. I readily agreed because I was planning a trip to New York from Florida to see my new grandchild and I could not afford the fare without the bonus. What came in the mail, however, was a shock: two $25 bonuses. I called them up only to get a runaround from many different customer service people who swore up and down that I had never been promised $100 bonuses, just the $25 ones."

2. "It's not my problem." "I rented a children's video for our son. It got lost amongst his toys, so I forgot we had it until it surfaced six days later. We called our video store, which we have been patronizing for five years, and told the manager our story, sure that he would acknowledge the honest error by a valued customer and give us a break. He told us, 'Sorry, not my problem, it's your problem and the rental will cost you eighteen dollars.' I said, 'But it costs twenty dollars to buy that same tape brand-new. Would you agree to at least let me purchase the old rental for eighteen? That way I don't lose out entirely and neither do you.' He said, 'Sorry, store policy says you have to pay for the late rental.'

3. "I never get what I ordered" "I ordered a dining room set. At the start, they told me it would take the typical twelve weeks to deliver. That would have been barely tolerable if they had delivered the entire set. The delivery men pulled up to my door with half the order. I said, 'Where's the other half?' They shrugged their shoulders."

4. Rent-a-car fiasco "The family rented a car for a three-day sight-seeing vacation only to find out on the road that the trunk and car doors wouldn't lock. So, every time we wanted to leave the car, we had to take all five bags with us. We spent most of our weekend hauling luggage. Considering what it costs to rent cars in this city, we were furious!"

Here are the ways we told our clients to resolve these problems:

1. Solution to the deal that was not a deal "I called back the bank, this time demanding to talk to representatives of higher authority, and took down their names and exactly what they said to me. I continued to get negative responses from both a supervisor and a manager. I finally spoke to the president's office, and explained the situation to his secretary, giving her the list of people I had talked to. She got her boss on the phone in a flash who instantly recognized the potential for losing a customer. He had two $100 bonus certificates in the mail to me that same day."

(There is an interesting sidebar to this story. When the bank solicited our client, they asked if she would agree to let them record on tape her saying that she was willing to become a member of the travel club. She should have said yes, but only if she could also record the name of the representative she was talking to and the fact that they were offering her two $100 bonuses. If she had gotten no satisfaction in the end, we would have told her to call the Consumer Affairs Department to find out if she had rights in this matter.)

2. Solution to "It's not my problem" "We told the manager of the video store that we were disappointed he did not respond favorably to a good faith effort to reach an equitable settlement regarding an honest error ... that we were surprised he didn't have more allegiance to loyal, long-standing customers ... that if he saw all his customers as unworthy of special attention no matter what the circumstance, then what would keep his customers from going to the competition down the street? We'd like to think we enlightened him just a bit; he finally let us buy the video we had rented."

3. Solution to "I never get what I ordered" "The Intrepid New Yorker told us we have rights to exercise regarding furniture delivery. The Consumer Affairs Department advises not to accept partial delivery. (If you accept partial delivery, the only recourse you have is to give them thirty more days to deliver the rest, or just get that portion of the money back.) If you don't accept partial delivery at all, you have the option, thirty days hence, if they still haven't delivered, to cancel the order completely and get a full refund. So we refused partial delivery, and to tide us over, we convinced the company that the least they could do for the inconvenience was to loan us a dining room set until the new set arrived."

4. Solution to rent-a-car fiasco "When we returned the car, we went for broke, went right to the manager, explained our problem in detail and requested a full refund for the car that took the 'vacation' out of our weekend—and got it! The manager was totally agreeable right from the start, but he would never have volunteered the refund if we hadn't implanted the idea firmly in his head."

(By the way, whenever you rent a car, never leave the

garage before making sure that everything, from headlights and gas gauges to locks and tires, is in good working order.)

INTREPID'S FOUR RULES TO DEMANDING EXCELLENCE

"Since 'consumer cops' can't be everywhere in this time of budget austerity, it's essential to empower and educate consumers to defend themselves in the marketplace. Only when each consumer feels like he or she is Consumer Affairs Commissioner will predatory businesses be motivated to comply with the law and do the right thing."
—Mark Green, Commissioner of the New York City Department of Consumer Affairs

You can demand excellence, but you may not get it. There is truly an art to receiving proper service. The Intrepid New Yorker has four basic rules we follow. If you follow them religiously you will never succumb to mediocre service again.

Intrepid Rule #1: Getting good service starts with being informed. If you go armed with knowledge and the attitude that you are the consumer and that excellent service is your right, you *can* obtain it—in all areas of your life. Service people will respond much more attentively when they realize they have met their match.

Intrepid Rule #2: It's up to you, not service people, to come up with creative problem-solving ideas. Most service people are not programmed to come up with solutions to your problems, so if you want a satisfactory outcome, you are going to have to come up with the ideas *for* them. Once you do, they will most likely respond favorably; don't forget, service people don't want to lose your business.

Intrepid Rule #3: You will only attract bees with honey. Treat people well. Make them feel competent and important. Appeal to their human side. It is a surefire way of getting exactly what you want.

Intrepid Rule #4: Speak up for yourself and be confident. Your only limitation to getting exactly what you want out of this city is your own apprehension that it can't be done. You don't have to be the CEO of Mobil Oil to get the kind of attention or service that is your right as a paying customer!

Let's examine Intrepid Rule #1: Being Informed.
It's really simple. The more informed you are and the more aware you are that you have rights, the less chance of being taken advantage of or deceived. There are organizations in New York that have been set

up for the sole purpose of informing and protecting you! And it will cost you nothing, or next to nothing, to use them. There's just no excuse for not taking advantage of them.

The Department of Consumer Affairs
This government agency was created for you and is paid for by your tax dollars—all to enforce the Consumer Protection Law forbidding "deceptive or unconscionable trade practices in the sale, lease, rental, or loan of any consumer goods or services or in the collection of consumer debt." This agency is one-stop assistance for the consumer. So use it! Here's how:

☞ **Business and Service Inquiries:** By calling the DCA at (212) 487-4444, employees will advise you as to whether a business has a record of previous complaints or violations on file. They will not, however, recommend a particular business or product.

> •
> DCA Bank Advisory: The 1990 consumer bank scorecard publication put out by the DCA ranks banks according to consumer fees and interest payments. Eighteen of the twenty banks with the lowest fees and highest interest on demand-deposit accounts are savings banks. In contrast, virtually all of New York City's largest commercial banks rank among the fifteen most expensive of the forty-nine banks surveyed. Banks can raise fees without worrying about extensive consumer backlash because bank customers tend to remain loyal, too loyal. If lots of New Yorkers began leaving these banks, they would start moderating their charges.
> •

☞ **Information:** The DCA helps consumers prevent complaint situations before they arise. The Public Affairs staff produces a continuous flow of consumer advisory pamphlets, booklets, and fact sheets free of charge (see below). They also provide a tape library service called Tel-Consumer/Tel-Law that enables consumers to call in at (212) 487-3938 and hear tapes in important legal and consumer issues like "Credit Bureaus—Somebody Is Talking about You," "Buying a Used Car," "Your Rights in the Supermarket," etc.

☞ **Investigation and Mediation of Your Complaint:** If you feel you have been mistreated you can contact the DCA complaint line at (212) 487-4444 from 9:30–4:30 P.M. Advisors will answer questions or give referrals over the phone concerning situations as diverse as destruction of a video store's rental tape to cancellation of tours booked through travel agents. Once the consumer completes and returns the form that the advisor has sent him, the advisor will work with the consumer and vendor to iron out the problem.

☞ **Licensing of Businesses:** In order to further protect consumers, the DCA has the authority to license and regulate eighty-two different

City of New York Consumer Affairs Free Publications

Clearly print your name and address on a sheet of paper, along with the title(s) of the material you are requesting, and send it to:

Mark Green, Commissioner, Consumer Affairs, 80 Lafayette Street, New York, NY 10013.

Booklets
____ The Consumer Affairs Information Guide*+
____ A Consumer's Guide to Home Improvement*

Brochures
____ Furniture: From Purchase to Delivery*+
____ The Small Claims Court*
____ Supermarket Checklist*
____ Tel-Consumer/Tel-Law
____ Used Cars*+

Fact Sheets
____ Auto Rentals: How to Avoid Getting Taken for a Ride
____ Buying Beef: Trimming Fat from Your Diet and Budget*
____ Buying Milk: Getting a Fresh Wholesome Product*
____ Choosing an Auto Repair Shop and Mechanic*+
____ Credit Bureaus*
____ Debt Collection Rules*
____ Food Poisoning from Meat and Poultry: Prevention in Your Own Home*+
____ Garages and Parking Lots
____ The Generic Drug Law*+
____ Home Equity Loans*
____ Lead Poisoning: Protecting You and Your Family
____ Lower Bumper Standards
____ Mail Order Buying*+
____ The New Prospective Payment System for Medicare: Your Rights as a Medicare Patient (DRGs)*
____ Refund Policies*+
____ Saving Money on Pharmaceuticals+
____ Storage Warehouses
____ T.V., Radio, Phonographic and Audio Equipment Repair*+
____ Tips for Food Shopping*+
____ What You Should Know About Tax Preparers in New York City*+
____ When Choosing a Private Business or Trade School*

Miscellaneous
____ A Guide for People in Business
____ How to Obtain a Home Improvement Contractor's License
____ Speakers Bureau Request Form
____ Summary of the Consumer Protection Law Regulations
____ Ten Consumer Commandments

* Available in Spanish
+ Available in Chinese

types of businesses, thereby requiring them to meet certain specifications of integrity, honesty, fair practices, and safety. You can call the DCA to find out which businesses are required to be licensed, or request "The Consumer Affairs Information Guide," which lists them.

Better Business Bureau

The BBB is a nationwide, private, non-profit corporation funded by the responsible business community. It offers membership to companies that meet their own high standards of business practice and ethics. It also offers a refuge to consumers giving them information they need to protect themselves against faulty and dishonest practices and a place to take their complaints and get help in resolving their disputes.

☞ **Reliability Ratings:** The BBB gives companies reliability ratings that you the consumer can use to make an informed choice about whether to do business with that company. You can call the BBB at (900) INFO-BBB and, for 85¢ per minute, get information about a company. For general inquiries about how to use the BBB, call (212) 533-6200.

☞ **Consumer Advisories:** The BBB offers advisories for consumers on topics such as getting refunds, delivery rights, mail order, credit cards, home improvement, new- and used-car lemon law, etc. Call (900) INFO-BBB to hear a ninety-second tape or to order a printed copy.

DCA Travel Advisory: You may be paying hundreds of dollars more for your summer vacation if you rely on airfares quoted by only one travel agent, according to a survey conducted by the DCA. The "lowest" round-trip fares for flights to nine destinations quoted to the department by forty-nine travel agents varied by as much as 115 percent. The main reason is simple: Some travel agents are lazy, negligent, or poorly trained. It can take up to half an hour to search properly for the lowest fares to some destinations. Good agents are creative and resourceful and will know about special deals and rules not provided on their computers, and will explore every channel open to them.

DCA Furniture Advisory—From Purchase to Delivery: Make sure that the contract has a detailed description of your furniture, including the type of material, the color, and any style or model numbers. Also, find out if there is a cancellation fee and how much it is. Contracts that say you cannot cancel violate New York law.

☞ **Mediation/Arbitration:** The BBB is not a law enforcement agency like the DCA, which means they cannot take legal action against a company or close it down. But they can mediate or arbitrate a customer's complaint. If you have a complaint, they will give you a case number and send you forms requesting information that you will read, fill out, and send back. Your mediator or arbitrator will then contact the company in your behalf and try to work out a settlement between you and the company in question.

The Consumer Resource Handbook

It is published by the United States Office of Consumer Affairs. It provides:

> DCA AUTO REPAIR ADVISORY: Don't authorize any work unless you understand exactly what you are signing. Always read the small print. No work may legally be done without your permission. Get an itemized bill. Check it against any estimate or authorization forms so that you are certain that you have been charged only for work you wanted to have completed. If you think you have been overcharged for parts, you may want to ask to see the supplier's parts price list, which gives retail and wholesale prices.

☛ **Smart Consumer Tips:** How to get the most for your money, and how to handle your own complaints.

☛ **Contacts for Consumer Problems:** Lists of offices you can contact for help with consumer problems or questions, including corporate consumer contacts, car manufacturers, Better Business Bureaus, state, county, and city consumer offices, trade associations, and other dispute resolution programs.

You can send away for it to:
Consumer Resource Handbook
Consumer Information Center
Pueblo, Colorado 81002

You can also ask for the "Consumer Information Catalog," which lists more than two hundred consumer advisory publications that are available for free or for a small fee.

> BBB Car Rental Advisory: Advertised rates are not always the price you will pay. Some firms require renters to pay an additional amount for fuel, additional driver insurance, or an airport fee. The BBB maintains that the advertised price should be the price consumers can expect to pay. Required fees should be disclosed in print. Not all firms comply with these standards so always inquire about additional fees.

INTREPID APPROACH
Use the Intrepid New Yorker "preventative checklist" to avoid fraud or negligence.

☐ Read up about the product or service you are about to purchase.

☐ Compare stores, services offered, product brands, and prices.

☐ Is the store or service required to be licensed? You can call the DCA at (212) 487-4444 to find out.

☐ Call the BBB to make sure the company is reliable.

- ☐ Know your rights up front. Get any advisories the BBB or DCA might have on the service or product you are requesting.
- ☐ What are the store's or service's policies regarding everything from returns, prices, and refunds, to warranties and guarantees.
- ☐ Read the fine print on all contracts and receipts.
- ☐ Make sure everything you agreed to including delivery date and cancellation agreement is in writing.
- ☐ Check for any extra charges such as delivery fees, installation charges, servicing costs.
- ☐ Put big purchases on a credit card so that if there is a problem, you haven't paid for it yet.

⚫ INTREPID APPROACH
You can get results by following our step-by-step approach to handling complaints.

If it's too late to prevent the problem, here are ways to deal with it:

☞ **Start a file about your complaint.** Keep copies of sales receipts, repair orders, cancelled checks, contracts, etc.

☞ **Go back to where you made the purchase.** Talk to the sales person and if you don't get help on that level, talk to the manager, or supervisor—even the owner or the president. Sometimes quiet but public venting is effective. Be firm but always treat people kindly and with respect. *Keep a record of every person you have talked to and all the efforts you have made.* This is critical. Save copies of any letters exchanged between you and the company.

> Emphasizing customer satisfaction is economical because it costs five times more to win new customers than to keep existing ones coming back.
> —Better Business Bureau

☞ **If you still aren't satisfied, don't give up.** Call the person responsible for consumer complaints at the company's headquarters. Describe your problem, and what you think would be fair compensation. Do you want your money back? The product repaired? Exchanged? Many companies have toll-free numbers. Sometimes those numbers are printed on the product's package. Or call the 800 directory at (800) 555-1212 and ask.

☞ **If necessary, write a complaint letter. As recommended by the U.S. Office of Consumer Affairs, here's how:**

SAMPLE COMPLAINT LETTER

```
                    (Your Address)
                    (Your City, State, ZIP Code)
                    (Date)

(Name of Contact Person)
(Title)
(Company Name)
(Street Address)
(City, State, ZIP Code)
```

Dear (Contact Person):

On (**date**), I purchased (**or had repaired**) a (**name of product with serial or model number or service performed**). I made this purchase at (**location, date, and other important details of the transaction**).

Unfortunately, your product (**or service**) has not performed well (**or the service was inadequate**) because (**state the problem**).

Therefore, to resolve the problem, I would appreciate your (s**tate the specific action you want**). Enclosed are copies (**copies—NOT originals**) of my records (**receipts, guarantees, warranties, canceled checks, contracts, model and serial numbers, and any other documents**).

I look forward to your reply and a resolution of my problem, and will wait (**set time limit**) before seeking third-party assistance. Please contact me at the above address or by phone at (**home and office numbers—with area codes**).

```
                    Sincerely,

                    (Your name)
                    (Your account number)
```

- describe your purchase
- name of product, serial numbers
- include date and location of purchase

- give the history
- state the problem

- ask for specific action
- enclose copies of documents

- allow time for action or response
- include how you can be reached

KEEP COPIES OF YOUR LETTER AND ALL RELATED DOCUMENTS

☛ **If all else fails, call the DCA or BBB.** The DCA's number is (212) 487-4444; the BBB's is (900) INFO-BBB (85¢ per minute).

Let's examine Intrepid Rule #2: Being Creative.

Service people, unfortunately, can be extraordinarily shortsighted when it comes to customer relations. They usually follow store policy to the letter and make no exceptions for valued customers. The old axiom "the customer is always right" is all but dead and buried in New York City.

But don't take everything handed to you at face value. With persistence and a sense of fairness, you can change almost any situation that's unacceptable to you. There are ways to push the system, ways to get an answer that service people are not programmed to give, ways to get bureaucrats to bend the rules for you, ways to make people accountable for their actions.

You can't enact Intrepid Rule #2 without enacting Intrepid Rule #3: Being Pleasant.

You will only attract bees with honey. We cannot emphasize too much how important your approach is with the service people from whom you are asking something. You must appeal to their human side, you must make them feel competent and important. Abraham Lincoln agrees with us:

> "It is an old and a true maxim that a drop of honey catches more flies than a gallon of gall. So with men. If you would win a man to your cause, first convince him that you are his sincere friend.... On the contrary, assume to dictate to his judgment, or to command his action, or to mark him as one to be shunned and despised, and he will retreat within himself, close all the avenues to his head and his heart."

When The Intrepid New Yorker put into action Rules 2 and 3, here are some of the wondrous things that happened:

The Missing Cheese
That Didn't Ruin the Meal

The Intrepid New Yorker went to a gourmet food store to buy food for a client's dinner party. We got home, only to find out that they had failed to include the Parmesan cheese in the package; the dinner party was starting in an hour and the store was twenty blocks away. We called to ask them what they could do to help us out of

---

Call **Consumer Reports** magazine toll free at (800) 234-1645. They will send you any issue from the past year that you request on a particular product about which you are interested in becoming informed.

---

a jam. There was nothing to be done, they said, short of our finding a way to come back down. We opened their minds to two solutions that never would have occurred to them. Wouldn't they think it reasonable, as the Parmesan cheese was integral to the meal, to either give us a full refund for the whole meal or to have one of their employees jump in a cab at store closing time and bring it to us? They suddenly liked the second solution a lot.

The Delayed Fabric That Actually Arrived on Time
We had ordered fabric from Paris for a client and it had been promised to us by a certain date. However, when we went to pick it up, it had not yet come in. The sales ladies shrugged it off saying we'd just have to wait. The Intrepid New Yorker surmises that if we can watch the Gulf War live from our own living room every day, we can find a way to get fabric delivered on time from France. We asked them nicely if they would have it overnight expressed. "What a good idea," they said.

The Meat That Took a Taxi All by Itself
The Intrepid New Yorker buys our meat wholesale in bulk from a butcher on the Upper East Side. One of us lives way down in the West Village, out of his delivery range. Rather than having to take a round-trip taxi to pick it up, we had the brilliant idea of having our butcher put the box of meat in the back of a taxi and send it on its way. At first our butcher thought we were crazy, but then became intrigued with seeing if it would actually work. We told him to give the taxi driver the address, to take down his license number and name before driving off, and to have the driver buzz the apartment when he arrived. The meat arrived on time, safe and sound, and it only cost one taxi fare.

The above three stories are examples of not taking no for an answer, coming up with solutions the service people can reasonably act on, all while treating people with respect. If you refuse to back down, 90 percent of the time you will get the solution you are asking for. It is important, however, that you don't look at these situations as isolated or chance moments of triumph. Part of your assertiveness training is making a point of establishing long-term relationships with critical service people in your area with whom you don't have to constantly negotiate because they will care enough about you and your repeat business to want to bend the rules and store policies for you as a matter of course.

Let's examine Intrepid Rule #4: Speak Up for Yourself.
Your only limitation is thinking you don't have the authority or clout

to get what you want, the way you want it. You really don't have to be a celebrity or a tycoon in order to make the earth shake a little bit in this town. The key to getting special attention is to assume a front-row-center posture and speak up for it—you have nothing to lose and everything to gain. The only thing to remember is to always demand to speak to someone in charge who is high enough up to be able to make spontaneous decisions on your behalf. The following stories might enlighten you.

From Steerage to First Class

"We were flying home to New York City from Shreveport, Louisiana, with a stop in Nashville. Our plane to Nashville was delayed by weather causing us to miss our connecting flight. With two exhausted toddlers on our hands we went to the flight director to see what could be done to make our situation more bearable. They had nothing to offer us except the next flight out leaving in three hours. We told them we knew that the delay was not the fault of the airline, but that under the circumstances perhaps they could bump us to first class so that there was room for the family to sleep. The flight director would never have volunteered the idea, but agreed to it. We were the only passengers to speak up and the final leg home was a pleasure."

From Rejection to Red Carpet

"I wanted to take my wife to a very exclusive, expensive restaurant in the City. When I called I was told there was no available reservation on the date we wanted. At first I was disappointed, but then I decided to take some action. I took a very different approach. I called the next day, asked to speak to the chef about a special meal I wanted prepared for my wife on our anniversary. The chef was on the phone in an instant. We talked about possible menus and then told him which night I wanted a reservation. He not only gave me the reservation immediately, he gave us his best table and prepared a delicious meal that was not on the menu."

Justice Prevails

"I was dropping off a large TV to be repaired and couldn't find a parking space anywhere close by, so in exasperation I double parked illegally for an instant in front of the repair shop—and of course, got a ticket. Rather than accept my two choices of going to court to plead my case or just cave in and send in my check for the fine, I decided to see what would happen if I wrote a letter appealing to the court's human side. I explained in detail my sincere attempts to abide by the law, my appreciation for traffic cops trying to do their job, but couldn't they see the justice in reducing my fine? They did—by 50 percent."

USING LOGIC AND PERSEVERANCE TO PREVAIL

There are more specialty stores and services, cultural institutions, restaurants, support groups, schools, professions, fine craftsmen, hot-lines, experts, academics, and advanced technology under one skyline than anywhere else in the world. It is ironic how little New Yorkers take advantage of, how passive and defeatist many New Yorkers have a tendency to be, how little many New Yorkers think they can accomplish or find on their own. Our clients call us regularly with tasks they think are going to overwhelm them.

❢ INTREPID APPROACH

Look at the task in front of you as an interesting exercise in logic and common sense, and as a bit of an adventure. The reality is that the anxiety about the task is usually far greater than the actual difficulty in completing it. If you realize that there are countless numbers of interested human beings and organizations in New York willing to assist you, then ye shall find and conquer. Here's what we mean:

☛ **Using your foreign connections:** A client came to us desperate to find some antique French china called *Compare* that was made some time in the early 1900s. It was to be a birthday present for her mother who had only a few pieces left of a set. Our client had no idea how to proceed beyond looking in some French antique stores. We took over the project, immediately calling The French Bureau of Trade, who told us who does commerce in this particular trade both in New York and in France. We not only found the right antique store in New York to help us, but we found a store in Paris that sent us pictures of exactly the china we wanted. If we hadn't found the china so quickly using this route, we would have called the auction houses Sotheby's and Christie's and asked to speak to their French-antique experts.

☛ **Heading straight for the source:** One client came to us looking for a top-notch travel agent who specialized in travel to Bali. She was sick of mediocre travel agents who had no imagination or vision to put together a truly one-of-a-kind vacation, but didn't know how to find one. We thought logically about which person or organization might steer us in the right direction. We called the Indonesian Consulate here in New York. They certainly want to see Americans spend money in Bali. They immediately suggested an Indonesian travel agent in New

Jersey. We also called a well-known travel magazine and asked to speak to an editor who writes about that area of the world. We got through to the editor immediately, who gave us the names of the magazine's favorite three travel agents and sent us all her articles on the area.

☛ **Using magazine editors as experts:** An exasperated client couldn't locate a school called The Outdoor School that they knew was somewhere in this country and that was supposed to be something like Outward Bound. It took us five minutes to come up with the answer. First, we called a well-known sporting goods store in New York City called Eastern Mountain Sports. As the great outdoors is their specialty, we thought they might have an idea. They weren't open yet. So then we called the 800 number directory—(800) 555-1212—to see if the school had a toll-free number; it did not. So we tried another avenue. We knew there was a magazine on the newsstands called *Outdoor Magazine*. We didn't know where they were located in the United States either, so we again called the 800 directory and sure enough they had an 800 number. We called the magazine headquarters, asked to speak to one of the editors, and told him what we were looking for. He had not only heard of it, but instantly gave us the telephone number and the address. Persistence pays off.

☛ **If you persevere, A will always lead to Z:** One client called us because he was interested in buying an island off Manhattan near Roosevelt Island. But he had no idea what it was called or whether it was for sale. We decided our first step was to call the developers of Roosevelt Island. They didn't know of the island, but they did know what assembly district they were in—the sixty-fifth. We called that district. They said they saw no island on their district map. We called the Manhattan Borough President's office who told us to call the Board of Elections of Manhattan. The Board of Elections told us the island was called Belmont Island and that it was in the sixty-fifth assembly district. We called back the sixty-fifth and they found it on a bigger map, but they couldn't tell us the status of the island and told us to call New York City Finance and Taxation to find out who pays the taxes on the island. Several people there told us the information wasn't public. We pleaded our case nicely and they finally told us: The island is "block 1373, lot number 2," is owned by New York State, and is not for sale. It was originally built as a conduit for a bridge that never went up. This task took us about an hour. We found it fun and adventurous, and everyone we encountered along the way got caught up in the search and was very helpful.

COMMUNITY LEADERS ARE HERE TO SERVE YOU

Many New Yorkers blame inadequate service from their city government for increasingly unlivable neighborhoods. And when they've really had it, they move out. Well, the fact is that in New York it takes citizen action to maintain a community in which you are proud to live. Municipal services are already stretched to the max in this needy city and you simply cannot expect them to anticipate and plan for every problem. The good news, however, is that your tax dollars don't just get swallowed up into a black hole of city services, they also go to a community board whose sole reason for being is to see that you get your neighborhood exactly the way you want it. Community boards are there at your service, so if you don't take advantage of them, you share the blame if you aren't happy with the state of your particular community.

> Recently a group of mothers in the West Village filed a complaint with their community board that there was only one small playground for all the kids in the neighborhood to use. And at night it was being used for drug transactions and for vagrants sleeping off drinking binges. Because of the swift and collective action of the neighborhood mothers and their community board, within six months the playground was expanded, cleaned up, and locked up every night by dusk.

Intrepid Approach
You can turn your neighborhood into a manageable small town by actively working with your community leaders. Community boards really can resolve issues quickly and efficiently. They know where to go, whom to talk to, and how to get the job done. *Your* job is to voice your complaint professionally and publically to them, with as much support from the rest of the community as you can get. They will do the rest.

How a Community Board works

There are fifty-nine community boards throughout New York's boroughs. Each has up to fifty nonsalaried members who are appointed by the borough president, with half nominated by city council members of the board district. Board members are selected from among active, involved

> If you are new to the neighborhood and you want to get to know your community board, go to one of their meetings. It is the best way to find out what they do and to introduce yourself to them and them to you.

HOW COMMUNITY BOARDS RELATE TO THE CITY

COMPTROLLER
- City fiscal officer
- Keeps City books
- Audits agencies

CITY COUNCIL PRESIDENT
- Presides over council
- Ombudsman on City services

MAYOR
- Chief executive officer
- Makes City policy
- Proposes City budget
- Appoints City agency commissioners

CITY COUNCIL
(51 Members after 1991)
- Passes local legislation
- Monitors service delivery
- Approves City budget
- Reviews decisions approved by City Planning Commission
- Member of Community Board and District Service Cabinet (ex-officio)

BOROUGH PRESIDENTS
(5 in New York City)
- Oversees boroughwide delivery of City services
- Assists preparation of City budget
- Each BP appoints 1 member to City Planning Commission
- Reviews ULURP applications
- Chairs Borough Board and Borough Service Cabinet

CITY AGENCIES
Decision-Makers
- City Planning Commission
- Brd of Standards & Appeals
Service Providers
- Police, fire, parks, sanitation, highways, traffic, etc.

DISTRICT SERVICE CABINET
- Plans and coordinates local service delivery to public improvements

COMMUNITY BOARDS
(59 in New York City)
- Land-use
- Zoning
- Service Delivery
- Community Welfare

DISTRICT MANAGER
- Runs district office
- Complaint resolution
- Service delivery improvements

PUBLIC
- Votes for elected officials.
- Suggests board members
  - Civic groups
  - Merchants
  - Tenants
  - Individuals
  - etc

Appoints Commissioners Directors, etc

Appoint local managers for agency's services

Proposes 1/2 of the Board members

BP with CB can appeal some of CPC's land-use decisions

Appoints board members

Consults & advises on land-use, ULURP, service delivery and City budget

Presides over Cabinet

Resolves problems and coordinates services

Hires, cooperates with, provides support, information

Input and advocacy

Information and assistance

Local problems, City service complaints

Provides information and assistance

> It is one-stop-shopping government —your little city hall which takes care of your neighborhood. But if you the citizen don't involve yourself, the board is a flop. A community board's sole purpose is to represent and advocate the citizens they serve to the government. The citizens of our Community Board Number 2 are very active; we get on average, 2,500 complaints a year that we help resolve. Your board is the place you go if you want to: Open a sidewalk cafe; get your park cleaned; get a traffic light installed or fixed; get a playground built; get a bus stop on your corner; plant trees on your block; quiet down a noisy disco; or get a crack house closed.
>
> —Rita Lee, District Manager, Community Board Number 2

people of each community. Their job is to monitor service delivery in the district, consider zoning and land use proposals, recommend budget priorities, and *function as your community information and complaint center.*

The person you should call if you have any complaint at all is your community board's district manager. District managers function as ombudspersons, information sources, community organizers, mediators, and municipal managers. They are, above all, public servants with the most direct ties to your local community.

Boards usually meet once a month to address items of concern to the community. Board actions and decisions are basically advisory. Board meetings are open to the public and the public must be allowed to speak and express opinions during a portion of the meeting. However, only board members may vote. Board committees will then implement what has been acted on at the meetings.

INTREPID TIP

To apply to become a member of your community board, call your borough president's office. The number for the Manhattan office is (212) 669-8300. They will send you an application in the mail.

THE INTREPID PAGES
OF
TAKE-ACTION NUMBERS

COMMUNITY BOARD DISTRICT MANAGERS IN MANHATTAN

COMMUNITY BOARD # 1

Mr. Paul Goldstein
49–51 Chambers Street
(South of Canal Street to the Battery—river to river)
(212) 374-1421

COMMUNITY BOARD # 2

Ms. Rita Lee
3 Washington Square Village
(14th Street to Canal Street, The Bowery to Hudson River)
(212) 979-2272

COMMUNITY BOARD # 3

Ms. Martha Danziger
59 East 4th Street
(East River to the Bowery, 14th Street to the Brooklyn Bridge)
(212) 533-5300

COMMUNITY BOARD # 4

Mr. Edward J. Kleifgen
330 West 42nd Street
(14th Street to 26th Street from Avenue of the Americas to Eighth Avenue, and 26th Street to 59th Street from Eighth Avenue to Hudson River)
(212) 736-4536

COMMUNITY BOARD # 5

Ms. Joan E. Ramer
118 East 28th Street
(14th Street to 59th Street, Lexington to Eighth Avenues)
(212) 686-7806

COMMUNITY BOARD # 6

Ms. Carol Pieper
330 East 26th Street
(14th Street to 59th Street, Lexington Avenue to East River)
(212) 679-0907

COMMUNITY BOARD # 7

Ms. Penny Ryan
250 West 87th Street
(59th Street to 110th Street, Hudson River to Central Park West)
(212) 362-4008

COMMUNITY BOARD # 8

Mr. Edward Benson
309 East 94th Street
(59th Street to 96th Street, Fifth Avenue to East River, and Roosevelt
Island)
(212) 427-4840

COMMUNITY BOARD # 9

Ms. Mildred Duran
565 West 125th Street
(110th Street to 155th Street, Hudson River to Edgecomb Avenue)
(212) 864-6200

COMMUNITY BOARD # 10

Ms. Linda Wood
215 West 125th Street
(110th Street to 155th Street, west side of Fifth Avenue and east side
of St. Nicholas Avenue)
(212) 749-3105

COMMUNITY BOARD # 11

Mr. Glen E. Williams
55 East 115th Street
(North 96th Street to East 142nd Street)
(FDR Drive to east Fifth Avenue)
(212) 831-8929

COMMUNITY BOARD # 12

Ms. Brenda Rosado
711 West 168th Street
(North side of West 155th Street to 220th Street)
(Edgecomb Avenue to the Hudson River)
(212) 568-8500

OTHER PROBLEM SOLVERS

THE CONSUMER AFFAIRS DEPARTMENT ★ (212) 487-4444

THE BETTER BUSINESS BUREAU ★ (212) 533-7500

"SHAME ON YOU" ★ (212) 975-4321

Consumer advocate television show with TV anchor Arnold Diaz.

THE INTREPID NEW YORKER ★ (212) 534-5071

The Intrepid New Yorker has acted as ombudsmen and trouble shooters for the last ten years. We will track down a rare book, argue a bill, research offbeat vacation ideas, write a complaint letter, or just advise you on how to do it yourself.

PART TWO

INTREPID FILES

T·H·R·E·E
STREET-
SMART
SHOPPNG

Thereisliterally no city comparable to New York when it comes to shopping—for absolutely anything. You don't have to leave this city to find whatever it is you are looking for and at the price you can afford. However, New Yorkers have become disenchanted with shopping. They find the experience fre-

NTREPID PHILOSOPHY

ATTITUDE As a consumer you have rights and protections in the marketplace. Get smart about what they are. Merchants can smell a street-smart shopper a mile away, and they don't want to mess with you.

APPROACH Find a method of shopping that really suits you. You may want to be a bargain hunter, but the reality might be that you need the convenience and peace of mind of full-service, retail shopping. If you try to be the kind of shopper you are not, you will eventually resent the exercise.

KNOWLEDGE If you don't want to you really don't have to pay retail for anything in this city. But you need to know the pros and cons of both full-service, retail shopping and bargain hunting in order to make an informed choice about which route to take.

ECONOMICS There is a difference between a "perceived" deal and a real deal. Sometimes it might actually cost you less to pay retail and more to get a bargain.

netic, time consuming, and costly, and they're tired of inadequate service and badly made merchandise. We are here to tell you that you can turn shopping into a pleasurable, successful experience, but you have to make it your responsibility to tackle shopping the right way.

TERMS YOU NEED TO KNOW

☛ **Retail:** This is the price marked up for sale to the consumer. It could be anywhere from a 100 to 1,000 percent markup from what it cost to make the product. The markup will fluctuate according to what the market will bear.

☛ **Wholesale:** This can be double or more what it cost to actually make the product, but half or slightly less than half of what it will cost you at the retail level.

☛ **Cost:** This is what it actually costs to make the product, with no additional markup.

RETAIL SHOPPING

When you shop full-service retail you are buying a product at the highest price you can pay. The reason for this, theoretically, is that you are getting the most complete service along with that product.

We have a client who has established such a good relationship with a saleslady in her favorite store that when the store holds a sale, the saleslady puts aside several outfits she knows our client will like, and then calls her up during the sale days so she can buy the items at the discounted price. Establishing strong relationships between a customer and a store means everything in terms of what kind of service you will receive.

INTREPID TIP
There are advantages to shopping full-service retail:

❑ Small specialty stores or department stores will have the most complete line of a particular product.

❑ They will get a product into their stores first (before it hits the factory outlets, sample sales, etc.).

❑ They can usually get you the size, model, or style you need from one of their other stores if they don't have it in stock.

❑ If you are buying clothes, there are changing rooms so that you can try them on.

- You can usually get a refund or a store credit if you want to return the item, often at any time. Department stores are usually more than willing to give cash refunds; small specialty stores or boutiques are more likely to give you credit instead because their volume of business is so much smaller.
- You will usually get better service and more knowledgeable salespeople.
- The products you buy come complete with guarantees and warranties.
- Services might include delivery, installation, and repair—and sometimes all for free.
- Some department stores and boutiques in particular offer the most luxurious way to shop. Boutiques are more apt to pamper you—let you make phone calls, order you lunch, do free alterations, and let you take home goods to try before purchasing, for example.
- Even though department stores are considered by many to be frenetic and overwhelming to shop in, they do truly offer one-stop, full-service shopping.

> A wonderful old tradition in New York worth participating in at least once is to go to Lord & Taylor just before the doors officially open at 9:30 A.M. for free coffee and a chance to join the employees in singing the national anthem.

INTREPID TIP

The most compelling reason to shop retail is the guarantee that the store stands behind the product and offers warranties, delivery, and installation. In most cases, the amount you pay is in direct proportion to the degree of coddling and free service you will get. Many full-service, retail stores think nothing of picking up your broken VCR, repairing it, and returning it to you, at no extra cost! Just make sure you ask what kind of service goes along with the product and if delivery and installation costs are included in the price.

INTREPID TIP

The second best reason to shop retail is that time is money. There is a lot of legwork involved in finding a "good deal" when you bargain hunt. And once you buy the product, you

> Merchants must give refunds on unused undamaged goods within twenty days of purchase unless they post an easy-to-read sign that tells you about their refund policy. Signs must be posted in any of the following four locations: (1) Attached to the cash register or wherever sales are completed; (2) In a place visible to the consumer from the cash register; (3) At each store entrance; (4) On a tag attached to the item.
> —Department of Consumer Affairs

still have to figure out how to get it delivered to your home and installed. If your "bargain" purchase needs servicing, guess who has to take it to a place to be repaired? If you don't have the time or stomach to shop this way, then for you full-service shopping is the "real" deal, regardless of what it costs.

WHEN RETAIL GOES ON SALE

INTREPID TIP
There are publications that will keep you informed about sales:

☞ Our own Intrepid Pages of Yearly Sales, page 97
☞ *New York* magazine, which lists sales and bargains weekly
☞ Advertisements in *The New York Times* and other local newspapers that regularly announce all major sales coming up

☞ **Clothing Sales** There are scheduled months when clothing lines begin to arrive in the stores:

✔ Spring clothes begin to arrive mid-December.
✔ Summer clothes begin to arrive in March.
✔ Fall clothes begin to arrive mid-July.
✔ Winter clothes begin to arrive mid-August.
✔ Holiday/cruise wear begins to arrive mid-November and December.

Sales begin about *60 days* after clothes arrive in the store, which means that sometimes the clothes are discounted even before the season begins.

Clothes will get progressively marked down throughout their season. So, although there is never as full a line of clothes in the stores to choose from as there is when they first come in, you can save considerable sums if you wait for the sales to start—and you still won't miss the season.

Some very frugal buyers only buy their clothes at the end of the season and save those items to wear the following year. Those are diehard "out of season shoppers." You have to like this kind of bargain hunting because it is very hit-or-miss, and you have to have a good eye for what will still be in style and look good on you one year from now.

THE INTREPID PAGES
OF
YEARLY SALES

You can get great deals at stores you normally couldn't afford to shop at by visiting them during their yearly sales. Be sure to call first, as some of these stores change their sale times from year to year.

JANUARY

BON POINT (children's clothes) ★ 1269 Madison Avenue (at 91st Street) ★ (212) 722-7720
Sales are January and July; up to 50 percent off.

BOTTEGA VENETA (shoes, bags, and belts mostly for women) ★ 635 Madison Avenue (at 59th Street) ★ (212) 371-5511
Sales are January and July; up to 50 percent off.

EMMANUEL UNGARO (women's clothing) ★ 803 Madison Avenue (between 67th and 68th Streets) ★ (212) 249-4090
Sales are January, April, June through July; discounts from 30 to 50 percent.

PAUL SMITH (men's and women's clothing) ★ 108 Fifth Avenue (at 16th Street) ★ (212) 627-9770
Sales January through February, late July to August; starts at 15 to 25 percent off, reaching 50 percent off.

POLO/RALPH LAUREN (men's, women's, and children's clothing) ★ 867 Madison Avenue (at 72nd Street) ★ (212) 606-2100
Big sales early January and early July; different departments run sales at different times.

PRADA (leather goods) ★ 45 East 57th Street ★ (212) 308-2332
Sales are January and late June through July; 30, 40, and 50 percent off seasonal items only.

SAINT LAURENT RIVE GAUCHE (men's and women's clothing) ★
for women ★ 855 Madison Avenue (between 70th and 71st Streets) ★ (212) 988-3821
for men ★ 859 Madison Avenue (between 70th and 71st Streets) ★ (212) 517-7400
Sales in January and July; up to 40 percent off.

SAKS FIFTH AVENUE (department store) ★ 611 Fifth Avenue (between 49th and 50th Streets)
★ (212) 753-4000
Sales are January and July.

SULKA & CO. (men's clothing) ★ 430 Park Avenue (at 55th Street) ★ (212) 980-5200
Sales are end of January and end of July on selected items only.

FEBRUARY

SONIA RYKIEL (women's clothing) ★ 729 Madison Avenue (at 67th Street) ★ (212) 744-0880
Sales are February and end of August; 30 percent off.

EMPORIO ARMANI (men's and women's clothing) ★ 110 Fifth Avenue (at 16th Street)
★ (212) 727-3240
Sales in February and August; up to 50 percent off.

MARCH

VALENTINO (men's and women's clothing) ★ 823 Madison Avenue (between 68th and 69th
Streets) ★ (212) 772-6969
Sales are in March, May, and November; sales begin at 40 percent and
can go up to 60 percent.

APRIL

HERMES (leather goods, pillows, men's and women's clothing) ★ 11 East 57th Street
★ (212) 751-3181
Ask to be put on their mailing list for an invitation.

MAY

MISSONI (women's and men's clothing) ★ 836 Madison Avenue (at 69th Street) ★ (212) 517-9339
Sales are end of May; discounts of 20 to 40 percent off.

TAHARI (women's clothing) ★ 802 Madison Avenue (between 67th and 68th Streets)
★ (212) 535-1515
Sales in May and December; up to 50 percent off.

CERUTTI (children's clothing) ★ 807 Madison Avenue (between 68th and 67th Streets)
★ (212) 737-7540
Spring sale at end of May, after-Christmas sale; up to 50 percent
off.

CARTIER (jewelry) ★ 2 East 52nd Street ★ (212) 753-0111
Sale on some jewelry in May; up to 30 percent off.

FENDI (leather goods, clothes, furs) ★ 720 Fifth Avenue (at 56th Street) ★ (212) 767-0100
Sales are from mid-May through July, winter sale also; up to 50 percent off.

JUNE

GIORGIO ARMANI (men's and women's clothing) ★ 815 Madison Avenue (between 68th and 69th Streets) ★ (212) 988-9191
Sales are June through July and late December; up to 40 percent off.

SUSAN BENNIS WARREN EDWARDS (women's and men's shoes) ★ 22 West 57th Street ★ (212) 755-4197
Sales start early June and January; up to 33 percent off. Mid-July and mid-February; up to 50 percent off. July finds some samples at 65 percent off.

SALVATORE FERRAGAMO (men's and women's shoes, bags and clothing) ★
for women ★ 717 Fifth Avenue (at 56th Street) ★ (212) 759-3822
for men ★ 730 Fifth Avenue (between 56th and 57th Streets) ★ (212) 246-6211
Sales in June and January; sales start at 30 percent and go up to 50 percent.

BROOKS BROTHERS (men's, boys', and women's clothing) ★ 346 Madison Avenue (at 44th Street) ★ (212) 682-8800
Sale items are in mid-June through early July; men's suits 35 percent off, other items 25 to 35 percent off.

CHARLES JOURDAN (women's shoes) ★ Trump Tower 725 Fifth Avenue (between 56th and 57th Streets) ★ (212) 644-3830
June 15th sale and after-Christmas sale.

MANOLO BLAHNIK (women's and men's shoes) ★ 15 West 55th Street ★ (212) 582-3007
Sales in the third week of June through August; starts at 33 percent off and goes to 50 percent or more off.

MAUD FRIZON (women's shoes) ★ 49 East 57th Street ★ (212) 249-5368
Sales are in late June and late December.

GIANNI VERSACE (men's and women's clothing) ★ 816 Madison Avenue (at 68th Street) ★ (212) 744-5572
Sales at the end of June and December; up to 50 percent off.

GUCCI (men's and women's leather goods and clothing) ★ 683 Fifth Avenue (at 55th Street) ★ (212) 826-2600
Summer and winter sales; markdowns to 50 percent.

SMALL CHANGE (children's clothing) ★ 1021 Lexington Avenue (between 70th and 71st Streets) ★ (212) 772-6455
Spring and after-Christmas sales; up to 50 percent off.

JULY

GIVENCHY (women's clothing) ★ 315 Fifth Avenue (at 75th Street) ★ (212) 239-0043
Sales are early July and early January.

KENZO (women's clothing) ★ 824 Madison Avenue (at 69th Street) ★ (212) 737-8640
Sales are the end of July through August; from 30 to 50 percent off.

LIBERTY OF LONDON (women's clothing) ★ 630 Fifth Avenue (at 51st Street) ★ (212) 459-0080
Sales at the end of July and after Christmas.

NICOLE MILLER (women's clothing and some men's accessories) ★ 780 Madison Avenue (between 66th and 67th Streets) ★ (212) 288-9779
Sales in July and January through March.

FURLA (bags) ★ 157 Columbus Avenue (at 67th Street) ★ (212) 874-6119
★ 705 Madison Avenue (at 64th Street) ★ (212) 755-8986
Sale in July, leftovers at end of August, also winter sale; 30 to 60 percent off.

OCTOBER

AQUASCUTUM OF LONDON, ENGLAND (men's and women's clothing) ★ 680 Fifth Avenue (at 54th Street) ★ (212) 975-0250
Late September through early October; up to 40 percent off.

UJA-Federation's annual benefit sale in June is a fashion feast for shoppers in the know. Sponsored by one of New York's largest philanthropies, the sale features new and current merchandise by over forty leading designers and manufacturers at prices way below wholesale. From classics to active wear to after-dark dazzlers, in a full size range by Carol Little, Leslie Fay, Evan-Picone, and French Connection. Proceeds go to UJA-Federation for humanitarian services in New York, Israel, and thirty-four countries worldwide. Clothes are restocked daily. For details about date, time, place, and entrance fee call (212) 836-1115.

NOVEMBER

J. PRESS (men's clothing) ★ 16 East 44th Street ★ (212) 687-7642
Sales in mid-November through January, and the end of June through August.

DECEMBER

BURBERRY'S (men's and women's clothing) ★
9 East 57th Street ★ (212) 371-5010
Sales at the end of December through February and mid-June; 25 to 50 percent off selected items.

Sales often start one or more days before the advertisement date, so you can beat the crowds and get the pick of the litter. When you hear of a sale coming up, call ahead and ask.

THE **I**NTREPID PAGES
OF
DEPARTMENT STORE CLEARANCE CENTERS

Most department stores have permanent clearance centers outside Manhattan. The majority of them carry home furnishings and a few carry just clothes. We'll tell you who carries what. You can save anywhere from 30 to 70 percent. Most of them are open seven days a week.

ABRAHAM & STRAUSS ★ 155 Glencove Road, Carleplace, LI ★ (516) 742-8500
Furniture, electronics, bedding, and rugs are all sold here. Open Monday through Friday, 11:00 A.M. to 9:30 P.M., Saturday 9:30 A.M. to 9:30 P.M., and Sunday noon to 5:00 P.M. A&S accepts MasterCard, Visa, and personal checks.

> Don't get trapped by false "going out of business" sales. Some shops advertise that they are going out of business in order to lure customers; some ads and signs say "lost our lease" or "everything must go." Once inside, customers may discover that merchandise "on sale" costs more than the same merchandise at the regular price in other stores. Ask other stores in the neighborhood how long the sign has been up, or call the BBB.
> —Better Business Bureau

BARNEY'S ★ 243 West 17th Street ★ (212) 929-9000
Barney's warehouse sale is a week-long event that begins the last Monday in August. It opens at 8:00 A.M. People begin to line up very early because it's a chance to buy good up to 40 percent off the retail price. Barney's accepts all major credit cards and personal checks.

BLOOMINGDALE'S ★ 155 Glencove Avenue, Carleplace, LI ★ (516) 248-1400
They sell mostly furniture, rugs, and bedding. They're open Mondays and Thursdays from 10:00 A.M. to 9:30 P.M., Tuesdays, Wednesdays, Fridays, and Saturdays to 6:00 P.M., and Sundays noon to 5:00 P.M. Bloomingdale's accepts all major credit cards and personal checks.

FORTUNOFF ★ 1300 Old Country Road, Westbury, LI
★ (516) 832-9000

They sell outdoor and indoor furniture. Open Monday through Saturday, 10:00 A.M. to 9:30 P.M., Sunday noon to 5:00 P.M. Fortunoff accepts all major credit cards and personal checks.

LORD & TAYLOR ★ 3601 Hempstead Avenue, Levittown, LI ★ (516) 731-5031 ★ 839–60 New York Avenue, Huntington, LI ★ (516) 673-0009

They sell clothing for children and adults. Both stores are open Monday, Tuesday, Wednesday, and Saturday from 10:00 A.M. to 6:00 P.M., Thursday and Friday until 9:00 P.M., and Sunday from noon to 5:00 P.M. Lord & Taylor accepts L&T cards only and personal checks.

MACY'S ★ 174 Glencove Road, Glencove, LI
★ (516) 746-1490

Furniture, electronics, bedding, and rugs are sold here. Open from 11:00 A.M. to 9:00 P.M. Monday through Friday, Saturday from 10:00 A.M. to 8:00 P.M., and Sunday from noon to 6:00 P.M. They accept all major credit cards and personal checks.

If you are shopping for a particular brand of an expensive item, it pays to ask a customer service person to find out when that brand goes on sale. One of our clients discovered when picking out her own wedding china that her pattern went on sale every year in August. Even though her wedding was scheduled for July, many of her family and friends bought china pieces for her after the wedding when that pattern went on sale across the country—and saved 40 percent.

Stores that have several different branches around Manhattan may sell their products at slightly higher or lower prices depending on what type of neighborhood they are located in and what the market in that neighborhood will bear. So it pays to ask if a different branch store sells the product you want at a lower price.

If you buy an item at the retail price and that item goes on sale shortly thereafter, you can bring that item back to get the full discount. Also, as a goodwill gesture, department stores that have similar goods at similar prices will often match the price of an item you saw at a lower price elsewhere if you bring it to their attention.

It is important to consider putting big-ticket purchases on a credit card. If there is a billing problem or a problem with the product, the delay in payment protects you while the problem is being investigated. Billing errors for which merchants are responsible include charges for items you did not order or never received; items delivered to the wrong address, in the wrong quantity, or so much later than promised that the bill arrived before the item; items that turned out to be different from what you ordered.
—Consumer Reports **Complete Guide to Managing Your Money**

Discount Shopping

INTREPID TIP
Discount shopping isn't for everyone. Know thyself before setting out to become an expert in this method, because it may not be for you. Beware of all the potential pitfalls of bargain hunting:

$ It requires much more homework to make sure you are truly getting "a deal."

$ It is much more hit or miss in terms of finding what you are looking for. Usually discount merchandise isn't as neatly laid out and there are fewer items to choose from.

$ You will get less service with this kind of shopping so don't expect to get expertise from a salesperson; you may not even find a salesperson to help you—period!

$ You may not get the same guarantees and warranties that you would shopping full-service retail.

$ The service people in this type of shopping arena are much less likely to offer goodwill gestures to customers, because they care less about long-term customers and more about the volume of customers every day.

Different types of discount shopping have different advantages and disadvantages. Below is a rundown of these:

SAMPLE SALES
Sample sales are unique to this city because New York is where most designers and their showrooms reside. Sample sales are sales of the designer's leftover inventory—anything from furniture to clothes to jewelry to shoes. Designers hold sample sales throughout the year but the predominant months are November, December, April, and May.

> •
>
> The stores on the Lower East Side around Orchard Street that are run by Jewish proprietors have a custom. If you are the first customer of the day, you will get a discount. The idea is that the first sale of the day is the most important, and therefore it will bring them good luck if they give you a break. Try it.
>
> •

The pros:

★ Prices start at wholesale and can go all the way down to cost. It is possible to get incredible deals.

The cons:

★ Small selection of leftover inventory
★ Chaotic, cluttered atmosphere
★ If you are going to a clothing sample sale, you often can't try them on or are forced to do so behind a clothing rack.
★ You have to pay cash.

★ Consumers have a tendency to overbuy when they think they are getting a bargain. A bargain is not a bargain if you never use what you purchase.

★ Some sample sales may also be selling inventory from previous seasons.

★ Most sample sales are only held Monday through Friday, 9:00 A.M. to 5:00 P.M.

The homework you need to do:

★ In anticipation of a sample sale, you should check out the merchandise at the retail stores (if it's clothes, try them on), take down the style or model numbers of those items you want to purchase, and take that information with you to the sale.

★ Examine the merchandise before buying it to check for any flaws. If you are buying clothes, be aware that the fabric might not be precisely the quality of the fabric on the same outfit you saw being sold at retail.

INTREPID TIP

There are publications that will tell you about upcoming sample sales. Designers do not advertise their sample sales. The only way to find out about them is by calling up your favorite designer yourself or by subscribing to one of the following publications:

Fashion Update

1274 49th Street, Suite 209; Brooklyn, NY 11219; (718) 377-8873

A quarterly that lists up to 150 sample sales; costs $50 a year.

The S & B Report

112 East 36th Street; New York, New York 10016; (212) 679-5400

A monthly that will tell you every major designer showroom sale from jewelry to furniture going on in New York; costs $50 a year.

> "Before buying retail or discount items, compare the terms and conditions of warranties on products or services before you buy. How long is the warranty and when does it start and end? What is covered? Which parts? What kinds of problems? Will the warranty pay 100 percent of repair costs? Will it pay for parts, but not labor? Will it pay for shipping or for a loaner? What do you have to do, and when? Are regular inspections or maintenance required? Do you have to ship the product out of state for repairs? Who offers the warranty? How reliable are they? Keep sales receipts and warranties in a safe place.
> —**Consumer Resource Handbook,** United States Office of Consumer Affairs"

> "Credit card fees and rates are very high in the New York area. You should consider out-of-state options. You are not limited to cards offered by banks or issuers in your state. Cards issued in other states may be less expensive and offer different protections. Contact the "Bankcard Holders of America" at (703) 481-1110 for their up-to-date information on which banks offer the lowest rates nationwide.
> —Better Business Bureau"

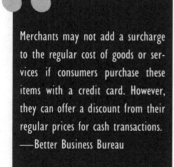

Sample sales and factory outlets can run your life if you let them. The trick is to know precisely which designers or manufacturers you like and go first to the retail stores to look at the inventory and see what you want. If it's clothes, styles and sizing will change somewhat from year to year, so try the clothes on in the retail stores first so you know what designers look good on you. This will remove the urge to hit every sale and outlet "just in case you miss something," which is time consuming, money wasting, and exhausting.

Merchants may not add a surcharge to the regular cost of goods or services if consumers purchase these items with a credit card. However, they can offer a discount from their regular prices for cash transactions.
—Better Business Bureau

"OFF-PRICE" OR "DISCOUNT" RETAIL STORES

Discount retail stores like Sears, Caldors, and K mart have been available to suburbanites for years, and have recently become a way of life for many New Yorkers. These are stores that sell merchandise about 20 percent below retail like Loehmann's for clothes, Yaeger Watch Corp. for watches, 47th Street Photo for electronic equipment, Toys "R" Us for toys. The really good discounters like the ones mentioned above pride themselves in selling quality merchandise at lower prices with all the same guarantees.

The pros:

◇ You generally get a 20 percent discount on all goods.
◇ You get the same warranties and guarantees.
◇ They will often match or discount any price you saw for the same product at their competitor's store down the block.

The cons:

◆ You may not find the more obscure brands.
◆ The environment tends to be frenetic.
◆ The service will not be as good.
◆ They are more likely to have to order an item for you because it isn't in stock.
◆ With discount clothes shopping often the selections of styles, models, and sizes are limited, and you have to search for a particular designer or manufacturer because they're all thrown in together. It's real hit or miss.
◆ If you are buying clothes you often have to try them on in one big common room with everybody else.
◆ They usually won't give you a cash refund, just a store credit.

INTREPID TIP
Here are some discount shopping guidelines:

☞ Stick to the reputable discount stores that do offer some guarantees. You can get badly burned by the many fly-by-night discount operations that proliferate the City.

☞ The reputable discounters are not full-service operations. They most likely won't deliver, wrap or ship, install or repair, and certainly not for free. So keep in mind those costs when deciding to purchase a product. You might find that the product you want is not only on sale at a full-service retail store, but that they will give you that full service for free. It pays to shop around first!

There is an organization called "Shop the World by Mail," which, if you request it, will send you a brochure free of charge listing dozens of catalogs from around the world. These catalogs enable you to buy clothing, handicrafts, jewelry, linens, rugs, silver, etc., at great savings direct from factories, retail shops and craftsmen worldwide. Once you pick out the catalogs you want from the brochure, for a small fee they will be mailed to you. "Shop the World by Mail" can be reached at (919) 467-3165.

THE INTREPID PAGES

OF

GOOD DISCOUNT SHOPPING

BOOKS

BARNES & NOBLE ★ 600 Fifth Avenue (at 48th Street) ★ (212) 765-0592
Other locations throughout the City. They discount all the best-sellers by 30 percent.

CLOTHING, CHILDREN'S

DAFFY'S FIFTH AVENUE ★ 335 Madison Avenue (at 44th Street) ★ (212) 557-4422
★ 115 Fifth Avenue (at 18th Street) ★ (212) 529-4477
For designer and European imports of girls' dresses (on a hit-or-miss basis) try Daffy's.

FOR KIDS' SAKE ★ By Appointment: (212) 772-9214
Rene Birnbaum has a buying service for children's clothing. She carries eight to ten lines, including sweats, leggings, hand-knit sweaters, designer outfits, bomber jackets, and more. Infant to size 7 for both boys and girls. The price is anywhere from 20 to 40 percent less than the retail boutiques in the city. You order from the samples that she brings to your home or office. You are shopping a season ahead; you will place your order for the fall in June.

KRAZY KIDS ★ 239 East 86th Street ★ (212) 410-7266
You have to come here with a good eye and some time to sift through the merchandise. You can find the best selection of children's underwear, socks, discounted Fusen Usagi, raincoats, and more—and forget the latest trends, i.e., Ninja Turtle shorts and Little Mermaid socks. Great swimsuits for under $5, pants for under $12.

RICHIE'S CHILDREN'S SHOES ★ 183 Avenue B (11th and 12th Streets) ★ (212) 228-5442
A family-run business whose emphasis is on quality and knowledge and, most of all, fair prices. They won't attempt to oversell you and they believe that most kids need only one pair of shoes.

CLOTHING, MEN'S

DAFFY'S ★ 115 Fifth Avenue (at 18th Street) ★ (212) 529-4477 ★ 335 Madison Avenue (at 44th Street) ★ (212) 557-4422

Daffy's is a good bet for men's designer sportswear. Here you can find Calvin Klein, Ferre, Paul Smith, Adolfo, and others at good discount prices in a well-laid-out manner.

DOLLAR BILLS ★ 99 East 42nd Street ★ (212) 867-0212

This is the place to go if you are in search of European designer clothing at fair prices. Be prepared to spend some time looking through the racks but if you do, you should find Armani, Ferre, and Byblos, just to mention a few.

KEEP IT FAIR ★ By Appointment: (212) 754-2199

Designer label suits at wholesale prices. Here you will find the latest models and styles all in 100 percent wool. Sizes range from 38 to 48 and the price is 50 percent off retail. Both traditional American and stylish European designers can be bought here with a money-back guarantee.

L. S. MEN'S CLOTHING ★ 19 West 44th Street ★ (212) 575-0933

L. S. stocks some of the best and most well known domestic designer labels for more than 40 percent off retail and they are usually the current styles. We have seen Ralph Lauren, Hickey Freeman, and Daks at low prices.

MOE GINSBERG ★ 162 Fifth Avenue (21st Street) ★ (212) 982-5254

Throughout this four-floor store you will see over 25,000 suits, all of which are 100 percent wool. The price range is from $180 to $360. Traditional suits on one floor, European on the next floor, and so forth. A great selection in a well-laid-out store.

CLOTHING, WOMEN'S

AARON'S ★ 627 Fifth Avenue, Brooklyn ★ (718) 768-5400

It is a little hard to get to, but it is worth the trip. Tahari and Calvin Klein are just two of the top designers that abound in this well-laid-out shop. The clothes are all grouped by designer so you don't have to weed through piles of clothes searching out your favorite label.

BEST OF SCOTLAND ★ 581 Fifth Avenue (47th and 48th Streets) ★ (212) 644-0415

Here you will find the lowest prices on fine cashmere in the City. They carry a wide variety of dresses, pants, scarves, shawls, gloves, and sweaters. The sweaters sell from $170 and up, but remember, cashmere from Scotland is the best.

DAFFY'S ★ 335 Madison Avenue (at 44th Street) ★ (212) 557-4422 ★ 115 Fifth Avenue (at 18th Street) ★ (212) 529-4477

All the major designers of women's fashions can be spotted here at one time or another. The store is appealing and well laid out. You don't feel like you are shopping in a bargain basement even though the prices are quite low.

DOLLAR BILLS ★ 99 East 42nd Street ★ (212) 867-0212

Women can also find good buys on fashionable European designer clothing at low prices. Very well known names can be found on the second floor, but remember, you must be prepared to spend some time sifting through the merchandise. We have spotted Armani, Ungaro, Fendi—need we say more?

TERRE GRAFF ★ By Appointment: (212) 288-3336

You won't believe this but you can buy couture Chanel, Armani, Ungaro, and more at half price. Twice a month the Graffs go to Europe and bring back these designer items, that they in turn sell to you. Each month they have a newsletter in which they tell you what they have. If you want to buy, just call them and make an appointment. They now sell to you from the comfort and luxury of a hotel suite.

THE LOFT ★ 141 West 36th Street ★ (212) 736-3358

Designer clothes at rock-bottom discount prices. Expect to find Donna Karan, Anne Klein, and other well-known American sportswear designers.

ONE NIGHT STAND ★ 905 Madison Avenue (72nd and 73rd Streets) ★ (212) 772-7720

If you need a smashing evening outfit you can rent one here. (Now *that* can be a great savings!) Everything is dry cleaned and fitted to your body.

HOSIERY AND UNDERGARMENTS

UNDERWEAR PLAZA ★ 1421 62nd Street, Brooklyn ★ (718) 232-6804

Dior, Eve Stillman, Calvin Klein, Vassarette, Bali, and Natori all can be found in this discount shop. Lingerie, slippers, and undergarments at low, low prices. It's worth the trip, and remember, with prices this good, buy in bulk.

Women are always in need of stockings. Here are three places that are happy to sell to you in bulk quantities with the best possible price:

NO NONSENSE DIRECT ★ By mail: 300 Dougherty, P.O. 26095, Greensboro, NC 27420-6095 ★ (800) 334-1633
Ask for Carol Burke

L'EGGS BRANDS ★ By Mail: P.O. Box 748, Rural Hall, NC 27098 ★ (919) 744-1790

NATIONAL WHOLESALE COMPANY ★ By mail: 400 National Boulevard, Lexington, NC 27294 ★ (704) 246-5904

SHOES FOR MEN AND WOMEN

PASSARELLA SHOE ★ 275 West 39th Street (12th Floor) ★ (212) 764-1408
The best thing about Passarella is their attention to organization and their incredible low prices. Top Italian name-brand women's shoes: Fendi, Valentino, and more. Call to check what is in your size.

STATESMAN SHOE ★ 6 East 46th Street ★ (212) 867-0450
This store is mostly for men. They stock sizes 5AA through 15EEE and are accommodating in trying to get you your size. Bruno Magli, Bass, Rockport, Nunn Bush, Stacy Adams, and Bostonian.

ORCHARD STREET
This is New York City's original shoe bazaar. It is hit or miss but women in particular will have over ten stores to choose from.

COSMETICS AND PERFUME

COSMETICS PLUS ★ 275 Seventh Avenue (at 26th Street) ★ (212) 924-3493
★ 518 Fifth Avenue (at 43rd Street) ★ (212) 221-6560
★ 515 Madison Avenue (at 53rd Street) ★ (212) 644-1911
★ 1201 Third Avenue (69th and 70th Streets) ★ (212) 628-5600
The most comprehensive discount perfume and cosmetic store in New York City. Their merchandise is fresh, which is important for cosmetics.

17TH STREET BETWEEN BROADWAY AND FIFTH AVENUE
This is the perfume store mecca of New York City. Just walk and price the bottles. Be sure to check that the merchandise is fresh.

ELECTRONICS

EAST 33RD STREET TYPEWRITER AND ELECTRONICS ★ 42 East 33rd Street
★ (212) 686-0930
Good buys on computers, fax machines, and copiers. They have a technician in the store if you need help with the installation of your computer or other electronic equipment.

47TH ST. PHOTO ★ 67 West 47th Street ★ (212) 398-1410
★ 115 West 45th Street ★ (212) 398-1410
★ 38 East 19th Street ★ (212) 921-5200
★ 116 Nassau Street ★ (212) 608-8080

Everyone knows about 47th St. Photo and for good reason: They really are one of the best discounters in the city. Their attitude can be a bit sharp, but just push it aside because they carry all major brand names at good prices.

VICMARR STEREO AND TV ★ 88 Delancey Street (Orchard and Ludlow Streets) ★ (212) 505-0380

This is a first-rate discount shop that is run by a friendly well-informed gentleman, Mel Cohen. He keeps his prices low and his sales staff does not give you a hard sell. He is well stocked with telephones, stereo equipment, microwaves, and more.

THE SHARPER IMAGE ★ 89 South Street Seaport ★ (212) 693-0477
★ 4 West 57th Street ★ (212) 265-2550
★ 900 Madison Avenue (73rd and 74th Streets) ★ (212) 794-4974

Every Sharper Image store around the country holds an auction every week at 12:30 P.M. on Tuesdays (except for the month of December). Here you can bid on discounted and returned merchandise that is in good condition. You can expect to find gadgets of all kinds, even robots. The merchandise changes weekly—so enjoy.

The following two shops are not really discount—but it is next to impossible to find full-service electronic stores in the City. Their expertise and quality of service make it an easy way to shop and sometimes that is the bargain:

INNOVATIVE AUDIO ★ 77 Clinton Street, Brooklyn ★ (718) 596-0888

This is a real find when you are looking for stereo equipment. Not only is Elliot Fishkin one of the nicest, most accommodating people, he is also one of the most knowledgeable. His prices can be negotiated and he does know exactly what system you need and will never try to oversell to you.

MPCS VIDEO INDUSTRIES ★ 514 West 57th Street ★ (212) 586-3690

A special salesperson wil be assigned to you according to your needs. They deal with both sales and rentals of VCR, camera, TV, musical equipment, and more. They have no problem getting the more unusual, hard-to-find items.

GENERAL STORE

CENTURY 21 ★ 22 Cortland Street (Broadway and Church Street) ★ (212) 227-9092

A discount designer department store selling everything from clothing for men, women, and kids to general household appliances. You can find some great inexpensive gifts. We call it the "Thrifty Man's Bloomingdale's."

ODD-JOB TRADING ★ 149 West 32nd Street ★ (212) 564-7370
★ 66 West 48th Street ★ (212) 575-0477
★ 10 Cortland Street (Broadway and Church Street) ★ (212) 571-0959
★ 7 East 40th Street ★ (212) 686-6825

The merchandise changes daily and is similar in all stores. They have household items, toys, clothing, accessories, and more. They buy closeouts from manufacturers and sell them for about 75 percent of what they are sold for in other stores.

GIFTS

JERRY SAMUEL ★ By mail: (203) 327-5851

Silver, china, crystal, and jewelry at discounted prices, even Baccarat. All you need to do is call and tell them what you want and they will ship it. Friendly and timely service.

JOMPOLE COMPANY, INC. ★ 330 Seventh Avenue (at 29th Street) ★ (212) 594-0440

You can expect at least a 20 percent discount off major name brands of china, crystal, cutlery, sterling, pens, and more. You can either order over the phone or go to their showroom. Don't hesitate to ask if they can get you balloons, appliances, and even award plaques.

MICHAEL C. FINA ★ 3 West 47th Street ★ (212) 869-5050

It is very hard to get anyone at this store on the phone due to the incredible volume of business that they do. However, they have a great selection of china, crystal, silver, pewter, and good baby gifts. They do have a mail-order business, which might be the way to go.

ROBIN IMPORTERS ★ 510 Madison Avenue (52nd and 53rd Streets) ★ (212) 753-6475

All major brand names in crystal, china, and flatware at discounted prices are sold here. Why walk three blocks north to spend 20 percent more for Baccarat, Lalique, and more?

LINENS

GRAND STREET ON THE LOWER EAST SIDE

This street is lined with shops. While browsing you should be comparing prices. Don't be afraid to bargain!

HARRIS LEVY IMPORTERS ★ 278 Grand Street (Eldridge and Forsythe Streets) ★ (212) 226-3102

One of the more "upscale" linen and bath shops located on the Lower East Side. Their emphasis is on quality merchandise and their prices are less than uptown. All major brand names including down comforters.

Large department stores have fairly good "white sales" where you can get good deals. So check their prices before going discount shopping. In particular:

BLOOMINGDALE'S ★ 1000 Third Avenue (at 59th Street) ★ (212) 705-2000

MACY'S ★ 151 West 34th Street ★ (212) 695-4400

PAPER GOODS

GEMINI PAPER GOODS ★ 449 Third Street, Brooklyn ★ (718) 768-5568

For paper napkins, matchbooks, place cards, ribbons, and envelopes (all can be monogrammed) at excellent prices. Just give them a call and they will be happy to fill any order by mail.

RECORDS, TAPES, AND CD'S

HMV RECORDS ★ 1280 Lexington Avenue (86th and 87th Streets) ★ (212) 348-0800 ★ 2081 Broadway (at 72nd Street) ★ (212) 721-5900

HMV is the largest music store in the city, with over 40,000 square feet of space. Their sales staff is more than accommodating in guiding you through this well-laid-out store. They encourage questions and will even play the album that you want to hear. Due to its size and volume of sales they keep their prices low compared to other music stores in the city.

TOWER RECORDS ★ 692 Broadway (at 4th Street) ★ (212) 505-1500 ★ 1961 Broadway (at 66th Street) ★ (212) 799-2500

Tower Records was the first to open a massive music store in New York City. They sell a complete range of music and try to be as helpful as possible. Their large size allows them to offer quite good prices.

TOYS

All the following stores sell toys way below the full retail toy stores in New York City. Some major brand-name items sell for 50 percent less than other stores. Unless you are looking for a specific European or a unique toy, you should always check at these stores first.

KAY-BEE TOY INC. ★ 901 Avenue of the Americas (32nd and 33rd Streets) ★ (212) 629-5386

LIONEL KIDDIE CITY TOYS ★ 24–34 Union Square East (at 15th Street) ★ (212) 353-0215
Call for other locations.

TOYS "R" US ★ 1293 Broadway (at 33rd Street) ★ (212) 594-8697

WATCHES

JC WATCH AND JEWELRY COMPANY ★ 37 West 47th Street ★ (212) 869-5250
All well-known designer names in watches are sold at JC's. Look around before you come here to buy. You will be sure to save at least 30 percent off retail.

YAEGER WATCH CORPORATION ★ 578 Fifth Avenue (at 47th Street) ★ (212) 819-0088
All major American and European designer watches are sold here at 33 to 40 percent off retail. You might have to wait a few weeks till they can get your watch in, but your savings can be thousands of dollars. Of course, they come with all the original guarantees and warranties.

FACTORY OUTLETS

These designer and manufacturer outlets are usually located in clusters about twenty miles outside the City, although The Intrepid New Yorker has seen a few open right in Manhattan. In theory, these stores are stocked with excess inventory. It has been rumored, however, that some manufacturers produce merchandise just for their outlets. There are two kinds of factory outlet stores:

1. Stores that the designer or manufacturer opened himself to sell his inventory at a discount.
2. Stores that sell a lot of different brands of a particular type of product at a discount.

The pros:

✔ Like off-price stores you get about 20 percent off retail.

✔ They are much more shopper-friendly than other types of discount stores—the merchandise is well laid out and the stores feel more like a full-service retail store in terms of shopping convenience and sales help.

✔ Outlets have a lot more inventory than a sample sale or off-price store because it's the designer's own store. Remember, however, that you still won't get the vast selection to choose from that you would on the retail level and they may not stock the same items you would find retail.

✔ They usually take credit cards and have a pretty good refund policy.

The cons:

☞ You have to travel out of the city to get to them.

☞ There are so many outlet stores to choose from that unless you know exactly what you want, you can quickly become overwhelmed and indecisive.

☞ You are buying the clothes six to eight weeks after they have hit the department stores, although we have heard that with the current dismal retail sales some designers may be sending their inventory to the outlets sooner.

☞ You may not find the styles and sizes you want.

> " A multibillion dollar industry has emerged around "gray market" goods. They are not counterfeits but "parallel imports," which are not made for U.S. consumption but may bear a valid U.S. trademark, and are imported into the States without the U.S. trademark holder's consent. The goods (which are primarily electronics) find their way into local stores where they compete with domestic versions. They are usually less expensive, but for the most part they do not have U.S. warranties, aren't eligible for manufacturers' rebates, and their instructions are written in a foreign language. In New York State, any retailer offering these goods must post a visible sign listing their limitations. If a merchant violates this law, the buyer has up to twenty days after the purchase to request a refund.
> —Better Business Bureau "

THE INTREPID PAGES
OF
FACTORY OUTLETS

SECAUCUS OUTLET ★ Secaucus, New Jersey ★ (201) 866-3516 for Directions
Although Secaucus is the closest outlet center to New York City, we find it a bit depressing and certainly hard to navigate your way around. They do have a lot of well-known brand names, but we found much of the merchandise to be tattered and old. *Some of the better ones in the Secaucus Outlet:*

THE GUCCI OUTLET ★ 50 Hartway ★ (201) 392-2670

CHURCH'S ENGLISH SHOE FACTORY STORE ★ 1000 Castle Road ★ (201) 863-9209

CALVIN KLEIN WOMEN'S DESIGNER SPORTSWEAR ★ 50 Enterprise Avenue ★ (201) 330-0373

THE CHELSEA GROUP OUTLETS
Our pick for outlet shopping are the ones owned and operated by The Chelsea Group. The merchandise we saw in these outlets appeared to be in tip-top shape. They make an effort to design their centers for convenience. There are benches for resting, restaurants to dine at, walkways that are easy to manipulate with strollers, and a peaceful ambience. The Chelsea Group manages the entire operation, setting strict guidelines that all of their stores must follow. At both of the locations below you will find some of the latest designers' apparel, brand-name sportswear, coats, furs, shoes, intimate apparel, accessories, fine china, crystal and silver, home furnishings and housewares, jewelry, gifts, luggage, and leather goods. They both have brochures detailing all their shops and can be reached from the Port Authority. *Call either of the following outlets for directions and brochures:*

LIBERTY VILLAGE ★ Flemington, New Jersey ★ (908) 782-8550
Fifty-five miles from New York City.

WOODBURY COMMON ★ Central Valley, New York ★ (914) 928-7467
Fifty-five miles from New York City.

WILLIAMS-SONOMA ★ 231 Tenth Avenue (at 23rd Street) ★ (212) 206-8118

Right here in Manhattan, in this 15,000 square foot store you will be able to buy items discounted 30 to 70 percent from Williams-Sonoma's four stores: Chambers Gardener's Eden, Hold Everything, Pottery Barn, and Williams-Sonoma.

WHOLESALE SHOPPING

In New York there are wholesale districts and then there are wholesale districts—you need to choose them carefully. We are going to tell you about only those districts that we think sell retail-quality items at wholesale prices. Here, again, you will forfeit some service, guarantees, and shopping ease.

But, there is one exception to that rule: If you are formally introduced to a wholesaler who doesn't normally open his doors to the public and accepts people by appointment only—such as the top wholesale jewelers and furriers—you will experience the finest full-service shopping there is, at wholesale prices.

> Every written appraisal of jewelry must state the standard of monetary value used (e.g., retail replacement). Persons engaged in the sale or appraisal of jewelry may not misrepresent the nature of an article of jewelry and must disclose that jewelry appraisals may vary as much as 25 percent. For sales of more than $75, very detailed and accurate sales slips must be given. Note: "Jewelry" means unset rare gems, precious and semiprecious stones, and articles for personal wear containing such gems or stones. It does not include gold, silver, platinum, or other precious metals.
> —The Department of Consumer Affairs

FURS AND JEWELRY

❗ INTREPID APPROACH
When buying wholesale furs and jewelry, take note of the following:

- DO NOT walk in off the street to just any wholesaler; you don't know who they are or what they are selling, and there is the potential for being taken—badly. Most of the top reputable wholesalers won't let the public in without a referral anyway. They sell primarily to dealers and retail stores so onetime-only walk-in customers are not worth their while.

- DO get an introduction to one of those furriers or jewelers from someone you know. When you are introduced formally, the wholesaler is going to eye you as a long-term customer, and now you have become important to them. In fact, your relationship with them should last a lifetime. Many of these wholesale businesses are family owned and get handed down through generations, so your children might end up dealing with their children.

> One reason to pay retail at a signature jewelers such as Tiffany, Harry Winston, or Bulgari is that when you sell one of the pieces you bought there, you could get what you paid for it back, maybe even a little more. Example: You could buy an imitation "Cartier rolling ring" for $100 wholesale and sell it back for the scrap weight of the gold for about $55. However, the real Cartier ring sells for about $500 today. If you had bought it some years before, let's say, for around $100, you could possibly sell it to a jeweler today for about $200. If the ring was discontinued and is now considered a collector's item, you might sell it for considerably more than what you paid for it.
> —Brad Reh, wholesale jeweler

Wholesale Furs: Seventh Avenue in the 30s

- You should never pay retail for a fur coat. Chances are the furs you are looking at in the retail stores came from the wholesale district to begin with.
- The best wholesaler will take care of your every need, change the style of the coat when you want to, let you trade in your coat for a new one, etc.
- If you don't know anything about furs, start learning! With a big-ticket item like this you'd better be informed. Go to the top retailers, look at dozens of furs, and ask questions. Call the American Fur Industry, (212) 564-5133. They also sell a booklet called "Fur Naturally" that tells you everything you need to know about furs. When you are capable of making an informed choice, you are ready to buy your fur.

Wholesale Jewelry: 47th Street between Fifth and Sixth Avenues

- Make sure the wholesale jeweler you settle on has a policy that allows you to trade your jewelry or possibly even get a cash refund.
- If you develop that all-important relationship with the jeweler, you should not only be able to buy all your jewelry from him but sell it back to him when you want to.
- Again, homework is critical. Look at stones in their settings at the top retail jewelers first. Get an idea of what you want. Call Jewelers Of America at (212) 489-0023 and get their booklets on everything you need to know about jewelry.
- When you talk to your wholesaler, ask him if the stone has been certified by the Gemological Institute of America, which is the last word on gems. If it hasn't, he will give you a letter of introduction to them, so you can take the stone there to be graded. Their number is (212) 944-5900.

THE INTREPID PAGES

OF
THE BEST WHOLESALE JEWELERS AND FURRIERS

WHOLESALE JEWELERS

BRAD REH INC. ★ 572 Fifth Avenue (46th and 47th Streets) ★ (212) 869-4259
A quality family business that now spans three generations. Brad, who is the youngest, is capable and accommodating. They even come to your home or office. Not only do they deal with high-quality stones and jewels, they also run one of the premier estate jewelry businesses in the country. How can you go wrong? By appointment only.

FRIMAN & STEIN ★ 58 West 47th Street ★ (212) 246-7920
This is one of the finest family-run businesses on 47th Street. The quality of their goods, combined with their knowledge and expertise, is unmatchable. They are ostensibly "wholesale only," so be sure to call ahead to see if they can handle your request. By appointment only.

WHOLESALE FURS

B. SMITH & SONS ★ 333 Seventh Avenue (28th and 29th Streets) ★ (212) 736-2423
Mark Smith has a fabulous eye for helping you choose a coat that looks great on you and that suits all your needs. They have a good selection of furs and styles. By appointment only.

CHRISTIE BROTHERS ★ 333 Seventh Avenue (28th and 29th Streets) ★ (212) 736-6944
Longevity is the name of the game here. Five generations of the Christie family have made this one of the finest furriers in the country. You can be sure of getting exactly what you want—whether it is a traditional style or one that is more contemporary. By appointment only.

OTHER WHOLESALE DISTRICTS

Wholesale Plants: Sixth Avenue from 24th to 28th Streets
Plants, trees, flowers—real, dried, or fake. It's here and all at wholesale prices. The service isn't great and you may want to repot the

plant once you get it home, but the bargains can't be beat. We recently came home with $75 worth of goods that would have cost us $150 uptown. Throw in the cab fare there and back, and it was still well worth it. If you can't get it all in a cab, they will deliver for a small fee. Just make sure you get a receipt and hold onto it until you get your delivery.

Wholesale Lighting: Third Avenue from 7th Street to Houston, Bowery from Houston to Chinatown's Chatham Square

This is a mini-lighting town with serious wholesale bargains. Dozens of lighting stores line the streets. Most have a large selection of inventory, are nicely laid out, and are shopper friendly.

Wholesale Restaurant Supplies: Third Avenue two blocks above Houston Street, and Bowery several blocks below Houston

These wholesale stores sell commercial-grade kitchen appliances, ovens, sinks, bar stools, chairs, butcher block tables, glassware, china —you name it—to restaurants, diners, and delis. They will also sell to the consumer with no minimums. It's an experience not unlike rummaging through a garage sale, so don't expect the red carpet treatment, but you can find extraordinary buys.

Wholesale Clothing

A wholesale clothing district exists, but it is not open to the public, period! You can gain access but only through the professional services of a personal shopper (see page 136).

Wholesale Gifts, Toys, and Accessories

Buyers come in to place their orders with the dozens of showrooms that are housed within the following:

The Gift Building
225 Fifth Avenue

The Toy Building
200 Fifth Avenue

The Accessories Buildings
320 Fifth Avenue
330 Fifth Avenue
389 Fifth Avenue
393 Fifth Avenue
417 Fifth Avenue

> •
> If you call (212) 675-3535, the people who manage the Toy Building will tell you when certain showrooms are having sample sales and when they will be open to the public. They often occur during the holiday season and before and after the big toy fair conventions in New York City.
> •

Theoretically, they are closed to the public because they only sell in bulk and only to stores. But if you need to buy certain items in bulk, let's say a dozen of a particular belt to give as Christmas presents, or half a dozen bracelets as bridesmaids gifts, they might be willing to sell to you. It's up to the discretion of an individual showroom. Your savings will be considerable. It is absolutely worth a try. Nothing ventured, nothing gained.

Another way to get in and not have to purchase in bulk is by hiring a personal shopper (see page 136) who by profession is permitted access to these "to the trade only" showrooms. Just be aware that personal shoppers have agreements with a specific group of showrooms; they can't access all of them.

ALTERNATIVE SHOPPING METHODS AVAILABLE IN NYC

NONSTOREFRONT "DESIGNER LABS"

New York City is the mecca for every type of fashion designer. Many unknown, up-and-coming designers start out as cottage industries designing hats, jewelry, clothes, belts, etc. hoping to become the next Elsa Peretti or Carolina Herrera. Most of them work out of their homes or small office spaces.

INTREPID TIP

If you can find these designer laboratories, it is a one-of-a-kind way to shop. They sell to specialty stores and large department stores, but if you make an appointment they will most likely be willing to have you down to their "shop" to either sell you one of their designs or actually design an original for you—and usually at wholesale or somewhere below retail prices. Imagine being able to go directly to the workroom of a favorite designer to have something made specially for you.

Here's how to find them:

- If you spot a designer's products you haven't seen before on display at a boutique or department store, ask the buyer at the store if the designer is located in New York City. You can probably find them in the phone book or ask the buyer if they would give you their telephone number.
- These designers have a tendency to show up at flea markets and street fairs where they might try to sell their leftover inventory for the season. They don't have enough inventory to actually hold a sample sale, but in effect, that's what they are doing here.
- Browse through the trade publications like *Women's Wear Daily* to find their picks of new designers. And in the Sunday *New York Times* Life Style section, there is a column called "Stylemakers" that writes up new designers of all types.

THE INTREPID PAGES
OF
NONSTOREFRONT DESIGNER LABS

To meet with these designers, you must make an appointment.

IN NEW YORK CITY

ALAN THOMAS ELECTRIC ANTIQUES AND TOPIARIES ★ (212) 245-6835
This company makes the most unusual and well-designed dried flower arrangements. They customize. Price range—$5 to $200.

BALI VISIONS, INC. ★ (212) 260-3583
Melanie Gouldon sells small to large bags made from colorful Balinese fabrics, floral island designs, and geometrics. Price range—$25 and up.

BOMBALULU'S ★ (212) 473-0752
He makes the cutest 100 percent cotton T-shirts we have seen. Mostly for kids, the designs included dancing pigs, fire fighters, and great scenes of New York City. If you give him a call, he will tell you the next street fair at which he will be. Price range—about $10 per shirt.

CAROLA ★ (212) 627-0599
Custom-made women's clothing that can be completed within a week. Carola has trained with Halston and she specializes in velour. Price range—$50 and up.

CYNTHIA C. & COMPANY ★ (212) 255-6161
Cynthia specializes in designing bridal gowns and special occasion dresses for all ages. The cost is $400 and up; bridal gowns average $1,500.

DEBORAH JOHNSON STUDIO ★ Usually through a Personal Shopper (see page 136)
If you are a woman and you plan on investment dressing here is the place for you. This is the way clothing should be made and should fit. Price range—$250 and up.

FERN DEVLIN ★ (718) 462-6059

Fern designs scarves, shawls, and handwoven neckties. Prices start at $40.

FRONK & MOSLER COUTURE ★ (212) 243-9221

A small custom business that designs mostly women's business suits. The customer has the option of supplying the fabric and design, which lowers the price. Average cost $500. If you want them to do the leg-work of getting the fabric the cost goes up. They have recently ex-panded to accommodate men.

HATS BY JO LAURIE ★ (212) 460-9299

For men or women, her hats lean toward the funky, but best of all she really knows what will work for you. As she says, "A hat completes the outfit." Price range—$50 and up.

HATS BY SARA GAVAGHAN ★ (212) 353-0349

For women, her materials are straw and felt; all hats have an upbeat, nontraditional feeling. Her studio is fun and functional, and anyone will have a great time going to buy a hat. Price range—$45 and up.

IDENTICAL COUSINS ★ (212) 535-5639

Roberta Chiarella designs and hand-makes earrings, pins, and pen-dants. All pieces are made from first-quality Austrian crystal and set in metallic resin, which is nearly weightless. Price range—$15 and up.

ISABELL TOLEDO ★ (212) 563-4960

Isabell produces two collections for women a year. Her fabrics span from denim to silk; her styles include unusually shaped coats and dresses that do stay in style. Price range is $50 for a cotton dress and up to $1,200 for evening wear.

JANE CROSS SCARVES ★ (212) 222-3901

Jane Cross creates limited-edition scarves and shawls for men and women made from imported, luxury fabrics. No more than forty of any one design is made and each piece is numbered. Price range— $40 and up.

JEWELRY BY MIRIAM ★ (212) 772-2595

Unusually designed bracelets, rings, necklaces, and earrings—silver and gold, with or without stones. Price range—$90 and up.

LAINEY'S KIDS, LTD. ★ (718) 859-0392

From infant layettes to toddler clothing, she designs with an eye for the delicate and detailed. She also designs and manufactures and hand-paints frames, baby baskets, and Lucite boxes. Price range—$20 and up.

LISA HAMMERQUIST ★ (212) 463-8172

Lisa has a terrific trained eye for knowing just what fabric and design will look good on her clients. She makes special-occasion dresses and everyday wear for women. Price range—$300 and up.

MR. JOBOUR ★ (516) 627-2588

Mr. Jobour knows that people still care about having beautiful house-coats, slips, and petticoats, bed linens, towels and tablecloths. He comes into New York City on Tuesdays and Thursdays and visits his customers at their homes. Call for prices.

PERSONALIZED CHILDREN'S BOOKS ★ (914) 965-0467

If you call, an order form will be sent to you. For only $14 you can choose from over eight different books, all of which can be personal-ized throughout with the name you provide.

RONALD FURST DESIGNS ★ (212) 686-8219

Creative leather bags, vests, and belts. Mostly designs for women but will be expanding to men. Price range—$40 and up.

SHIMODO ACCESSORIES ★ (212) 491-6726

Donna Emanuel creates interesting jewelry, mostly in the style of the Native American and African. Her materials include semiprecious stones, glass beads, and even bones. Price range—$15 to $600.

SWERVE DESIGN ★ (718) 383-1896

She hand-paints frames, furniture, mirrors, and more. Her finishes include polka dots, marbleized, and sponge. A five-by-seven-inch frame sells for $15.

TELE-FUN ★ (212) 319-1247

Leslie Levitan has a functional and beautiful line of home decorative accessories including telephone book covers, laminated trays, aprons, placemats, and more. Price range—$20 and up.

THE WESTMINSTER LADY ★ (212) 243-6891

Diane designs dresses exclusively for large and supersized women. She uses a multitude of fabrics, even 100 percent cotton knits. Best of all, she can design lingerie and exercise wear. Price range—$45 to $160.

All of these craftspeople will speak to you on the phone. Some have a catalogue that they can send to you, others will describe their goods over the phone. Most will sell directly to you. However, a few prefer that you buy from them when they are at a craft fair in New York City and will tell you the next time they will be in town.

ALISON PALMER ★ (914) 277-8078

Alison sells over 100 different spoon-rest designs. Her designs include: fried eggs, chickens, vegetables, fruits—all whimsical. Her price is about $20 per spoon rest.

ANDERSON EDUCATIONAL DESIGNWORKS ★ (412) 357-7613

This company designs and manufactures fine-quality, wooden educational puzzles and learning aids. Each puzzle piece has its own handle for easy removal. Price range—$20 and up.

ANNETTE HOLLANDER—BOOKCRAFTS ★ (203) 281-3135

Annette makes notepads, picture frames, boxes, wastebaskets, blotters, pen holders, and more—all covered in beautiful Italian marbleized paper at half the cost you'd find in the City. She will send you a piece but prefers to see you in New York City at a show. Items start at $15.

BiG DIPPER CANDLES ★ (914) 469-9442

Jerome and Paula Specter make the most interesting array of candles. Their designs include red peppers, sushi, long, delicate shapes, and more. We're sure if the order is big enough they can be commissioned to make anything you want. Price range—$10 and up.

CASTERWELL ★ (607) 587-8558

Robin Caster makes whimsical jewelry—earrings, pins, bracelets, and more. She comes into New York City twice a year but will ship to you. Price range—$18 to $150.

DEEP SPRING STUDIO ★ (304) 257-4356

Collapsible wooden baskets are cut from a single piece of fine-quality exotic or domestic hardwood. The handle is cut integrally with the basket body to ensure proper fit when collapsed. It doubles as a trivet. Price range—$28 and up.

GINNY'S ★ (602) 830-2666

This talented craftsperson has two passions: (1) Hand-appliquéd and painted blue jean jackets for men, women, and kids that can be custom ordered to depict your own theme; average price is $200; and (2)

Silk wedding bouquets and boutonnieres designed in conjunction with the bride's color and flower choices; bridal bouquets average $300. She can also design the flowers for an entire wedding.

HEATHER BELL DESIGNS ★ (617) 320-0956
Hand-painted silk on one-of-a-kind pieces such as silk earrings, scarves, jackets, and vests. Price range—scarves: $18 to $59; vests: $98 to $120; jackets: $300.

HEISE AND SON SCULPTURE ★ (802) 658-9328
Bill Heise is a contemporary folk artist who creates shapes of birds, animals, and people indigenous to the hillsides of Vermont using discarded metal tools as his materials. The beauty of Bill's work is that he is able to animate old, rusty, otherwise-useless objects. His work can be found in major stores and galleries in the United States. Price range: $85 and up.

KERR HOUSE ★ (203) 966-5523
Mary Lou Kerr makes hand-painted wicker baskets, chairs, tables, and more. Her patterns are floral and colors are pale pink, blue, and peach. She will customize. Hand-painted wicker magazine basket is $65.

LAURA D'S FOLK ART FURNITURE INC. ★ (914) 228-1440
Laura Dabrowski sells her colorfully animated furniture to major stores around the country and she will also sell direct to you. You can call her direct for custom work. Originally her furniture was all geared to children—from Peter Rabbit to abstract design chairs—but now she has branched out to adult pieces. Call for prices.

MELODIOUS ★ (207) 774-5519
Melodious music boxes present music and animation in irresistible combinations to delight music-box lovers of all ages. The size is approximately five by seven inches. Average price $36 and they have music clocks for $60.

MOMMY MADE ★ (214) 270-8329
Mercedes Meier makes the most adorable children's clothing, especially for girls. Appliqué dresses and patchwork pants all at moderate prices. Even though she lives in Texas, she regularly does business in New York City, or tell her what you like and she will send it to you.

BOB MORRIS, TOYMAKER ★ (201) 522-1651
Bob makes the most charming and playful wooden mobiles. Jack-in-the-box designs, clowns, moon, and stars. Price range—$22 to $36.

PAMELA MORIN, INC. ★ (914) 831-2200

Pamela designs hand-painted accessories—wearables, clocks, furniture, and custom-interior pieces. Her style is that of whimsical contemporary primitives using bold, bright colors. All at moderate prices.

WHEEL WOODEN TOYS ★ (804) 295-0534

Robert Stoh designs these sturdy wooden objects for kids. Lamps that have dinosaurs or fish at the base, coat racks, counting beads that are held together with dinosaurs, and an animated assortment of pull toys. Price range—$6 and up.

WOODEN EVE ★ (207) 549-3932

The Wooden Eve Company is dedicated to the creation of high-quality, hand-crafted, wooden rocking animals. Each colorful animal is made from hard woods, painted with nontoxic paints, signed and numbered by the artist. The design choices include rabbits, cows jumping over the moon, pigs, fish, and custom designs of your own pet. Size: twenty-five inches high, thirty-six inches long, and eleven inches wide. All are $300 except your pet, which is $375.

THE INTREPID PAGES
OF
STOREFRONT DESIGNER LABS

The next level of success for emerging designers are storefront labs. They are more expensive than the nonstorefront laboratories because of their overhead and because they are farther along in their careers, but there is still room for some price negotiation.

INTREPID TIP
There are areas of the City where storefront designer laboratories are most likely to be found. You'll find them in the artists' districts of Manhattan such as SoHo, NoHo, and the East and West villages. The designers often run the stores themselves, and if you don't see exactly what you want there, they might actually make something up for you.

BARNEY'S and **BENDEL** both like to discover young designers. Every now and then go and browse through the store; often they will have the designer there promoting and selling their designs.

BIJOUX WOLF ★ 346 East 9th Street ★ (212) 529-1784
Greg Wolf designs and manufactures exquisite sterling silver jewelry. His bold, handcrafted fashions are influenced by the ancient past. Prices start at $40.

DAPHNE ★ 473 Amsterdam Avenue (82nd and 83rd Streets) ★ (212) 877-5073
Daphne designs clothing for the larger woman using a multitude of fabrics such as silk, wool, and rayon. Dress prices go up to $225.

EDDRIS SHOES ★ 274 Columbus Avenue (72nd and 73rd Streets) ★ (212) 787-4198
Eddy is the maker of these stylish, comfortable shoes for women only. Everything is custom-made in sizes 4 to 11. Prices range from $79 to $129.

EMPIRIAL HOUSE ★ 119 St. Mark's Place ★ (212) 533-2895
Edward Erlikh designs beautifully made, forward-thinking clothes for women, from blouses to coats, in natural fibers such as silk, cotton,

and wool. Winter jackets from $300 to $700. Summer jackets from $100 to $300 in linen and silk. He has two collections, winter and spring.

FAD ★ 117 Perry Street (Hudson and Greenwich Streets) ★ (212) 242-4614
Fashion Art Design is filled with designs for women by Donald Witkewicz. His taste is fun, functional, and colorful. Jackets range from $400 to $500. Skirts are around $180.

JADED ★ 1048 Madison Avenue (at 80th Street) ★ (212) 288-6631
Jaded manufactures and designs contemporary jewelry, using coins and stones, which is sold throughout the country. They will accommodate all your needs. Prices start at $50.

> One of the biggest mistakes people make when shopping for clothes is always going for the familiar, more expensive designer labels. New York City is the fashion laboratory capital for young, up-and-coming designers who tend to set up shop in the lower rent districts and neighborhood fringes of Manhattan. If people spend more time looking for them, they will get far more value for their dollar buying high-quality clothes from lesser-known designers.
> —Susan Dresner, image and wardrobe consultant, *Successful Ways and Means*

J. MORGAN PUETT ★ 527 Broome Street (Thompson Street and Sixth Avenue) ★ (212) 274-9485
Morgan designs clothes for women, men, and children. You shop from her floor samples and then she makes the item for you. Her pants and shirts are unisex and she designs two collections a year. Linen dresses: $200; jackets: $300; pants: $80; baby clothes: $50.

JANICE FARLEY CERAMICS ★ 175 Franklin Street ★ (212) 226-4425
Janice handcrafts the most festive, functional ceramics that we have seen. She has animal motifs that come to life. A ceramic cream and sugar set of giraffes, zebras on top of cookie jars, turtles that swim on plates. A plate costs about $30.

KILIMA ★ 69 West Houston Street ★ (212) 473-8509
Dresses by Kilima are custom-made designs. The material of choice is silk and she has four collections a year. Prices start at $150.

KATINKA ★ 303 East 9th Street ★ (212) 677-7897
Jane Williams works with materials that come from India. She designs shoes, vests, and sportswear. Her emphasis is not on customization, but she will do it. Prices start at $50.

LA LUMINA ★ 253 Church Street (Leonard and Franklin Streets) ★ (212) 966-3923
Jackie Sencion is the owner and designer of this boutique that sells

---

mostly contemporary casual clothing for women. She likes to use all types of fabrics. A dress runs about $100.

LOLA MILLINERY ★ 102 St. Mark's Place (First Avenue and Avenue A) ★ (212) 979-1005
Lola can design anything from the classic to the funky. Her attention to detail in both her hats and her customers can't be beat. She can accommodate men looking for the offbeat. Average price is $175.

MICHELE NICOLE WESLEY ★ 126 Prince Street (Greene and Wooster Streets) ★ (212) 334-1313
You can buy everything from fantastic lingerie to gorgeous evening wear all designed by Michele Nicole Wesley. Her materials of choice are cotton knit and lace in mostly one size. Price range—$7 to $200.

ONLY HEARTS ★ 386 Columbus Avenue (78th and 79th Streets) ★ (212) 724-5608
Helena Stuart is the designer of this comfortable and fashionable line of lingerie and sleepwear. Most items are made from cotton or silk. Only Hearts is sold other places but this is the main outlet for her merchandise. Prices are moderate.

SHRIMPTON & GILLIGAN ★ 70 East 1st Street ★ (212) 254-1249
Angel Zimick and Alpana Bawa make coats, jackets, skirts, and blouses all of which are intelligent, sophisticated, and well made. Prices range from $75 to $500 and they have two collections a year. They also carry a line of their own home furnishings: sheets with matching men's-style pajamas, neck rolls ($30), duvet covers, and pillow shams. All are white cotton with different cuts, embroidery, and appliqués.

THE DRESS ★ 103 Stanton Street ★ (212) 473-0237
Amy Downs designs free-form hats in bright colors. She is known as the "mad hatter." Mary Adams handles the clothing end (special occasions and bridal)—very feminine linen, princesslike silk organzas, layers of iridescent color. She works directly with the customer to design something dramatically special. Hats—$50 to $150; dresses—$150 to $800 (nonbridal).

TRACEY TOOKER HATS ★ 1213 Lexington Avenue (at 82nd Street) ★ (212) 472-9603
Tracey has a wonderful eye for designing traditional hats for all heads and occasions. She uses a wide variety of silk flowers and straw, and she does custom orders. Prices start at $75.

YOURS ALONE SWIMWEAR ★ 14 Roosevelt Road, Chatham, NJ ★ (201) 701-1777
Just forty minutes from New York City, you can get a bathing suit custom made to hide all your flaws. It's all made possible by computers. All you need to do is pick out your fabric. Prices start at $75.

THE INTREPID PAGES
OF
NONSTOREFRONT SHOPS

There is a category of people who have a passion for collecting certain types of items—it could be anything from quilts to dried flowers—and sell them by appointment out of their home. Needless to say, they are hard to find because they don't advertise and they don't have storefronts, but we have a growing list that we will continue to update for you.

JANE SYBILLA CROSSLAND ★ By Appointment: (212) 734-4216
Jane creates true-to-life silk flower arrangements. Usually she expects you to bring your own vase and color swatches of the room in which you plan to place your flowers. Price range—$200 and up.

JUDY CORMIER ★ By Appointment: (212) 517-3993
Judy specializes in antique decorative prints—book plates and copper-plate engravings. Designs include birds, flowers, agricultural, and garden scenes. Price range—$98 to $5,000.

FANCY THAT ★ By Appointment: (212) 838-1201
Customized party supplies, invitations, tabletop accessories, even party favors can be found here. Prices vary according to what you want.

VICTORIA HOFFMAN ★ By Appointment: (212) 794-1922
Victoria collects antique quilts that come from the Northeast, South, and Midwest. They date from the 1880s to 1935. She also has white Marseilles bedspreads, hook rugs, and shawls. Price range for quilts is $300 to $700.

PANTRY AND HEARTH ★ By Appointment: (212) 532-0535
Here in Gail Lettick's home you will be able to browse through her wonderful collection of kitchen-related folk art. American-country painted furniture and more. Price range—$25 and way up.

Regularly, foreign retailers will come to New York to promote their business by setting up shop in a hotel suite to sell their products. Depending on the strength of the dollar against foreign currency, you can make out quite well. You can find out about them by looking in your local newspapers and **New York** magazine. If you are really intrepid, you can also check in with the concierges of the major hotels. For instance, a representative from the British department store Harrods is a regular visitor, as well as tailors from Hong Kong, children's clothing designers from Europe, and so on.

MRS. JOHN L. STRONG ★ By Appointment: (212) 838-3848

Here you will find some of the more expensive and nicest hand-engraved stationery and invitations.

TROUVAILLE FRANCAISE ★ By Appointment: (212) 737-6015

Here you will find a large collection of antique and vintage lace goods—pillow shams, linens, even baby clothes. Average price of a pillow sham is $85, other prices range from $12 to $200.

KAREN WARSHAW LTD. ★ 167 East 74th Street ★ (212) 439-7870

Karen deals mainly with nineteenth-century oil paintings, porcelain, wood boxes, furniture, and silver. She does carry a few eighteenth-century pieces. Just tell her what you are looking for and you can be sure she will eventually locate it for you. Her prices are reasonable and her turnover is frequent.

PERSONAL SHOPPERS AND WARDROBE CONSULTANTS

The Intrepid New Yorker is surprised that more people don't take advantage of personal shoppers and wardrobe consultants, professionals who make it their business to know everything about the fashion industry, clothing stores, and dressing properly.

Personal shoppers and wardrobe consultants are a gold mine for people who either don't have the time to shop, hate to shop, or need help making sense out of their wardrobe. These experts come in all shapes, sizes, and prices—you don't have to be Ivana Trump to use them. In some cases, it will actually cost you nothing to use them.

Department Store Personal Shoppers

There are a few things left in life that are free—travel agents and department store personal shoppers. If you get overwhelmed at the thought of shopping at a department store, this is the way to go for both men and women. Their jobs are to shop with you, give you guidance on styles and fashions, and help you find what you are looking for. They will also do all the shopping for you. You tell them what you are looking for and they will go from floor to floor pulling together items for you to try on. In fact, once you have established a working relationship, they should know your style and taste so well that all you have to do is call up to make a date at the store and everything will be waiting for you when you arrive.

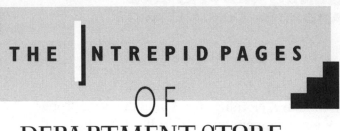

THE INTREPID PAGES
OF
DEPARTMENT STORE
PERSONAL SHOPPERS

BERGDORF GOODMAN ★ 754 Fifth Avenue (at 58th Street) ★ (212) 872-8812
★ Men's Store: (212) 339-3383
Bergdorf's personal shopping department has five people who can assist you. It's best to make an appointment about one week in advance. You should plan to spend at least one hour there.

BLOOMINGDALE'S ★ 1000 Third Avenue (at 59th Street)
Bloomingdale's has various departments of personal shoppers:
    At His Service (for Men): (212) 705-3030
    At Your Service (High-end Women's Clothing): (212) 705-3135
    Beatrice Dale (Household Merchandise): (212) 706-2378
    Corporate Gifts: (212) 705-2380
    Hope's Corner (Women's Clothing and Gifts): (212) 705-3375
Make an appointment one week in advance and plan to spend at least one hour in the store.

LORD & TAYLOR ★ 15 West 38th Street ★ (212) 391-3675
★ Men's Fashion Advisor: (212) 391-7607
Their personal shopping office is on the third floor. They are happy to consult with you on the phone. To make an appointment call one week in advance and plan to spend at least one hour in the store.

MACY'S ★ 151 West 34th Street ★ (212) 560-4181 ★ Macy's for Men: (212) 560-7460
"Macy's by Appointment" is organized slightly differently from the other stores. You call and tell them your requirements and then they have a personal shopper call you back to make arrangements with you. You are assigned to a specific consultant who will take care of your every need.

SAKS FIFTH AVENUE ★ 611 Fifth Avenue (49th and 50th Streets) ★ (212) 940-4145
★ Saks for Men: (212) 940-4056
The name of Saks's general personal shopping department is One on

---

One. They have about seventeen people able to help you and they have their own private fitting rooms located on the fifth floor. Men and women are both welcome. Call ahead for an appointment and plan to spend one hour.

Independent Personal Shoppers

These are independent shoppers you hire to get into the designer showrooms to buy clothes for you at wholesale prices. Some access more expensive lines and designers than others, but they stick primarily to the better designers. Your shopper will probably require a minimum order from you to make it worthwhile, and you will pay a fee of about 20 percent of the cost of the clothes. You still come out ahead, however, because you will be getting your clothes wholesale. There are two ways these independent shoppers work:

1. There are those who take you into the showrooms before the clothes hit the retail stores. That means, for example, that you will be buying your fall clothes in June. The advantage is that you will get first pick of the season and you get to see the whole line. The disadvantage is that you usually cannot try on the clothes. But a good shopper should be able to spot what will fit you or only have to be altered slightly. You must pay by check and you cannot return anything.

2. There are those to whom you simply give the name of the designer, size, and style of the clothes you want, and they will get them for you. The advantage to this route is that you will have already tried the clothes on in a store, and know they will fit. All you have to do is wait for delivery. The disadvantage is that this route forces you to wait until the clothing lines hit the retail stores; and that means that the designer might not have what you want in stock anymore.

Independent personal shoppers are in direct competition with the department stores and boutiques, and therefore they prefer to remain anonymous. The only way to find out about them is by word of mouth so call The Intrepid New Yorker at (212) 534-5071. Tell us what you are looking for and we will match you up with the appropriate personal shopper.

WARDROBE AND IMAGE CONSULTANTS

These are professionals who actually come into your home, look at the clothes you have in your closets, help you plan a wardrobe in keeping with your needs and your life-style, and then go out and shop for it. Some of them also have access to the showrooms in the wholesale district. They can be pricy because they are offering such full service, but are well worth it in terms of giving your look and your closets an overhaul. For a lot of people it's a very valuable one-time-only expense. By the time the consultant is done with you, you will have a wardrobe chart and a definitive style that you can follow on your own from that point on.

THE INTREPID PAGES
OF
WARDROBE AND IMAGE CONSULTANTS

CAROLYN GUSTAFSON ★ By Appointment: (212) 755-4456
Carolyn is a former model who knows how to dress and where to go to buy clothes. She is great at accommodating your needs and budget. She works on an hourly basis, which means that she does not have a vested interest in seeing you spend thousands of dollars. Her fee is $100 per hour and she is well worth it.

DOWNTOWN WITH BARBARA ★ By Appointment: (212) 807-5757
Barbara Singerman guides you through your closet and then the stores. She helps you sort out what you want to look like and what you feel comfortable in, and then takes you to her special haunts. Her hourly rate is $50.

LISA GREENBERG ★ By Appointment: (212) 288-2990
Lisa has extensive training in wardrobe planning and shopping from having been a television clothing stylist for the past ten years. She recently left the world of TV to pursue her craft among individuals. Her taste is impeccable and best of all she really knows what looks good on you and never tries to oversell you. She charges $100 per hour with a minimum of two hours.

SUCCESSFUL WAYS AND MEANS ★ By Appointment: (212) 877-1417
Susan Dresner charges a yearly membership fee of $225 and provides her clients with their own personal profile, plus body analysis, color and wardrobe analysis, yearly budget, and referrals for shopping services during the year should the client suddenly need a special pair of shoes or an evening dress. She charges $50 an hour to take you shopping.

CLOTHES MAKERS

INTREPID TIP
There are advantages to having clothes made for you. It's a good alternative to shopping because:

☛ **You are paying for a perfect fit and lastability.** You'll get a piece of clothing that is absolutely tailor made to your specifications. Nothing you will ever buy off the rack will look as good or last as long, which more than makes up for the price of the item.

☛ **You can order a piece of clothing exactly the way you want it.** For men— What kind of lapels do you want? How wide do you like them? Do you want a vest? Do you want pencil, wallet, or watch pockets added? How about cuffs for the trousers? Slit pockets or flapped? Suspender buttons? An extra pair of trousers for your suit? For women—What skirt length? What type of sleeve or collar? A flared or narrow skirt? Pleats? How many and how wide?

INTREPID APPROACH
Don't just walk into any tailor's or seamstress's shop and ask them to make you a suit; you want to look for the right one.

- You are looking for a very talented craftsman with an eye for fashion.
- Different tailors and seamstresses have different styles. One might be an expert in sportswear, another in evening wear or suits.
- You can find them through word of mouth; just make sure you get some serious recommendations before hiring them. Most fabric

stores keep a list of clothes makers and can recommend them according to your needs.
- Interview the clothes maker in person. Ask to see samples of his/her work.
- Make sure you get price ranges depending on the fabric and patterns you are interested in. Write them down.
- Find out if the clothes maker will assist you in choosing fabrics and patterns. Will that be a separate charge? And do you also have to purchase the thread, lining, interfacing, etc? There's so much to pick from, you might want them to handle these types of details.
- You might want to have your clothes maker make an inexpensive item first to see how it turns out.

THE INTREPID PAGES
OF
DRESSMAKERS AND TAILORS

DRESSMAKING CONSULTANT

ARIEL LAWRENCE ★ 526 East 5th Street ★ By Appointment ★ (212) 529-2889

Ariel is the link between you and the dressmaker/tailor. If you don't have time or are not confident about your color or design choice, Ariel is the person you need. She has impeccable taste and has a background in design. Ariel will meet with you at your home or office, discuss styles and fabric choices to fit into your life-style and needs. She then finds the appropriate dressmaker or tailor. She "holds your hand" the entire way. All compliments, complaints, and payment are made to her. For this hassle-free approach to getting your clothes made you will pay more, but it is sure worth it.

DRESSMAKERS

MRS. DELGADO ★ 50 East 81st Street ★ (212) 628-6975

Original creations and alterations are done from this comfortable town house. Don't expect to walk in off the street. Mrs. Delgado takes her work quite seriously and books way in advance. Her work is quite good and her prices moderate.

SURANG YAMNARM'S ★ 134½ East 62nd Street ★ (212) 371-4842

Surang does both creating and copying. She gets calls from all over the United States so be sure to make an appointment well in advance. She can copy a Chanel as well as judging what original creation will look good on you. Her prices are moderate.

TAILORS

DYNASTY TAILOR ★ 6 East 38th Street ★ (212) 679-1075

Although Hong Kong is far away, some of their best tailors are here. Joseph is one of them. He has an incredible understanding of fabric and style and his prices are reasonable. Don't be afraid to have him copy your favorite suit. He can also make you an original.

L.N.C. CUSTOM TAILOR COMPANY, INC. ★ 83 Baxter Street (near Centre Street) ★ (212) 406-9527

This tiny shop on a small street does fabulous custom tailoring at moderate prices. Their attention to detail, style, and timeliness is impeccable. Their fabric selection is excellent and they do their best to explain to you all your options.

MID CITY TAILOR ★ 1188 Sixth Avenue (46th and 47th Streets) ★ (212) 719-2215

The entire fashion industry seems to use these old-world tailors. Their alterations are done promptly, accurately, and inexpensively. Best of all they don't try to overalter your clothes.

CUSTOM SHIRTS

NICKY BELLANI ★ 72 Narrows Road South (Staten Island) ★ (718) 447-7653

There is nothing that fits better, wears better, or looks better than a custom-made man's shirt. Nick knows that and so do his customers. His prices are $45 per shirt (minimum order five shirts) poly and cotton; $48 per shirt (minimum order five shirts) Egyptian cotton; $65 per shirt (minimum order five shirts) Sea Island cotton; $3 per shirt for a monogram. Shirts take about four weeks to make, so order early.

THE INTREPID PAGES

OF
FABRIC STORES FOR CLOTHES

B & J FABRIC ★ 263 West 40th Street ★ (212) 354-8150
If you are looking for a specific color and fabric go to B & J first. Their prices are reasonable and the selection is good.

BANKSVILLE DESIGNER FABRICS ★ Norwalk, CT ★ (203) 846-1333
Here they buy the best of the designer leftover fabrics, all natural fiber. All fabrics are labeled by designer and content and they are about one-third less than the price in New York fabric stores.

JERRY BROWN IMPORTED FABRICS, INC. ★ 37 West 57th Street ★ (212) 753-3626
Jerry Brown carries fabrics that no one else seems to get. He has fabric that designers have used in their "past lines." It is certainly high end with a little touch of snobbiness but it is well worth it. Try to get upstairs—that is where they keep the "better fabrics."

PARON FABRICS ★ 60 West 57th Street ★ (212) 247-6451
Paron sells fabrics at reasonable prices. They buy designer fabrics from jobbers. A good selection.

40TH STREET BETWEEN SEVENTH AND EIGHTH AVENUES
There are many stores that sell silks, wool gabardine, and wool crêpe in a tremendous array of colors.

THE INTREPID PAGES
OF
TRIM STORES

GORDON BUTTON COMPANY, INC. ★ 142 West 38th Street ★ (212) 921-1684
Incredible selection.

K TRIMMING & ZIPPERS ★ 519 Broadway (Spring and Broome Streets) ★ (212) 431-8929
Trimmings as well as hundreds of buttons. You must have an idea of what you want; otherwise you will be overwhelmed.

M & J TRIMMING COMPANY ★ 1008 Sixth Avenue (52nd and 53rd Streets)
★ (212) 319-9072
Everything you need to trim your outfit—beading, shoulder pads, feathers, patches, and much, much more.

TENDER BUTTON ★ 143 East 62nd Street ★ (212) 758-7004
Non–New Yorkers would never believe that a salesperson will happily search for just the right button for you, even if you are only spending 15 cents. And you are bound to find what you need.

FLEA MARKETS AND STREET FAIRS
This is a wonderful way to go if you like rummaging and taking your chances on not finding anything that day. It's pot luck so you have to enjoy the outing itself. You can find real treasures at great prices and you can bargain to your heart's content. But don't spend a lot of money at these places unless you absolutely know what you are buying.

INTREPID TIP
There are three types who set up shop at flea markets and street fairs:

- High-end to low-end antique dealers
- Young up-and-coming designers we've been telling you about
- Mom and pop yard-sale dealers

THE INTREPID PAGES
OF
FLEA MARKETS

ANNEX ANTIQUES FAIR AND FLEA MARKET ★ Sixth Avenue between 24th and 26th Streets ★ (212) 243-5343
Saturday and Sunday, 9:00 A.M. to 5:00 P.M.
Admission—$1

BATTERY PARK CRAFTS EXHIBIT ★ State Street between Bowling Green subway and Pearl Street ★ (212) 752-8475
Thursday, 11:00 A.M. to 6:00 P.M.
(Seasonal)

BRYANT PARK CRAFTS SHOW ★ 42nd Street between Fifth and Sixth Avenues ★ (212) 752-8475
Friday, 11:00 A.M. to 6:00 P.M.

PS 44 FLEA MARKET ★ Columbus Avenue between 76th and 77th Streets ★ (212) 678-2817
Sunday, 10:00 A.M. to 6:00 P.M.
(Outside as well as inside)

196 BLEECKER STREET ★ (outside The Little Red School House at Sixth Avenue) ★ (212) 564-1670
Saturday and Sunday, 9:00 A.M. to 5:00 P.M.

PS 41 SCHOOLYARD ★ Greenwich Avenue between Sixth and Seventh Avenues ★ (212) 751-4932
Saturday, 11:00 A.M. to 7:00 P.M.

PS 183 FLEA MARKET ★ 419 East 66th Street ★ (212) 737-8888
Saturday, 6:00 A.M. to 6:00 P.M.

SOHO ANTIQUE AND COLLECTIBLES ★ 465 Broadway (at Grand Street) ★ (212) 223-4590
Sunday, 9:00 A.M. TO 5:00 P.M.

TOWER MARKET ★ Broadway between West 4th Street and Great Jones Street ★ (718) 693-8702
Saturday and Sunday, 10:00 A.M. to 7:00 P.M.

YORKVILLE FLEA MARKET ★ 351 East 74th Street ★ (212) 535-5235
Saturday, 9:00 A.M. to 4:00 P.M.
(No market June through August)

THRIFT STORES

New York City is teeming with the well to do who are just as happy as the rest of us to get a tax break by bringing their "used" inventory to thrift shops. That means everything from once-worn designer ball gowns to an antique waffle iron. So don't pass by these stores without taking a peek. You never know what mint piece of clothing, furniture, or fine linen might be lurking there.

CONSIGNMENT SHOPS

These are places where the well heeled take their once-used gowns or Chanel suits to sell because they don't want to be seen in the same outfit twice. Most consignment shops have strict guidelines and only accept high-quality used clothing in near-perfect or perfect condition. You might even find clothes that have never been worn before. Most items are sold at one third or less of the original cost. In these hard times, it's a great way to shop smart. For those of you who feel uncomfortable wearing someone else's clothes, walk into one of these shops. You could find a $3,000 Bob Mackie gown reduced to $500, a Ralph Lauren winter coat for $200, or an Armani blouse for $100. We think you'll change your mind. See the Intrepid pages, page 232, in Chapter Six for listings.

To get a list of street fairs throughout the City, write to Lawrence Heller's Directory, Box 559, Van Brundt Station, Brooklyn, NY 11215-0010. Another great source is Lea Lerman who for $8 will send you twice a year a list of the antique shows, festivals, street fairs, and flea markets happening in New York City. You can write to her at 2 Lincoln Square, New York, NY 10023, or call her at (212) 874-4472.

Auctions

The Intrepid New Yorker wants to demystify the auction industry. It is a wonderful way not only to find one-of-a-kind items and treasures, but to furnish your home without spending a fortune. Yes, depending on the demand for the item, it can cost a good deal of money to buy it at auction. But veterans who know how to work them can get incredible deals.

> A dealer at a flea market must provide consumers with serialized receipts that must contain the date, total amount of money and tax paid, itemized, and the true name and address of the seller. The dealer must keep copies of all receipts for three years.
> —Better Business Bureau

You can find amazing deals when buying "seconds" or used goods from a private owner. Look carefully in the local papers for owners selling anything from pianos to furs. The Intrepid New Yorker had one client who wanted to sell his twenty-year-old Series-B Steinway piano, which is worth $35,000 new today. He put an ad in the paper and got dozens of calls from interested buyers who were thrilled at the idea of buying this vintage piano. Our client accepted $17,000. The buyer got an amazing deal and so did the seller, because Steinway was only offering $12,000 to buy it back. Before making a big purchase we advise you to take an expert with you to appraise the goods before writing the check.

INTREPID TIP

Anyone on any budget can access an auction. But keep your expectations in perspective. You don't know if you are going to walk away with the item you want or if someone else is going to outbid you. Some auction houses are more "high end" than others, some specialize in specific types of collectibles, but all auction houses in New York City are happy to have you.

Here are some additional tips to keep in mind:

☛ **Don't be intimidated** by the auction process. Their in-house specialists are there to guide you every step of the way, educate you about the pieces you are thinking about buying, and answer all questions you have—free of charge.

☛ **Look in the local newspapers** every Friday. There you'll find out when the next auctions are and what they are featuring. Or call an auction house and ask them what exhibits are coming up.

☛ **Auction houses hold "exhibit days"** prior to the auction itself. These are so that you can actually look at and touch the pieces that are going to be sold at the auction. After close inspection, you can decide on which piece(s) you want and what you are willing to pay for them.

☛ **You can buy a catalog that features the pieces being sold.** The catalog includes a detailed description of the pieces and their estimated cost. The experts at the auction house set an estimated price range they believe the item will sell for based on what they believe the piece is worth. In reality, the item could go for much less or much more depending on how much bidding activity there is.

☛ **Ask the expert what the "resale condition" of the item is.** This is a very important question to ask—they will honestly answer what kind of condition the piece is in. It is their job to know and they expect you to ask.

☛ **Stay within your budget.** When you go to the auction and bid on the item(s) you are interested in, know beforehand what you can spend and keep your hand down if the bidding escalates out of your range.

> For more information about collecting, a must read is **Duveen,** by S. N. Behrman, who was one of the great 'dealers' of the world. It is currently out of print but you can find it at your local library. It was published by Random House in 1951.
> —Helaine Fendelman, Fendelman and Schwartz, Fine Arts Appraisals

> If you decide that $1,200 is too much for an antique dining table in good condition, and you just want the look, you can pay half that for one whose legs have been replaced. Just be aware that the ones in pristine condition are the only ones that have a chance of appreciating in value. It really depends on your motive.
> —Karen Keane, Managing Director, Skinner Auction House

> •
> Once a year The Lighthouse for the Blind holds a fund-raising sale called The Posh Sale, which is considered the Tiffany of garage sales in Manhattan. What you will find at a fraction of the normal cost are "gently used" or even new merchandise donated by the crème of society. It is open to the public, and there is no entrance fee. Call The Lighthouse at (212) 808-0077 to find out when the next one is.
> •

> Auctions used to be the exclusive terrain of wholesale dealers and wealthy individuals going bankrupt who needed a place to sell their assets. As the public became more sophisticated, the auction world opened their doors to them; it is a way for people to circumvent the more expensive contemporary and antique retail shops. All auction houses are hoping to get the "big-ticket" item to auction off; but the reality is that getting that item is often contingent on also being willing to accept a lot of "lesser pieces" that go along with it. Also, the big-ticket items don't get offered to auction houses every day, so their bread and butter has to come from sales of less prestigious ones. Most of those items sell for less than retail value.
> —Karen Keane, Managing Director, Skinner Auction House

THE INTREPID PAGES
OF
AUCTIONS

SCHOOL AUCTIONS

Some of the auctions that are the most fun and have the best buys are held at fund-raising benefits for the various private and public schools throughout the City. The PTA of each school works for close to a year getting individuals and companies to donate cars, vacations, classes, merchandise, weekends away, professional services, summer camp fees, hot-air balloon rides, art work, and whatever else they can drum up. Ask your friends if their child's school has such a benefit. You can pick up great deals and give money to a good cause all at the same time.

AUCTION HOUSES

CHRISTIE'S ★ 502 Park Avenue (at 59th Street) ★ (212) 546-1000

High-end merchandise that usually sets the tone for what is considered to be valuable. Call for information on upcoming auctions.

CHRISTIE'S EAST ★ 219 East 67th Street ★ (212) 606-0400

There are more affordable buys here. Call to see what the next auction offers.

GREENWICH AUCTION ROOM ★ 110 East 13th Street ★ (212) 533-5550

Although they rarely hold auctions, they do keep a client wish list in their computers. If there is something specific you are looking for, let them know. If and when it arrives they will give you a call.

> Fendelman and Schwartz will handle appraisals of art or antique collections at a public sale or at auction. If you are considering buying art or antiques, Fendelman and Schwartz are prepared to help you. Call (914) 725-0292.

LUBIN GALLERIES ★ 30 West 26th Street ★ (212) 924-3777

Lubin auctions entire estates and individual pieces, so you never know what you might find. Some amazing deals have been gotten at auction estate sales. Auctions are held every other Saturday.

PHILLIPS ★ 406 East 79th Street ★ (212) 570-4830
Collectibles, toy soldiers, dolls, and animation art are auctioned here.
They hold about four auctions a year in New York City.

SOTHEBY'S ★ 1334 York Avenue (at 72nd Street) ★ (212) 606-7000
Sotheby's is considered to be the most powerful and influential auction house in the world. Call for upcoming auction dates.

SOTHEBY'S ARCADE ★ 1334 York Avenue (at 72nd
Street) ★ (212) 606-7245
At the arcade you will find some less expensive and valuable collectibles as well as merchandise that wasn't exclusive enough to make it into their specialized sales.

TEPPER GALLERIES ★ 110 East 25th Street ★ (212) 677-5300
Tepper handles estates of all sizes and quality as well as individual pieces. You can find jewelry, lamps, furniture, and paintings. Prices can go high but they do start fairly low. Auctions are held every other Saturday.

> If you are unsure of the name of a particular mail-order firm or where it is located, you can call Direct Mail Marketing at (212) 689-4977. They might be able to help you. Also, if you feel inundated with mail-order mail, you can ask for their "Mail Preference Service" Department and they will get you off certain mailing lists.

WILLIAM DOYLE GALLERIES ★ 175 East 87th Street ★ (212) 427-2730
William Doyle appears to fall in the middle of the auction houses.
Their goods tend not to compete with Christie's and Sotheby's yet
they seem more discerning than Tepper and Lubin. Auctions are usually held on Wednesdays.

TAG SALE (NEXT DOOR TO WILLIAM DOYLE GALLERIES) ★ (212) 410-9285
Doyle operates a perpetual tag sale of goods from estate sales that
could not sell at auction. A fun place to browse and buy.

TRADE SHOW SHOPPING
Manhattan holds about 1,000 trade show conventions a year such as
the Gift Show, Linens Show, Accessories Show, Stationery Show, and
Toy Show, to name a few. This is where hundreds of exhibitors set up
booths to present next year's products to the trade.

INTREPID TIP
*On the final day of the show, exhibitors may be willing
to sell their individual samples to save on the cost of
shipping it home.* You will pay wholesale or perhaps less. You
can find out when trade shows are being held by calling the New

York City Visitor's Bureau at (212) 397-8222 or the Jacob Javits Convention Center at (212) 216-2000. Trade shows are only open to the trade so you must have some business credentials to get in. When you walk in you should be prepared to:

- ☐ Fill out a form for accreditation.
- ☐ Present a business card and perhaps another form of I.D. If your business relates to any kind of personal service, party planning, gift buying, etc., you should get admitted. Sometimes they ask you what you do, sometimes they don't.
- ☐ Be professional as you ask each exhibitor if they are selling any of their samples that day. If they are, they will probably only accept cash. If you want to buy a dozen or so of a particular item, ask them if they are willing to take an order. Think of it as a way to get all your birthday or Christmas gifts for the year out of the way and at great savings.

SHOPPING BY PHONE

INTREPID TIP

You can get a substantial savings if you try to buy through the sister store in another city. Many of the more exclusive boutiques have franchises in other cities, and their products are priced according to what the market will bear in a particular place. *Here are some examples:*

You can subscribe to a published guide to wholesale, retail, and discount shopping by mail called the **Shop-by-Mail Report.** It is published by the same people who put out the **S & B Report.** It comes out four times a year and they list over 250 manufacturers and stores that offer shopping by mail. By knowing the manufacturer's name, style, and product numbers, it is possible to order merchandise at 40 to 70 percent savings. You can call the **S & B Report** at (212) 679-5400.

Baccarat Crystal

If the dollar is strong in Paris, call the Paris store and get the same crystal you wanted shipped from there. You will have to pay duty and shipping but you will still save a bundle. Credit cards make this possible.

Frette Sheets

The Intrepid New Yorker wanted to buy Frette sheets. We priced them here in New York at $300. We then called their store in Los Angeles to find they were selling for $170. The price was lower because that was all the market could bear in that area of the country. If you don't like the idea of having to wait for the shipment to come in, have them overnight expressed.

THE INTREPID PAGES
OF
FUN STORES

Here are some stores we threw in because we find them irresistible.

ABRACADABRA ★ 10 Christopher Street (near Sixth Avenue and 9th Street) ★ (212) 627-5745
Here you will find the largest selection of authentic-looking costumes for adults. Santa Claus, animals, cartoon characters, Dracula, and American Indians can be purchased or rented. They also carry an extensive selection of makeup, masks, and wigs.

DOT ZERO ★ 165 Fifth Avenue (at 22nd Street) ★ (212) 533-8322
For those of you who love modern, high-tech design items, this is the store for you. The owners, Kevin Brynan and Harvey Berstein, sell an unusual mix of everything from Slinkys and dice to high-tech gifts.

EAT GIFTS ★ 1062 Madison Avenue (80th and 81st Streets) ★ (212) 861-2544
EAT represents the love/hate relationship most people have with New York. The selection of gift items that they sell is wonderful and enticing, yet the salespeople and the prices are horrendous. You will pay 25 percent more for a T-shirt here than in the store next door. But people flock to buy here. Why? Because of its obvious exclusivity and style.

ELK CANDY COMPANY, INC. ★ 240 East 86th Street ★ (212) 650-1177
The world of old New York comes alive at Elk Candy Store. Here you will find European candy makers making marzipan in adorable animal shapes. During the holidays the store comes alive with Santas, Easter bunnies, and turkeys.

EMPORIO ARMANI ★ 110 Fifth Avenue (at 16th Street) ★ (212) 727-3240
If you always wanted to meander through a top designer clothing store but felt too self-conscious, fear no longer. Emporio is Armani's less expensive line yet it has all the flair and style of the couture collection and the staff is helpful and friendly.

LA FANION ★ 299 West 4th Street ★ (212) 463-8760

This store is stocked with beautiful French country antiques, pottery, and furniture. The owner, Claude-Nöelle Toly, is from the south of France, and if you didn't hear the traffic outside the store, you'd think you were in his birthplace. On July 14 they hold a Bastille Day party.

NEW YORK BOUND BOOKSHOP ★ 50 Rockefeller Plaza (Sixth Avenue at 49th Street) ★ (212) 245-8503

This store specializes in New York: books, architecture, guides, transportation, and more. They have an eclectic selection of prints and other rare collectibles.

PAPERS ETC. ★ 510 Broome Street (West Broadway and Thompson Street) ★ (212) 431-7720

Here you will find beautiful rice and lace paper from Japan, 100 percent linen paper, marbleized paper from Europe, and more. The paper comes in both letter size and art size.

PERFORMER'S OUTLET ★ 222 East 85th Street ★ (212) 249-3088

This store was originally dedicated to selling the crafts that were made by actors and actresses to make extra money. Now the store sells crafts made by a wide variety of people. You will find a large assortment of well-priced and well-made hand-loomed rugs, candles, boxes, jewelry, picture frames, and hand-carved, wooden toys.

POLO/RALPH LAUREN ★ 867 Madison Avenue (at 72nd Street) ★ (212) 606-2100

Even if you have no intention of buying, you must stroll through this store, a renovated mansion. The staff is gracious, the layout is superb. You will think that you are walking through Ralph Lauren's country estate (with his closets and bureau doors all open). Antiques abound while you browse through the home furnishings, men's, women's, and children's departments.

THE COMPLETE STRATEGIST ★ 320 West 57th Street ★ (212) 582-1272 ★ 11 East 33rd Street ★ (212) 685-3880 ★ 630 Fifth Avenue (at 50th Street) ★ (212) 265-7449

The store specializes in military games as well as science fiction, murder mysteries, and adventures. It is a great place to browse for those who love board games.

THE ELDER CRAFTSMAN ★ 846 Lexington Avenue (64th and 65th Streets) ★ (212) 535-8030

There are two wonderful things about the Elder Craftsman. The first is that this is a not-for-profit store whose merchandise is all made by people over sixty. The second is that their goods are quite well made. You will find sweaters, hand-carved and -painted wooden figures, needlepoint pillows, hand-sewn dolls, and more. A similarly made item in a department store might sell for three times the price.

F·O·U·R

REAL ESTATE: A GAME YOU CAN WIN

There is a bit of a carnival atmosphere around trying to buy, sell, or rent a home in Manhattan. And market trends shift like sand. Some years back, New Yorkers would have killed each other for a rental; now rentals are cheaper and landlords

INTREPID PHILOSOPHY

ATTITUDE You can make a successful real estate transaction if you are fully informed and fully in control of the process.

APPROACH By having a clear understanding of the market and recognizing what options are amenable to your circumstances and financial means, you can make a smart real estate choice.

KNOWLEDGE Knowing how to read a property's true value, knowing when a broker, a real estate attorney, and other real estate experts are necessary to use, and then knowing how to choose truly qualified ones will make all the difference in the outcome of the deal.

ECONOMICS There are great opportunities in today's real estate market, but knowledge of that market has never been more critical. Whether you are renting, buying, or selling, if you take the time to learn the subtleties of the game, you can come out ahead, if not way ahead.

are going begging. In the 1980s sellers literally made fortunes from selling apartments they never thought would have been worth anything. Today, the happiest New Yorkers are the buyers. Whatever the trends, New Yorkers obsess about beating the system and getting the best deal, and that goes for all the players in it—the brokers, the buyers, the landlords, the managing agents, the sellers, the developers, and the renters. There are smart ways to play the real estate game in New York City, but as the consumer, you need to know how the game works before you make your first move.

REAL ESTATE TERMS YOU NEED TO KNOW

Rent-Stabilized Apartments

☞ Apartment buildings containing multiple dwellings that were built between February 1947 and January 1, 1974, are rent stabilized. There are about 700,000 of them in New York City.

☞ The amount of increase on rent-stabilized apartments is determined yearly by the Rent Guidelines Board. It is announced every July and put into effect every October. You can read about the increase in the newspapers, or you can call the Division of Housing and Community Renewal at (718) 739-6400.

☞ In rent-stabilized apartments, tenants must be offered either a one- or two-year lease.

☞ A rent-controlled apartment becomes rent stabilized after the statutory tenant finally vacates. If you are the first tenant in that apartment when it converts, the landlord can charge you what he thinks is fair market value. From then on, the increases are determined yearly by the Rent Guidelines Board.

Rent-Controlled Apartments

☞ Most apartments built before February 1947 in multiple dwellings come under the New York City Rent Control Law. This law was enacted to prevent rents from skyrocketing and to stop other bad practices during the housing emergency that began during WW II.

☞ A tenant who moved into a rent-controlled apartment before July 1, 1971, is protected by the rent control law. This type of tenant (also called "statutory tenant") does not need a lease.

☞ Apartments can only be passed along to and occupied by family members, so few of the approximately 150,000 rent-controlled apartments ever become available.

☞ In New York City rent control operates under the Maximum Base Rent (MBR) system. A maximum base rent is established for each apartment and is adjusted every two years to reflect changes in operating costs. Owners can raise rents by 7.5 percent each year until they reach the MBR limit.

Nonrent-Regulated Apartments

There are many "free market" apartments in New York City. Many of these rentals can be found in co-ops and condos. They are not regulated. That means the landlords or owners can raise the rent whenever they want, and they don't have to provide you with a lease.

Condominiums

☞ You are the sole owner of the apartment that you occupy, and joint owner of the common areas such as the lobby and hallways.

☞ Each unit owner is responsible for paying his or her own monthly mortgage and real estate taxes. So the monthly maintenance (common charges) is small compared to a co-op because it just applies to the upkeep of the building.

☞ If an owner defaults on his mortgage payments and common charges, the other owners are only responsible for making up the difference on the common charges.

☞ A condominium board of directors is elected to run the building but they do not have the legal clout to tell any individual unit owner to whom they can or cannot sell or rent their apartment. There is much more autonomy and much less exclusivity in a condominium. If you are an individualist, you might prefer this atmosphere to a co-op.

Co-op

☞ Apartment dwellers in a co-op "own their apartments" in that they own shares of stock in the corporation worth the value of their apartment. The corporation actually owns the building. You get a proprietary lease.

☞ Your monthly maintenance will be a lot higher than a condo's because it covers the entire building's mortgage payments and real estate taxes as part of the common charges.

☞ In a co-op, if one owner defaults on his payments, or if any units remain unsold, all the other owners could ultimately be responsible for meeting those payments.

In rent-stabilized apartments, landlords are required to attach to apartment leases the former rent paid so that the new tenant can know if his or her rent is legal. The vast majority of landlords do not do this, and overcharging is widespread. New tenants who suspect overcharging can file a challenge form with the State Division of Housing and Community Renewal district office. If you aren't even sure what category of building you are in, write to the DHCR district office, give your name, date your lease commenced, address and apartment number, and ask for the status of your apartment. They will send you a form to file. Their general information number is (212) 519-5789.

—**The Tenant Fact Book,** Open Housing Center, New York City

---

☞ A co-op is much more exclusive. You have to pass the scrutiny of a co-op board before being accepted into the building. And once you are in, they have the authority to prevent you from selling your apartment to just anybody, and they may not let you sublet at all. They can also be much more restrictive about what renovations you can make on your apartment.

☞ Many apartment dwellers prefer buying into the exclusivity and the restrictiveness of a co-op because dwellers can choose the environment (a family building or a nonfamily building, for example) they want to live in, and they know that that environment will be protected.

CHOOSING A NEIGHBORHOOD

INTREPID APPROACH

You should choose your community before you choose your apartment. New Yorkers tend to miss this major point about finding a home in Manhattan: And by community, we don't just mean address. When you buy a home outside New York City, the first thing you do is research the communities you are going to choose from—the history, the life-style, the types of people, average incomes, the schools, community activity, the community's philosophy and priorities, etc. Why would you do it any differently here? The Intrepid New Yorker recommends several ways to do the research:

Get an Overview

Walking tours It may be hard for busy New Yorkers to take this exercise seriously, but there is no better way to learn about neighborhoods in Manhattan. These tours will make you realize that each area of Manhattan has its own origin, history, and life-style. As a result, you will get a real feel for an area that you wouldn't get otherwise.

We also suggest you walk around a neighborhood you are interested in at night. See if it seems comfortable to you then. Doing this will give you an idea of how active or isolated it feels during the late hours.

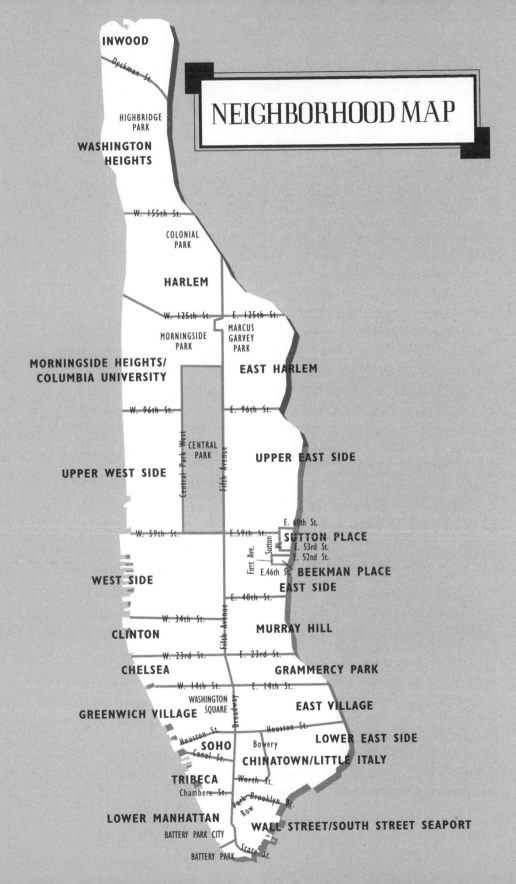

THE INTREPID PAGES
OF
NYC WALKING TOURS

THE MUSEUM OF THE CITY OF NEW YORK ★ (212) 534-1672, Ext. 206
Walking tours on most Sundays. They last about four hours. Different neighborhoods and themes. The fee is $10 for museum members, $15 for nonmembers.

92ND STREET Y WALKING TOURS ★ (212) 415-5599
To find out more about their tours, call for a copy of *The Whole Y Catalog.* Three times a week, they usually focus on a specific theme, and range from $15 to $35.

MANHATTAN NEIGHBORHOOD TROLLEY ★ (212) 677-7268
This brings people into lower Manhattan to see what these neighborhoods have to offer: Chinatown, Little Italy, Lower East Side, and the Battery Park Area. They can customize a tour for a group of people. A weekend tour is $4 and lasts about forty minutes (you can get on and off as much as you like).

•

If you are thinking of living on the Upper East Side, one organization that is a great resource for helping you decide is the Yorkville Civic Council, which brings together the leaders of the community's civic, cultural, educational, health, religious, and social service institutions to address the needs of the community. It functions as an advocate for the community's well-being. They can answer all your questions. They cover 59th to 96th Streets from Fifth Avenue to the East River and can be reached at (212) 427-5629.

•

A Publication That Might Help You
Michelin, New York City is a terrific overall guide to the City and its neighborhoods. It can be bought at any major bookstore.

Zero In on One or Two Areas.

Local Community Boards They can provide you with neighborhood directories that tell you about the local churches and synagogues, community organizations, libraries, schools, social services, recreational areas, major attractions, local newspapers, etc. Depending on the community board, some directories are more up to date and complete than others. But, if you have any questions, they will be happy to answer them. See page 87 for community board telephone numbers.

Neighborhood Associations and Local Precincts You can get an idea from these organizations how safe the neighborhood is, what the community is like, what its problems and strengths are. You can find out the names of neighborhood associations by asking the community affairs officer of the precinct (see page 306 for numbers), or the community board.

Local Community Newspapers Again, once you have narrowed your search, look through their local newspapers. They can really give you an idea of what is going on in a community.

THE INTREPID PAGES
OF
COMMUNITY NEWSPAPERS

THE DOWNTOWN EXPRESS ★ (212) 941-6888
Area covered: South of Canal to the tip of Manhattan including Battery Park City.

THE VILLAGER ★ (212) 420-1660
Area covered: All of lower Manhattan, the East Village, West Village, and SoHo.

THE CHELSEA AND CLINTON NEWS ★ (212) 989-4096
Area covered: From 14th to 59th Streets on the West Side.

THE WESTSIDER ★ (212) 989-4096
Area covered: From 59th to 125th Streets on the West Side.

UPPER WEST SIDE RESIDENT ★ (212) 679-4970
Area covered: 50th to 116th Streets west of Fifth Avenue.

UPPER EAST SIDE RESIDENT ★ (212) 679-4970
Area covered: 59th to 96th Streets east of Fifth Avenue.

MIDTOWN RESIDENT ★ (212) 679-4970
Area covered: 14th to 59th Streets east of Fifth Avenue.

OUR TOWN ★ (212) 439-7800
Area covered: East Side from 14th to 96th Streets, Fifth Avenue to the East River including Roosevelt Island and Central Park.

MANHATTAN SPIRIT ★ (212) 947-5511
Area covered: Most of Manhattan.

NEW YORK PRESS ★ (212) 941-1130
Calendar of events, day-to-day listings.

Renting in NYC

As of this writing, there are plenty of rentals available in the marketplace, and prices, which have decreased 30 percent since 1988, are stabilizing. They will most likely start coming back up if there is no new construction. The current market is a result of overdevelopment in the eighties, particularly of new condos and co-ops. Thousands of them have been placed in the rental market by owners and developers who have been unable to sell them. So, in addition to the classic "landlord" buildings, there is a whole new category of rental available that is more upscale and loaded with amenities. Many New Yorkers who aren't planning on living in one place for more than two or three years are more inclined today to rent because they can find very attractive rentals and because apartments are no longer the fantastic investment they were in the eighties. There's no such thing as making a quick "turnaround profit" today.

SECURING A RENTAL

INTREPID TIP

In today's rental market, there are many different ways to secure a rental in New York City. Take your pick of the one that suits you the best:

★ *Give a broker a 15 percent commission.* In this market, you really don't need a broker to find you an apartment. But, you should absolutely hire a broker if you don't have the time or inclination to find your own apartment. In this case they can be well worth the 15 percent commission on one year's rent that you will have to pay them. Good brokers will zero in quickly on exactly what you want, handle the negotiations for you, and help finalize the deal.

★ *Look at "no fee" apartments through a broker.* In this scenario you will ask a broker to find you a "no fee" apartment. And all you have to do is look in the paper to see that there are plenty of those. Because of the glut of rentals in New York City, managing agents are offering to pay the broker commission themselves as an enticement for you to rent their space. The catch here is that it is not always a deal. They may have already jacked up the price of the rental to factor in the

> •
>
> With a rental, even if you are shown a brokered apartment, you are not liable for the commission if you find it yourself. If you are told, however, that you have to go through a broker, but you don't want to lose the apartment, pay the commission, sign the lease, and **then** file a complaint with the Division of Licenses, New York Department of State, 270 Broadway, New York, NY 10007. Their number for more information is (212) 417-5747.
>
> •

broker's fee. Instead, it might be smarter to ask for other concessions such as a free month's rent, free use of the building's health club, etc. There is a lot of creative bargaining going on today.

★ *Look at "no fee," nonbrokered apartments you see in the paper.* You'll find many rentals in the papers that say "no fee" that aren't brokered—another way for owners and landlords to get you in the door.

★ *Negotiate your own deal with a managing agent or landlord:* In this scenario, and it can be a highly successful one, take a day and just walk into any apartment buildings that appeal to you and ask for the managing agent, superintendent, or landlord. Usually their names are posted. More likely than not they will show you what is available, and you can negotiate the best deal for yourself. Even if you are shown a brokered apartment, you are not liable for the commission.

Whichever method you choose, bring a checkbook with you! Be prepared to move fast to secure an apartment if you really want it. The smartest thing you can do is to write out a check for a deposit right then and there to take the apartment off the market. *Renters take note:* Write on your check "good faith" deposit. Legally it will help you to get your money back should you change your mind.

HIRING THE RIGHT BROKER

INTREPID TIP

Make sure you hire a broker who really earns the commission! There are thousands of brokers in the marketplace. You want to zero in on a reputable firm with an experienced broker. Once you have zeroed in on a good firm, call one of the principals or sales managers of that firm and request an experienced, knowledgeable real estate broker—never just settle on the first broker who happens to pick up your call.

The best rental agencies have a very large number of listings and brokers who are so familiar with those properties that they can match their clients up efficiently.

Good brokers will make sure you have communicated to them exactly what you are looking for and will show you only properties that are appropriate. Good brokers will also ensure legitimacy of the rental property, proper execution of the leases, mediate attending fees, and expedite the approval process.

UNDERSTANDING YOUR LEASE

INTREPID TIP

A lease is a legal binding contract that under most circumstances cannot be broken. Just make sure you read *everything* in that lease before you sign it. And pay attention to the following:

- Some leases have illegal clauses in them. These illegal clauses are not binding to you, even if you sign the lease.
- You and the landlord should *inspect everything* in the apartment together and make note of deficiencies. If some of them are not going to be fixed, make sure those are spelled out in the lease so you can't be held responsible later.
- Never sign a lease unless it contains all verbal agreements made between you and the landlord (for painting, repairs, etc.). Both the landlord and the tenant should put their initials next to any changes made in the lease itself. The lease should indicate that all repairs will be made before you move in.
- The lease should state when the rent is due, under what conditions it may be increased, and should include terms regarding lease renewal.
- Be suspicious of anything a landlord adds to a standard lease.

A landlord cannot "unreasonably withhold consent" to let you sublet your apartment in New York City. But the tenant must inform the landlord thirty days in advance by registered mail. The notice must include the sublessee's name, address, telephone number, place of business, occupation, income. You must tell the landlord where you are going, why, and for how long. You cannot sublease for more than two years in a four-year period. If, however, you have no intention of returning to the premises, and plan to renew the sublease, the landlord can regain possession by a housing court action if he can prove the apartment is no longer your primary residence. If you are the "sublessee," make sure you have a legal right to be there.
—**The Tenant Fact Book,** Open Housing Center, New York City

---

Most landlords require a new tenant to pay a security deposit of one month's rent against the possibility of the tenant's moving out without paying the last month's rent, or damaging the premises. By New York State law, this money must be deposited in an interest-bearing bank account. Further, the owner must notify the tenant, in writing, of the name and address of the bank. The interest (minus 1 percent for administrative expenses) is payable to the tenant no later than annually from the date the security deposit was originally paid. If your landlord fails to pay you, contact the consumer protection bureau of the New York State attorney general's office, (212) 341-2345.

—**The Tenant Fact Book,** Open Housing Center, New York City

SUBLETTING

INTREPID TIP
If you decide to sublet an apartment, the leaseholders cannot charge more than the rent they are currently paying unless it's furnished, and then the rent can only increase 10 percent. Make sure you get a written agreement stating all terms and listing anything you find that is already damaged. *The New York Times* and *The Village Voice* are the best sources for sublets. If a broker finds you a sublet with a lease for a year or more, she is due a commission from either you or the owner of the apartment.

SHARING

INTREPID TIP
You can find ads for roommate shares in **The New York Times** *and* **The Village Voice** *or you can call one of the roommate-finding agencies in the City listed below.* If you are the sole leaser of an apartment, you have a legal right to a roommate. Make sure that you get a written agreement with your roommate that states who has the rights to the apartment.

THE INTREPID PAGES
OF
ROOMMATE REFERRAL AGENCIES

LINDA CARROL'S ROOMMATES ★ 51 East 42nd Street ★ (212) 972-9899

Linda has been in business for twelve years placing educated, refined men and women in apartments. For $160 she conducts a half-hour interview and gives you names and numbers of people who have apartments and who are looking for a roommate. She supplies you with a list of questions to ask and then helps you and your roommate in writing up an agreement. If you simply want to register your apartment the fee is $10 and when you accept a roommate there is a $35 fee.

ROOMMATES/APARTMENT PLACEMENT SERVICES ★ (212) 288-9825

Elizabeth Greer has been in business for nineteen years and works out of her Park Avenue residence. The placement fee for finding you a roommate is $350 and she prides herself on making the perfect match. If you have an apartment and want to find a roommate there is a $150 fee once someone is placed.

ROOMMATE FINDERS ★ 250 West 57th Street ★ (212) 489-6860

This company appears to be the largest roommate referral business in the City. Since 1979 they have helped over 195,000 people find roommates. There is a $175 fee if you are looking for a roommate. If you want to list your apartment there is a $25 fee.

TENANT TROUBLESHOOTERS

There are organizations in Manhattan that are set up specifically to offer you guidance and information about renting in New York as well as help protect your rights as a tenant.

THE INTREPID PAGES

OF
ORGANIZATIONS TO HELP TENANTS

OPEN HOUSING CENTER ★ 594 Broadway, Suite 608 ★ (212) 941-6101
Whether you are an owner or a renter, this nonprofit agency assists anyone who feels in seeking housing they are meeting discrimination based on race, color, creed, national origin, sex, children, or marital status. The center provides investigators and legal assistance to help secure the right of equal access to all available housing. There is no charge for these services. They put out a valuable free booklet called *The Tenant Fact Book*, which explains the legal ins and outs of renting in New York City.

NEW YORK STATE DIVISION OF HOUSING AND COMMUNITY RENEWAL (DHCR) ★ Office locations vary according to your neighborhood ★ (212) 240-6008 ★ Rent Hotline (718) 739-6400
All rent regulation programs, including rent control, are administered by DHCR. Tenants should contact their borough office branch with complaints and questions. They also have a list of twenty-five free fact sheets on everything you need to know about renting in New York City.

The following organizations provide written information, information clinics, telephone advice, and in some cases advocacy for individuals and tenant organizations needing help with landlord-related problems:

GOOD OLD LOWER EAST SIDE (GOLES) ★ 525 East 6th Street ★ (212) 533-2541

LENOX HILL NEIGHBORHOOD ★ 331 East 70th Street ★ (212) 744-5022 ★ 11:00 A.M. to 5:00 P.M.

METROPOLITAN COUNCIL ON HOUSING ★ 198 Broadway, Room 905 ★ (212) 693-0550
Calls taken on Monday, Wednesday, and Friday from 1:30 P.M. to 6:00 P.M.

NEW YORK STATE TENANT AND NEIGHBORHOOD COALITION ★ 198 Broadway, Room 1000 ★ (212) 964-1274

OPERATION OPEN CITY ★ 165 West 133rd Street ★ (212) 281-8700

WEST SIDE TENANTS UNION ★ 200 West 72nd Street, Room 55 ★ (212) 595-1274

How THE BUSINESS OF BUYING AND SELLING WORKS

Almost all real estate agencies in the country are supported by a multiple-listing service, which means that every agency and every broker has the same shared list of all available homes in their area. The only city we know of that doesn't is New York. It seems archaic that brokerage agencies in such a huge city with so many thousands of homes on the market would not share their listings. The inherent flaw in omitting this step is that it is very hard to find out all that is available if you are a buyer, and it is very hard to get your apartment exposed to the most potential buyers if you are a seller. Here is how the system in New York City works:

AN EXCLUSIVE
You the seller can give the exclusive right to one real estate agency to try to sell your apartment, and to collect the full 6 percent commission if they do. For the right to obtain an exclusive from you, this agency, in theory, will pull out all the stops to market and promote your apartment, take photographs of it to place in real estate magazines, field calls from prospective buyers, zero in on the serious ones, give you regular, updated reports, and show your apartment, until it gets sold.

The hitch to this scenario is that it usually means they will "hide" the listing from other brokers, at least for a while. In most cases brokers will tell a seller that they will try to sell it through their own agency for x amount of weeks and then, if they haven't found a buyer, share the listing with other agencies and split the commission if one of those other agencies finds a buyer (see "Cobrokerage," below). Well, this is contrary to what the seller needs, which is total exposure and *immediate*, total exposure. Your apartment will go "stale" in the marketplace if it sits for weeks with one firm.

Another hitch that is important to note is that brokers aren't willing to take an exclusive on apartments below a certain price. In fact, in this market, many brokers aren't going to work very hard to sell a studio or one bedroom. You may have to offer to pay them a higher commission to make it worth their while.

OPEN LISTING

You the seller can give your apartment's listing to as many brokers as you want. The point to an open listing is that you are trying to expose your apartment to as many brokers and real estate agencies as possible. You pay a 6 percent commission to the broker who sells your apartment.

The hitch for the seller is that your apartment won't get the special handling and promotion that it would if you went in on an "exclusive" arrangement with a real estate agency, and you have to do a lot of the work that would automatically be done by an exclusive broker. You're the one who has to get the listing out to dozens of agencies, function as the coordinator of all the brokers and the showings, and keep up with what each broker is really doing to try to sell the apartment.

COBROKERAGE

This term is relatively new to the real estate process in New York, but became a necessity when the market went soft and brokers weren't making commissions. In this scenario, as we stated above, a broker with whom you have an exclusive decides to share their "exclusive" listing with other agencies, because at least they will get a 3 percent commission (as opposed to no commission) if another agency actually finds the buyer. This is where the concept of an "exclusive" gets tricky. You the seller get the benefit of dealing with only one broker, who handles all the details and coordinating for you, while the broker shares the listing with other brokers, thus giving your apartment maximum exposure.

INTREPID TIP
The seller should accept an exclusive with an agency only under the condition that they will cobroker immediately and with many of the other 200-plus agencies in the city.

❢ INTREPID APPROACH
You can greatly affect the outcome of your purchase or sale by doing your homework. There is a huge financial and emotional stake in buying or selling a home. And so much can go so wrong if you don't have the right players by your side. Before proceeding, make sure you have the following:

☛ **An Accountant:** Find one who is truly qualified to tell you what your financial limits are as a buyer, or how to manage a potential profit or loss if you are a seller.

☞ **A real estate attorney:** This is no time to just settle on a "friend of a friend." Too many buyers and sellers get into serious trouble because they hire an attorney who is not an expert in real estate. Inexperienced lawyers can blow the deal or deliver a deal that is nowhere near as beneficial to you as it should be.

☞ **A broker:** Good brokers have experience, know the marketplace, can match buyers and sellers quickly, and know how to finesse the closing of a deal. Inexperienced brokers can cost you time, loss of potential home profit, and missed opportunities.

☞ **A basic knowledge of the real estate game: Know the market and the process of buying or selling real estate.** Do as much of your own homework as possible by directing as many questions as you need to the experts you have chosen to be your players. See also The Intrepid Pages of Information Sources for Apartment Buyers, page 177, for our pick of resources that will help you make smart choices about real estate.

THE INTREPID PAGES
OF
FOUR DIFFERENT KINDS
OF REAL ESTATE COMPANIES

The following is a sample worth considering. There are many excellent firms in New York City. Just make sure to do your homework before settling on one.

BROKER/MANAGING AGENT APPROACH

SULZBERGER-ROLFE ★ 654 Madison Avenue ★ (212) 705-4725

This is a traditional brokerage firm that deals in the selling of condos and co-ops. They are also a building management company. This can be a plus if you live in one of their buildings and want to sell. They will know quite a lot about your building and are familiar with the board and its requirements. Sulzberger-Rolfe will cobroker immediately with an exclusive.

SEPARATE BUYER AND SELLER DIVISIONS

S. W. BIRD ★ 331 Madison Avenue ★ (212) 351-2400

Susan Bird has an innovative approach to the market. She divides her company into two divisions: buyer brokers and seller brokers. This way you are ensuring that a broker works solely for your best interest. Your broker will be able to negotiate the best deal for you because they do not have any conflict of interest. Depending on the cost of your apartment you will still be working with a 6 percent commission basis. With an exclusive, S. W. Bird will cobroker immediately.

COMPUTERIZED SCREENING APPROACH

SMILE, developed by S. W. Bird ★ (212) 351-2400

SMILE is basically a computerized way to preview apartments and homes that you want to see in the City, the rest of the country, and even the world. You make an appointment with a broker who will invite you to her office to spend an hour or so viewing apartments that meet your specifications on a computer. You will be able to see high-quality images of the apartment, an actual floor plan, as well as any other particulars that relate to each apartment. This is a wonderful time saver and a good way to know if you will want to work with your broker. And for those who are selling, it is a great opportunity to have people all over be able to view your apartment without setting foot in your home.

TRADITIONAL BUT TOP-NOTCH BROKER

THE CORCORAN GROUP ★ 645 Madison Avenue ★ (212) 355-3550

Barbara Corcoran of The Corcoran Group runs a first-class, aggressive brokerage firm. She keeps a handle on the market by constantly keeping up with the latest sale and trends. Her brokers, who both buy and sell apartments, have regular sales meetings and are kept abreast of all issues relating to the co-op and condo markets. This means that you as the buyer or seller will have a smart, well-informed person working for you and that is important when you are dealing with such a major transaction. The Corcoran Group will cobroker immediately with an exclusive.

ONLY DEAL WITH RENTALS

THE FEATHERED NEST ★ 310 Madison Avenue ★ (212) 867-8500

Nancy Packes created this very successful company that only deals with the rental market. Because she has decided to specialize, you as a potential renter will receive 100 percent of the company's attention when looking for an apartment. They were one of the first real estate companies to computerize, therefore giving themselves a leg up on the market and creating an efficient way to match clients with apartments. Whether you are looking for a sublease or a long term rental they will be able to provide you with a broker who specializes in your needs.

Buying in NYC

It is a great time to buy a home in New York City. Prices are much lower, which makes down payments more reachable. On top of that, mortgage rates are lower than they have been in years. And of course, a significant portion of ownership costs are tax deductible. So today it will often cost you less to buy than to rent. However, the experts will tell you that you should not be looking at your purchase as a fast profit-generating investment, but as a long-term home that will hopefully build equity over a period of time. In this uncertain market, you don't know what you will be able to sell your home for when the time comes. If, however, you are planning on living in a particular space for only two or three years, think twice—no, three times—about buying. You might find that with combined brokers' and lawyers' fees, accountant costs and closing costs (not to mention the hassle) that you will incur both when you buy and when you sell, even under the tax shelter of ownership, it might cost you less to rent.

INTREPID TIP
Whether you are buying or selling, there are good brokers and less than good brokers in just about every agency. Brokers are not rigorously trained, so don't ever choose a broker on the luck of the draw.

- *Word of mouth.* Ask people specifically *why* they were satisfied with a particular broker, not just *if* they were. That will tell you a lot about the broker's skill.
- *Call several reputable agencies.* First, as we have advised previously, ask to speak to a "principal" or sales manager of the firm. Second, brokers have specialties in different types and sizes of properties and know specific neighborhoods, so find one with the appropriate background. And third, insist on working with one of their more experienced and consistently successful brokers. They will put you in the right hands because they want to make a deal too.

INTREPID TIP
What good brokers do for the buyer:

- ◆ They are willing to share commissions with other brokers and will therefore show you a wider range of apartments listed with other agencies as well.
- ◆ They are skilled problem solvers, negotiators, and good facilitators able to handle buyer, seller, co-op boards, and lawyers with equal grace.
- ◆ They see a lot of the apartments before showing them to you so they don't waste your time.

- ◆ They know a lot about the type of apartment you are looking for and the neighborhood you are interested in.
- ◆ They really know the market.
- ◆ They can review a financial statement.
- ◆ They are good resource people and have real estate attorneys, mortgage brokers, etc. in their Rolodex. Good brokers want to know these people because they help close deals.

❗INTREPID APPROACH

Pay attention to our "buyer beware" checklist, below. As a potential buyer, if you do not carefully check into a building's status and stability, you can end up with a lemon of an apartment on your hands that not only hurts you financially but that might be unsellable when the time comes. Make sure you and your real estate attorney look into the following carefully:

☐ *Building's financial health:* Examine the building's "financial statements," which tell you what the building's assets and liabilities are, what money has been spent on what, and how large a fund is in reserve for repairs. Even if your building looks beautiful, it could be heading toward bankruptcy. Without a large reserve fund, any repairs or significant payments that need to be made will have to come out of your pocket.

☐ *Unresolved problems with the building:* In addition to looking at the financial statements, you should ask to see the minutes of the board meetings to determine what problems are outstanding or likely to occur. Boards are not legally obligated to give out the minutes, but you should always ask.

☐ *Monthly maintenance:* Determine as best you can what the scale of monthly maintenance will be one to ten years in the future. Be

> " The two biggest mistakes a buyer makes is to make an offensively low bid that alienates the seller and labels himself a wise guy, and falling prey to the classic "buyer's remorse." Many buyers, just before closing a deal, have thoughts of pulling out because they all of a sudden feel they are missing something better out there. We recommend that, instead, they take some time with their broker to take one more look at other apartments to compare. More often than not, they close on the deal.
> —Barbara Corcoran, The Corcoran Group, Real Estate Firm "

> " A common mistake that many buyers make is not looking into fifteen- to twenty-year mortgages. The monthly payments are not that much higher than on a thirty-year mortgage, yet you will save thousands in interest payments. Just have your accountant do the calculation for you. You'll be amazed.
> —Robert Goldstein, Real Estate Attorney, Berger & Kramer "

skeptical if the current fees seem low. If you compare monthly maintenance fees from year to year, you can get a good idea of what the trends have been.

☐ *Possible maintenance increases resulting from:*

1. Refinancing of the building's mortgage. The sponsor of the building might have started out with a low interest rate mortgage of 8 percent and then decided to acquire a wraparound mortgage for the building. All of a sudden the interest rate has jumped to 12 percent.

2. Leasehold renewal. Some co-ops do not own the ground they sit on. It is leased to them. If that lease comes due, chances are the renewed lease will be higher.

3. A sponsor who owns more than 50 percent of the units. During the conversion explosion in the eighties, many tenants elected not to buy their apartments but continued renting. This left the sponsors still owning those units. Many of those tenants pay rent that falls short of the monthly maintenance requirements so the sponsor has to make up the difference. If he still owns 50 percent or more of those units, and the tenants are paying less than is needed, it is wise to stay away from that building.

☐ *A sponsor-controlled board:* A sponsor controls the board if he has owned 50 percent of the units for five years or more. This sponsor may have a landlord mentality. He doesn't want to pay for the extra laborers, fix the boiler, etc., that the rest of the tenants want. So it automatically becomes an antagonistic relationship.

☐ *Co-op board rules and restrictions:* Co-op boards are notoriously strict. If you want to do construction on the apartment you are thinking about buying, make sure the co-op board will approve it. If you think it will be necessary to sublet down the road, again, make sure the board will let you. Many don't. If the restrictions are too severe, you might want to consider a condo instead.

☐ *The building's condition:* What does it look like? Is it well-maintained? Is the boiler room door covered in grease? Are the halls well lit and clean? Are the floors shined in the lobby? Does the elevator work well? You can tell a lot by eyeballing the building yourself. Then, have an engineer go through the building and your apartment carefully. That engineer will file an official report.

> Talk to the current owners in the building you are thinking of buying an apartment in. Get their perspective on problems there are with the building.

THE INTREPID PAGES
OF
INFORMATION SOURCES
FOR APARTMENT BUYERS

Before buying, arm yourself with as much knowledge as possible.
Here are some places to start.

THE NEW YORK COOPERATOR NEWSPAPER ★ 23 Leonard Street ★ (212) 697-1318
An information source for co-op or condo owners. *The Cooperator* is really in the business of publishing its monthly paper, but because they are experts in the field of co-ops, they are happy to try and answer any questions you might have about the co-op in which you live or in which you are thinking of buying. They also hold seminars to help teach and guide co-op boards and their members on how to run an efficient building.

HABITAX ★ 18 Branchbrook Road, White Plains, NY 10605 ★ (914) 997-0669
Habitax is a company that tells you if you can afford the apartment you want to buy. It has designed OWNET, a system capable of producing an in-depth analysis of your financials on the apartment you want to buy. You must provide John Tyrrell with the anticipated or actual purchase price, estimated amount of down payment, percent of maintenance deductible, interest rate you expect to pay on the loan, number of years of the loan, and your estimated tax bracket. The initial report is available for $25; any additional ones cost $10.

H S H ASSOCIATES ★ (800) UPDATES or (201) 838-3330
H S H compiles mortgage rates and terms nationwide on a weekly basis. For a fee of $20 you can receive the home buyers mortgage kit, which is a printout of current rates and terms in your area and a booklet on how the mortgage process actually works. If you already know the process, you can just buy the printouts.

SKYSCRAPER ★ 555 Fifth Avenue ★ (212) 490-1800
Neil Bader is a mortgage broker with whom you want to speak. This company obtains mortgages for home buyers at no extra cost to the

buyer. Rather than shopping around by yourself for the best deal, let Skyscraper do it for you.

SULZBERGER-ROLFE ★ 654 Madison Avenue ★ (212) 705-4725

If you are looking to buy a condo or a co-op you should attend their home buyers seminars. Here you can learn in four hours what usually takes about four weeks. The discussions include an overview of condo versus co-op ownership, tax benefits associated with your primary residence, red flags in buildings' financial statements, bank lending practices, and a discussion of popular prices and trends as well as legal considerations.

THE BOWERY MORTGAGE COMPANY ★ 110 East 42nd Street ★ (212) 953-8310

The Bowery offers approximated pre-approved mortgages at no extra cost. It's helpful to be sure of what you can spend before you go shopping for an apartment.

THE CORCORAN GROUP ★ 645 Madison Avenue ★ (212) 355-3550

They publish *The Corcoran Report*, which comes out twice a year and is a comprehensive study of the co-op and condo market trends in Manhattan. You can receive it by calling and putting your name on their mailing list.

SELLING IN NYC

These are hard times for a lot of sellers in New York City. Sellers are lucky to even get the price they bought their apartment for and many haven't been able to sell at all. The market has come back a little bit but not enough to ease the tensions of those would-be sellers who bought at the peak of the market in the eighties. When the market first softened, potential sellers just wouldn't believe the facts and insisted on putting their apartments on the market at overinflated prices. Today sellers are more realistic about the conditions in which they are trying to sell. And they may be dropping their asking prices, but they will also most likely be paying quite a bit less for their next home.

INTREPID TIP
Make no mistake. As the seller, you are the broker's client. Even though your broker will have spent 90 percent of their time with the buyer, you are the one paying them the commission. And in America, the guy who pays is boss.

INTREPID TIP
There are ways to sell your apartment in a soft market:

☛ **Fix it up.** The following is a list supplied to us by the real estate agency, The Corcoran Group, about the most important ways to enhance the appearance and value of your apartment:

- Scrub everything until it sparkles.
- Wash all the windows.
- Remove and repair any signs of water damage, mildew, and other deterioration. Repair holes and cracks in ceilings.
- Repaint with a "commercial double coat" of flat white on walls, eggshell white on ceilings.
- Repair existing wallpaper.
- Repair or restore floor surfaces.
- Regrout wall tiles.
- Clean floor-tile grout with a mild muriatic-acid solution.
- Restore or repair bathroom fixtures.
- Add new shower curtain, rod, and hooks.
- Repair kitchen cabinets, and make sure doors and drawers work.
- Increase existing lighting. Replace old ceiling fixtures.
- Eliminate odors.
- "Expand" bathroom size with visual ploys. Install a mirror opposite medicine chest.
- "Expand" closet size with visual ploys, such as thinning out clothes.
- "Expand" size of other rooms, with mirrors at ends of hallways, in corners, adjacent to windows.
- Replace broken window panes and mirrors.

☛ **Price to sell.** Get estimates from at least three brokers. If your brokers are experienced, they should be able to give you an educated appraisal on the first visit. A price is determined by "comparables"—

what equivalent apartments are going for within a ten-block radius. Be aware of the broker who tells you what you want to hear and basically lets you dictate the price. Also, a good broker will not let you take an inferior bid just to sell the apartment.

☛ **Get the best exposure.** The seller wants the broadest exposure in the shortest period of time. Make sure you hire a reputable real estate firm that is willing to take you as an exclusive but will cobroker with most other firms in New York City immediately—as soon as they get the listing.

> Unless the broker has a process that's tested for reaching more than at least one hundred firms, the firm is not serious about cobrokerage. And there should be a measurable program for frequent contact with other brokers. Each firm should be contacted about your property on a weekly basis. Only a firm whose agents work cooperatively to expose their own and each other's properties to buyers' brokers can do this for you.
> —Susan Bird, President, S. W. Bird, Inc.

> If you are open listing your apartment, try to get your broker(s) to agree to a written commitment stating that the broker will get a full commission if your apartment gets sold for the asking price, but that if it sells under that, he/she will agree to a smaller commission.
> —Robert Goldstein, Real Estate Attorney, Berger & Kramer

☛ **Choose the right broker in an exclusive.**

☛ They should tell you exactly how they plan to sell your property with a serious marketing strategy.

☛ They should cobroker immediately and tell you how many firms with which they will cobroker.

☛ They should have a clear strategy for how they will communicate with the other brokers about your property and continue dialogue with them.

☛ They should keep you informed by giving you detailed progress reports.

☛ **Give your broker all the facts.** *Never* hide any obvious problems that exist in the building or the apartment. They will come up sooner or later, and if it's later, the buyer might pull out of the deal. The following is a list of questions from S. W. Bird, Inc., one of the top real estate firms in the City, the answers to which you must communicate to a broker so he/she can work effectively for you.

☞ When did you acquire the property?
☞ In whose name is the title held?
☞ Is it a co-op or condo?
☞ Is there a flip tax, and how is it calculated?
☞ What is the maintenance? When was the last increase?

☞ What percentage of the maintenance is tax deductible?

☞ What is your board's current view regarding the percentage of financing they will allow a prospective applicant to undertake?

☞ Has there been a recent assessment of tenant shareholders? For what amount? For what purpose?

☞ Are you aware of any significant proposals under review by your board?

☞ Why are you selling?

☞ At what price have other apartments in your line sold for?

☞ When do you have to move out?

☞ What are the most convenient times to show your property?

☞ What are your expectations for how long it should take to sell?

☞ What are your board's procedures for reviewing an application?

☞ Is there a written or unwritten net worth requirement for prospective buyers?

☞ What types of applicants does the board like? Frown upon?

☞ How long has your property already been on the market? What has happened so far? In what ways are you expecting this broker to handle it differently?

☞ Are there special amenities that will enhance the property's values?

☞ What kind of services are provided by the building?

☞ I low does the board feel about pets, musical instruments, celebrities, etc?

☞ What rules will the new owner have to obey regarding home renovation?

☞ Do you want to sell furnishings? Are there any fixtures you plan to take?

☞ Will you spend money to give the apartment a fresh coat of paint? Do repair work?

There is a one-year-old company called the Real Estate Marketing Network, Inc., which has come up with an interesting idea for helping people get maximum exposure for their hard-to-sell apartments. For a flat fee ranging from $150 to $300 depending on the size of your home, they will market your apartment on a nonexclusive basis. After they have gathered detailed information, they pass it on to the listing departments of over 130 real estate firms in New York City, who in turn will contact you if they have a qualified buyer. If the information needs updating, they will forward that along too. The listing stays active with all these agencies until your apartment is sold. The incentive for the brokers is the full 6 percent commission they would receive. Call them at (212) 734-0199

TIPS FOR SELLING A SMALL APARTMENT

Many sellers who own studios and one bedrooms in this market can't find brokers willing to work on selling the apartment. The commission on a small sale isn't worth it to them. In this scenario, you can try to open list it, but it's a lot of work for you the seller, and you still may not get brokers to show it. It's next to impossible to get an exclusive with immediate cobrokerage, because most firms won't agree to work that hard for an apartment under $300,000.

INTREPID TIP

There are two main ways to sell your apartment, even if brokers are turning up their noses at it:

1. *Get an exclusive by offering to pay the firm a higher commission.* They might be willing to take it for a 10 percent commission, let's say. If they do, you want to make sure you know what they are planning to do with the extra 4 percent. They should be offering part of that to other real estate firms so that, once again, you are getting maximum exposure.

2. *Sell it yourself without a broker.* You may feel that it isn't worth it to you to fork over a 10 percent commission on an apartment that you won't be able to sell for very much anyway. If you are willing to do the work, you can save a bundle by finding creative ways of selling it yourself. Consider the following recommendations:

Place Your Own Ad

You can get a lot of mileage out of placing your own ad in the paper. The key is to make the ad so appealing that buyers have to see it.

- It is worth it to spend the money to make your ad big enough so that your eye is drawn to it on the page. Give the ad a big headline and extra lines.
- A catchy headline really attracts attention. Like: "Room with a View" or "Country in the City" gives a potential buyer a real feel for a place.
- Look at other ads in the paper. Notice the ones that appeal to you and figure out what it is about the writing and descriptions you like.
- Be specific and colorful in your writing. Instead of saying "lots of light," say floor/ceiling windows. "Old-fashioned country kitchen" sounds much more appealing than just eat-in kitchen. List the major selling points such as fireplace, eat-in kitchen, etc.
- Clarify what your apartment really contains —two bedrooms, one bath, dining alcove, etc.—so that you don't attract buyers who are inappropriate.
- If your home stays on the market for some time, change your ad. Buyers will otherwise start to wonder why you can't sell it. And you can focus on different selling points that might attract different buyers.

> There are two big mistakes sellers make. One is overpricing their apartment and then not bringing it down fast enough. The other is not going with a real estate firm that guarantees maximum exposure.
> —Barbara Corcoran, The Corcoran Group, Real Estate Firm

Target Your Buyer

Think logically about who your type of buyers are most likely to be and go after them aggressively. Yes, you have already placed your *New York Times* ad, but where else should you advertise? If you have a studio apartment, your most likely buyer is a young professional just starting out.

- Advertise on the bulletin boards of local hospitals. You might attract an intern or a nurse.
- Advertise in your alma mater's bulletin or in the bulletins of any other affiliations you might have.
- Advertise at graduate schools. Consider anyone about to graduate from law school, business school, or medical school. They are about to enter high-income jobs.
- Advertise in your community newspaper. You may find someone who wants to stay in the area.

Moving in NYC

Here is our tried-and-true checklist to follow in order to make moving as painless as possible.

☐ Always get at least three estimates and make sure the movers come to your residence.

☐ Always ask if they will put a cap on the estimate (a dollar figure that the estimate cannot exceed once the job is finished).

☐ Always take pictures of your belongings before the move; that way you will be able to prove if any damage has been done.

☐ Figure out who will be packing what; your moving company should be able to pack and unpack for you.

☐ Boxes, wrapping material, and tape should be dropped off by the company (of course, you need to pay).

☐ Confirm your move in advance.

☐ Offer the movers something to eat and drink. Your show of kindness will keep your movers motivated.

☐ There is always one mover who has been appointed as the leader. Take all your concerns to him.

☐ Don't forget to notify your building in advance that a move is going to take place.

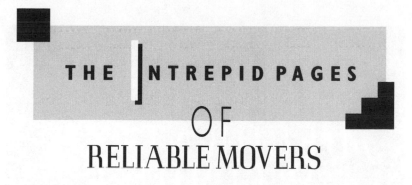

THE INTREPID PAGES
OF
RELIABLE MOVERS

Here are companies that The Intrepid New Yorker relies on for moving.

GENERAL MOVERS

CAREFUL MOVERS ★ (212) 584-3542
Contact Jim or Fred.

MANBER TRUCKING ★ (718) 937-4648
Contact Larry Berman.

SHLEPPERS ★ (212) 472-3820
Contact Moishe Kazaz.

FINE ART MOVERS

DUKE'S MOVING AND EXPRESS ★ (212) 289-0695

JOHN HUGHES MOVING AND EXPRESS ★ (718) 786-7340

PIANO MOVERS

FRED HINES PIANO MOVER ★ (718) 291-2644

BUN-RITE MOVERS ★ (212) 823-7533

F·I·V·E
RENOVATING AND DECORATING WITHOUT DESPAIR

What to Consider Before Renovating

When You Own

INTREPID TIP

Before undertaking a renovation, consider what it will mean to you financially in the future. The National Association of Realtors maintains that, as a rule, the amount you spend on remodeling added to the current market value of your home shouldn't exceed the value of the highest-valued homes in your neighborhood by more than 20 percent. You don't want it to be overpriced for your neighborhood. The only time this philosophy would not apply is if you are planning on living in your home for a lifetime and want to make improvements for your own satisfaction.

When You Are Selling

INTREPID TIP

There are improvements you can make to enhance the value of your home before selling. An interior face-lift can make a world of difference; paint or wallpaper the walls, refinish the floors, polish the wood. The kitchens and bathrooms should be in excellent shape—they are a major selling point. Make sure the interior and exterior look attractive enough for you to want to buy it. The American Institute of Real Estate Appraisers has found that wallpapering, painting, and carpeting are generally the best investments you can make to increase the resale value of your home.

When You Are Buying

INTREPID TIP
Make sure that before you buy an apartment that needs substantial renovation you thoroughly research what the renovation is going to cost. You may discover it will cost

---

NTREPID PHILOSOPHY

ATTITUDE You are much more capable of directing a home renovation than you think. The Intrepid New Yorker has watched client after client hire people for renovations that they could have done themselves and saved a bundle. We are not suggesting you shouldn't hire home improvement specialists; on the contrary—there are times when it is critical to do so. The trick is to know when. It's time to become home improvement activists so that you can make informed and successful choices. It starts with understanding the renovation process.

APPROACH Don't get intimidated by the idea of home renovating because you don't understand it. You can learn. Let's demystify the process, put it in layman's terms, and turn it into a comprehensible and manageable operation.

KNOWLEDGE Knowledge is the key to a successful renovation. Home improvement can be a massive undertaking and, for most people, one of the biggest expenditures of their lives. The Department of Consumer Affairs receives over 1,500 complaints from consumers every year on home improvement work. Most problems can be avoided, however, if you learn how to hire the right people and take the time to become knowledgeable about the renovation you are considering. The more knowledgeable you are, the easier the task becomes. And costly and time-consuming mistakes will be avoided.

ECONOMICS Even Alan Greenspan might get flummoxed by all the hidden costs in home renovating. If you don't learn what labor and materials cost and if you don't comparison shop, you can get taken to the cleaners and never know you've been there.

---

a disproportionate amount compared to the overall value of the apartment and therefore isn't worth it. It is well worth a small fee to have an architect, contractor, and/or decorator give you a ballpark estimate on the cost of the renovation you are considering.

When You Rent

INTREPID TIP
Even if you are in a rental it may be worth remodeling if you plan on being there for a long time. It's purely for your own satisfaction so it's your choice to make. At times, landlords are receptive to sharing some of the costs of the improvement because it adds to the future rental value of the apartment. Such improvements as painting are mandatory for your landlord; others, such as retiling a cracked bathroom floor, might be negotiable. For more information, talk to a tenants advocacy group (see page 168) before discussing renovations with your landlord.

Who's who in home improvement

☞ **Architect:** An architect has a degree from an architectural school and has to be licensed. He or she has the most knowledge regarding spacial relationships and a building's various systems, such as plumbing and electrical. An architect has the knowledge to design and construct a new building or space from scratch and knows precisely which types of laborers and materials to use for a particular job. He or she will oversee the contractor and other laborers. If you are going to be moving walls or fixtures, you need an architect to officially approve a plan that can get passed through New York's Buildings Department.

> Take "before" pictures of your home prior to a renovation for tax purposes. Also, keep all records and receipts of any home improvements you make. The cost can be added to the purchase price of your home to arrive at your "basis." The basis is subtracted from the selling price to determine your capital gain. Also, when doing capital improvement work, much of it will be exempt from sales tax so be sure your contractor supplies you with a capital improvement sales tax exemption form.

☞ **Interior Designer:** An interior designer is not licensed, although he or she has graduated from an interior design school. In addition to being able to create a look for your home, an interior designer can provide guidance on room layouts, drawings and specifications, and construction that has nothing to do with the building's systems.

☞ **Decorator:** A decorator is not licensed and does not need to have formal school training to be called a decorator. He or she gives your home a new cosmetic look by purchasing all furniture, rugs, fabrics, fixtures, etc. for you.

☞ **Contractor:** A contractor must be licensed. He or she is the implementer of all the plans put together by you and/or your architect or interior designer. A contractor will oversee the day-to-day task of buying construction materials, hiring the laborers, and getting the actual renovation and installation accomplished.

THREE DIFFERENT RENOVATION APPROACHES

We will walk you through three different economic approaches, using a kitchen renovation as one of the most typical examples so you can make an informed choice about which method is right for you no matter what area of your home you are improving.

In this scenario, a ten-by-ten-foot kitchen is being gutted, but all the cabinets and appliances will be installed in their original positions so there is no extra cost for moving gas and water lines. Also, no major electrical upgrades are required.

OPTION #1—THE $12,000 SOLUTION

❢ INTREPID APPROACH:
You act as contractor and decorator, the most difficult and time-consuming route. This option is only for those who like challenges and have the least money to spend. (No architect is involved because the kitchen is not in need of total restructuring.)

Pros:

★ Least expensive route because you aren't hiring a contractor and decorator.
★ Most self-satisfying in terms of putting your own skills to work.

Cons:

★ Most time-consuming.
★ Greatest potential for error because you are relying on yourself as the expert. Two of the hardest and most important parts of a renovation are: (1) coordinating of the trades, and (2) having enough authority over your subcontractors to get them to complete the job on schedule.

★ If anything goes wrong, you are responsible. The Intrepid New Yorker can be of help here. In our Intrepid Pages of Home Renovating Sources and Services, page 206, we have listed the names of quality laborers we know from our experience you can rely on and trust.

Requirements:

★ You put the rest of your life on hold and consider the renovation a full-time job.
★ You are the expert, so a great deal of homework has to be done.
★ You have to trust your own vision and taste.
★ You have to have self-confidence and a sense of adventure.

The Preparation

★ When planning a renovation, be aware that it might have to pass your building's codes and regulations as well as New York City's codes and regulations. Filing your plans with the city can take considerable time. We recommend hiring a professional expediter.
★ Determine what budget you have to live with. This one factor will set the guidelines for the project. Be realistic about your bottom line and stick with it.
★ Look at what's available in design by studying books and magazines on kitchen renovations and designs. Also, on the last pages of almost all the design magazines there is a long list of how-to booklets available for a small fee that you can send away for on everything from do-it-yourself decorating tips to how to hire a contractor.

★ Visit kitchen showrooms. This is the time to ask your questions and determine what materials you are going to use based on your budget. You will choose between ready-made and custom materials.

★ Put together a "checklist" of all the changes you want to make by using the Intrepid New Yorker kitchen checklist (page 244). Take proper measurements of your kitchen spaces.

★ *Have comprehensive plans!* This may be the most important piece of advice we give you. Having a plan from the start will prevent huge cost escalations due to day-to-day changes in the project. We recommend that you spend some extra money to hire an architect or interior designer on a consulting basis to draw up a plan for you. This may save thousands in the end.

> It is critical to learn what options you have in terms of materials and how much they fluctuate in price. A Formica countertop could cost you $600, a granite one, $3,000. Even faucets can vary by hundreds of dollars. It is also critical to understand that the slightest alteration can cost you hundreds—even thousands—of dollars more. One of our clients decided she wanted to round out the edges on the square granite countertop she had purchased, and that raised the cost 20 percent.

The Process

1. *Before hiring any laborer:* Get two or three references on him and call those references to find out whether they thought he was reliable and qualified for the job. If you are hiring a laborer for a big job, go and actually see the work he's done.

   Get at least three estimates. Most people have no concept about what labor should cost, so you have to get enough estimates to make an educated decision. You can get badly ripped off if you don't. And a very low estimate may not mean a good deal. You could be dealing with a dishonest laborer who is planning to use inferior materials. Make sure the laborers you hire carry the proper insurance for their work.

   You can find your plumber, electrician, and carpenter through word of mouth. Your building employees may have suggestions. You could call plumbing parts stores, lighting stores, and lumberyards and ask the owner or manager for recommendations. Yes, you can check the yellow pages; just make sure you get those references.

2. *Hire your plumber and electrician.* Then have them inspect your existing plumbing and electricity to see if it can accommodate the new fixtures and appliances you have in mind. If electrical alterations have to be made, it is always a good idea to add more electrical sockets.

3. *Hire a top-notch carpenter.* Make sure he is experienced in kitchen renovations. He is the one you are going to be leaning on all the way through the project. Go see some work he has done and make sure you like it!

   Have him do all the final and precise measuring of all your spaces. Discuss and agree on all the design possibilities. He will draw up a floor plan.

   Make final decisions with your carpenter on your cabinets, counters, and appliances. He should go with you to pick them out.

4. *Now pick out your appliances:* refrigerator, stove, microwave, dishwasher sink, faucets, and whatever else you may be replacing.

The best design bookstore in New York is Morton—The Interior Design Bookshop, 989 Third Avenue, between 58th and 59th Streets. The best place to buy design magazines is the newsstand in the D & D Building, 979 Third Avenue, between 58th and 59th Streets.

In apartment buildings, make sure before you proceed with the costly venture of redoing the plumbing and electricity in your kitchen that your building isn't already planning an overhaul of these systems in every apartment.

Make sure you order all your appliances and cabinets as soon as possible. We have had many a frustrated client who has paid installers to put them in only to find that they hadn't arrived by the installation date.

---

5. *Hire a demolition expert.* You will need to hire a demolition expert to re-move your old cabinets, for example. If you live in a large, well-staffed build-ing, maybe some of the workers will do the work for a little extra cash.

6. *Now the major work can proceed.* Your carpenter installs your cabinets and countertops. It's also the time to have your plumber and electrician install your appliances, and finally, your lighting fixtures.

7. *Install your floor.* You can go and pick out beautiful ceramic tiles but if you are trying to stay on budget, you can find some interesting designs in linoleum or vinyl. Either the floor experts that you buy from or your carpenter will install it.

8. *You are ready to paint or wallpaper.* If you don't have to do serious repairs to your walls and you want to save money, paint them yourself. If you do need to have your walls repaired, do *not* hire a cheap painter who will only do a patch job. You will pay dearly later when your walls start to crumble. You want a semi- or high-gloss washable paint. If you want wallpaper and are game enough to hang it yourself, go ahead!

•

Remember that ready-made mate-rials never fit as precisely as cus-tom work. Make sure the ones you have chosen are going to fit your space. Otherwise, you will be pay-ing your carpenter overtime so that he can cut them down to size.

•

•

As you hire each laborer, check what kind of insurance coverage he carries. Make sure it covers him for working in New York City. Many buildings in New York de-mand construction and alteration laborers to carry at least one mil-lion dollars in liability and work-men's compensation, which covers you, the building, and the manag-ing agent. However, it is often up to you to decide whether to hire laborers with or without insurance. Our guideline is that the riskier the job, the more you want to consider requiring it from the workers. Laborers that carry insur-ance can cost more, however.

•

OPTION # 2—THE $15,000-PLUS SOLUTION

INTREPID APPROACH
You hire a contractor; you only act as decorator. This middle route is for people who have more money to spend, and don't want the nightmare of doing it all themselves. We cannot put a ball-park ceiling on the cost be-cause it totally depends on whether or not you choose to use more expensive materials and/or go custom. In this scenario you will hire the contractor to carry out the day-to-day project. You don't have any extra money to spend on a decorator, so you're it.

Pros:

● You are no longer totally responsible for the renovation.

● Your contractor acts as foreman and is re-sponsible for getting all aspects of the job done, from hiring the laborers to getting and installing all the materials.

- You have a lot more free time.

Cons:

You are spending considerably more money than in Option 1.

Requirements:

✔ You have to make sure you hire exactly the right contractor. Hiring the wrong contractor will be an even worse nightmare than doing it all yourself.

✔ You have to rely on your own aesthetic taste.

INTREPID TIP
There are ways to start out on the right foot with your contractor.

- The more you know about what you want and what your options are, the more seriously your contractor will take you and the more he will be on his toes. He won't take the easy route with someone who is informed.

- The cost of contractors can vary by thousands of dollars. You should get three estimates before deciding on one. Be aware that a contractor is going to size you up as a client too. If he thinks you are going to be particularly difficult to work with—that you are going to be finicky, indecisive, and neurotic—he will factor that into the price of the job.

- For more tips on hiring a contractor, see page 196.

The Storefront Contractor Option
You can hire one of many storefront kitchen contracting companies (see the Intrepid Pages of Home Renovating Sources and Services, page 206). They will charge you a fee of about $300 to come to your home, look at your kitchen space, and do a floor plan design for you. If you like what they have done, that $300 is put toward the rest of the work and you do not need to hire an architect. You are not obligated to continue further with that kitchen contractor. In fact, you can take your floor plan and shop around for the best price.

A storefront contractor will do all the measuring, and have cabinets, countertops, and floors installed. Most of these stores have stock, ready-made items as well as more expensive materials to choose from. They also will do custom work. If you were to buy ten

Be aware that when choosing paints, a paint chip will read lighter than when that same paint is applied to a larger surface. So find a paint chip that looks lighter than what you actually want on your walls or ceiling.

" When buying a lighting fixture, make sure the light bulb is readily available and you know what it will cost. Light bulbs for certain types of lamps are not only expensive but hard to find.
—Karen Wenderoff, Lighting Designer Consultant "

custom cabinets versus ten ready-made, the difference in cost would be about $2,000. Remember that custom is made better and fits better.

Often you can buy your appliances through their showrooms. However, storefront operations deal directly with the consumer so they strictly sell retail. You may save some money by purchasing your appliances from an appliance store on your own to avoid the middle-man markup.

These kitchen "stores" will hire the carpenters, plumbers, electricians, painters, demolition experts, and oversee the day-to-day work. They subcontract their work out, which means they hire free-lance carpenters, electricians, and so on to do the work. These free-lancers have other commitments as well and you may have a little less control over their work routine.

If you have any reservations about your own judgment as decorator, the kitchen planners at these storefront operations will be very helpful in coordinating your look and having fresh ideas. But you should expect to be responsible for deciding what lighting fixtures, handles, wallpaper, and so on you want to use.

> It is critical in a place like New York City for laborers to have organizational and interpersonal skills. New Yorkers should make sure the laborers they hire have these strengths.
> —John Zebreski, Point Way Group, Contracting

•

Catch a mistake before it gets too big. Inspect the renovation work at the end of every day before the workers go home. Make sure you get the beeper numbers of all the laborers; they are not easy to track down without them.

•

Independent Contractor Option

These contractors work for themselves. They don't have storefronts, probably just an office and a telephone number. As long as you are sure you have hired a qualified, reliable contractor who has expertise in renovating kitchens, this is a fine way to go. In this scenario, make sure you have an architect draw up that all-important plan for you.

The independent contractor will provide the same expertise as the storefront contractor, and will show you pictures of all the kinds of designs you could have. He can get you ready-made or he will have your cabinets and countertops custom made. He will either subcontract the work out or he will have his own shop and staff laborers. The advantage to hiring a contractor who subcontracts the work out is that he can choose the best person for the job. The advantage to hiring a contractor who has his own staff laborers is that he will have more control over the time period in which the work will get done. The work could cost slightly less because staff laborers are generally less expensive than free-lancers employed by your contractor. Your choice.

Your independent contractor will have samples of everything from floor tiles to knobs for the cabinets to show you. He will not have every color and style, however, so it is up to you as the decorator to know what is really available on the market from which to choose.

OPTION # 3—THE "MONEY'S NO OBJECT" OPTION

❗ INTREPID APPROACH
You hire a contractor and decorator, maybe even an architect if you want to restructure your space. You have absolutely no inclination or time to get involved and you have plenty of money to spend. You are doing major alterations. You are requesting expertise and more original and creative designs—and you pay for it.

Pros:

☆ Your decorator will hire the contractor and oversee his job in addition to being responsible for the "look."

☆ Your contractor will hire all the other laborers and oversee the nuts and bolts aspect of the job.

☆ Every appliance, countertop, tile, and hinge will be found and brought to you for your choice.

☆ If you have to hire an architect, she will collaborate with your decorator regarding what to do with the space, get your approval, and then tell the contractor what to do.

> " It is wise not to live in your home during a major construction. Contractors factor that in and add it to the cost of the job.
> —Page Goolrick, Architect "

> " New York is extremely difficult for a laborer to work in because of the constant parking tickets, building hours limitations, high insurance premiums, long walks through buildings and up stairs with equipment, elevator size restrictions, and attitude problems from building employees. All these factors add to the price of the work.
> —Peter Rondash, carpenter "

> • Be aware that in the field of home improvement, there is a phrase called "padding the bill." These are markups that architects, decorators, contractors, and others may charge the client that are considered completely legitimate. They are charging you more for their time and the cost of materials in case they encounter any unforeseen problems such as overtime and materials that cost more than expected. You should ask them to break down the estimate for you. It is not inappropriate for you, the client, to ask if there is any money left over at the end of the project. •

Cons:

★ You have to pay the decorator, so add 20 percent to the cost.
★ If you hire an architect, add another 20 percent to the cost.

Requirements:

☆ Make absolutely certain that the people you hire are completely qualified, trustworthy, and reliable.
☆ Make absolutely certain that they share your taste, style, and vision.
☆ Make absolutely certain that you can get along together—you are going to be spending months of critical time under the same roof.

How TO MAKE THE RIGHT HIRE THE FIRST TIME

HIRING A CONTRACTOR

No matter how simple the job, only deal with a licensed contractor. They have to be licensed by the New York City Department of Consumer Affairs. You can call the DCA to make sure at (212) 487-4444. You can also call the Better Business Bureau to make sure no complaints have been filed against them. If complaints have been filed the BBB can tell you if they were justified, and whether or not they have since cleaned up their act.

> You will get what you pay for. One mistake that many people make is that their expectations are higher than their pocketbooks are deep. That is one major reason why relationships between the client and the laborer often turn sour. You can avoid this if you understand what you can get for the money you are spending. You cannot turn a Honda into a Rolls-Royce.

Make sure you get five or six referrals on several different contractors, and then *go and see their work.* Get estimates from two or three of them. This is the most important hire you are going to make. Don't overlook this step.

The law states that upon request, a contractor must furnish you with a written estimate of the work to be done. A low price might not necessarily mean a bargain. In fact, a big difference in price between estimates should alert you that something is wrong. One builder may be planning to use lower-grade materials or may have misunderstood what you wanted. Or he may have cut corners to entice you to hire him. Many contractors don't charge for an estimate.

INTREPID APPROACH
Ask a contractor these sixteen questions before hiring him:

1. How long have you been in business?
2. Is this the original company or did you buy the name?
3. Do you subcontract out all your crews or do you have your own staff laborers?
4. Do you have your own cabinet shop or do you contract that out too?
5. Do you carry insurance—Workman's Compensation and Liability? (Most buildings require insurance certificates to be filed prior to the work commencing.)
6. Will you allow me to buy my own appliances? (Sometimes you can buy your own appliances less expensively because your contractor might charge a markup if he buys them for you.)
7. Are the cabinets stock or custom made?
8. May I see some of your work?
9. May I have five or six references with whom I can talk?
10. Are there any liens against you? (You can also call the Better Business Bureau.)
11. Do you specialize in the type of renovation I am planning?
12. Can you really commit to my time frame for completing the job? (Make sure you find out from their references how reliable they are for finishing a job on time.)
13. Who is actually overseeing the job and how often will they be on site? (You don't want them farming it out to subordinates.)
14. How long will it take to get an estimate? (It shouldn't take more than a week or so.)
15. What is the payment schedule? What is the turnkey price? (Price of *entire* job.)
16. How will you charge for extras and changes? Will the fee include a penalty charge?

> "In a small town, a contractor will not survive if he does inadequate work. New York City, however, is such a big place that unqualified contractors can hide out in it and continue to get work from unsuspecting clients. It is critical to not only get five or six referrals before settling on a contractor, but to go and actually see their work. If you still aren't sure, you can call the Point Way Group, which will, on a consulting basis of fifty dollars an hour, look over your bids and determine whether they seem legitimate and reasonable. You can find us at (212) 517-5725.
> —Brooke Loening, Point Way Group, Contracting"

> "A proof of payment clause will protect you in the event the contractor fails to pay his subcontractors or suppliers. With this clause, you can withhold payment until proof of payment is submitted to you. Without this clause, the subcontractors and suppliers could put a lien on your home for the amount due them.
> —Department of Consumer Affairs"

> If your project is very big, involving hundreds of thousands of dollars, you will need a construction supervisor with a great deal of experience who can monitor and schedule all the subcontractors' work, keep you apprised on a daily basis of any potential hidden costs and problems, and handle all the bookkeeping.

> Think twice about hiring a contractor who is late with an estimate, who can't answer all your questions to your satisfaction, and who is hard to reach on the phone.

What the Contract Should Say

The contract should contain all agreements between you and the contractor relating to the work to be done. Any verbal agreements separate from the estimate should be included. By law, the contract must also include all advertised or verbal offers made by the contractor and all guarantees and warranties provided by the contractor. The contract must also contain items defining his responsibilities with regard to building permits, insurance, time in which he will complete the job, etc.

A complete description of the work to be done should be included. Be clear about the location of doors, windows, plumbing, and electrical outlets; the brand names and model numbers of appliances and materials to be used; and anything else required to complete the job. The written estimate should include these items in detail. Have all blueprints, photos, plans, or sketches made part of the contract.

Spell out the terms of payment that should be matched to the progress of the work. In many cases, payment of one-third of the total contract price is sufficient as a first payment. The next payment of one-third can be made while the work is in progress, and the final third upon completion of the work to your satisfaction.

HIRING A DECORATOR/INTERIOR DESIGNER

INTREPID APPROACH
Consider the following six points before hiring a decorator:

1. Hiring a decorator is a very personal choice based on mutual vision and taste. If you don't like her portfolio, don't hire her!
2. If you decide to go with a large, well-established firm, make sure that the person you choose to be your decorator is in fact the one who is going to show up at your home every day. You can get lost between the cracks in a big place if you don't make it clear what you expect in terms of time and commitment to the job. The advantage of a big firm is that they are capable

of handling more than one type of design and their resources are vast.

3. If you decide to go with a small, boutique agency make sure you like the decorator's portfolio. Because the firm is only made up of one or two people, your design choices might be limited to one or two decorators' particular style. The advantage of a small firm is that you will receive total, hands-on personal service.

4. Be sure you understand what percent commission the decorator will be charging you for the material he buys for you. On the low end, some decorators will only charge you 15 percent on top of the wholesale price. On the high end you might get charged 30 percent on top of the retail price.

5. You have to set the tone for the business relationship you want: that you expect them to finish the job within a certain time frame; that you expect them to be completely available to you for the duration of the project ... Make sure everything you agree to is in writing.

6. The best way to find a good decorator or designer is through word of mouth, through people who have had good experience with them. You can also call one of several referral services that operate in New York (page 206).

HIRING AN ARCHITECT:

INTREPID APPROACH
Before hiring an architect, follow these three steps:

1. Look at their work. Make sure you like it.
2. Talk to their clients and find out how their relationship worked out in terms of accessibility, finishing the work on time, and amicability.

If you have a small job and little money to spend, we recommend you look in the classified section of **New York** magazine under designers and decorators or call the New York School of Interior Design or Parsons School of Design and get their recommendations for a graduate student or teacher. (**New York** magazine's classified section also includes a listing of all types of home improvement laborers.)

You can also find a decorator or designer suitable to your tastes by attending the many designer showcases that are held throughout the City annually. These events allow the designers to show off their talents by designing "rooms" that the public can view. You can find out when these events are happening by looking in your local papers, **New York** magazine, or by calling up the American Society of Interior Designers at (212) 685-3480.

For help in finding an architect, call the American Institute of Architects at (212) 838-9670.

---

3. Architects can vary greatly in price. Get several estimates. When the housing market is soft, you often can get the very best "ungettable" architects to work on your apartment for a lot less. So, never shy away from at least asking.

┃NTREPID DO-IT-YOURSELF DECORATING TIPS

As we stated earlier, there are times it pays to hire experts in home improvement and times when you can do just fine on your own.

A Minor Kitchen Face-lift—Two New Cabinets

☛ **With the decorator:** You call a decorator. The decorator calls her carpenter. The carpenter takes measurements and drawings of the cabinets, counters, and so on to the wood shop and the shop makes them. The wood shop charges the carpenter $400 for the pieces. The carpenter includes his markup and charges the decorator $500. The decorator includes her markup, a 20 percent commission, and you could owe as much as $720 for the work. Sometimes the decorator might deal directly with the wood shop and bypass the carpenter. Sometimes she might get a break from the wood shop that you wouldn't get if you went yourself. Regardless, the decorator route will cost you a lot more.

☛ **Without the decorator:** Take your own measurements, and decide on the materials you want to use. Find a qualified wood shop yourself by asking friends, lumber shops, and others. Get several references on their work, then go to them directly to have them made. Your cost: $400. The only down side we can think of to this route is that it's your neck and pocketbook if the work isn't satisfactory. But if you have done your homework, you shouldn't have a problem.

Upholstering

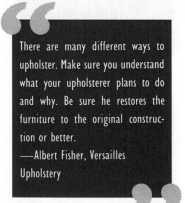

There are many different ways to upholster. Make sure you understand what your upholsterer plans to do and why. Be sure he restores the furniture to the original construction or better.
—Albert Fisher, Versailles Upholstery

When re-covering a few pieces of furniture or making curtains, pillows, and duvet covers, if you hire a very good upholsterer you might not need a decorator. You can rely on her to guide you through the process. In fact, some of the better upholsterers probably know more about the practicality and workability of a particular fabric than a decorator. Also, your upholsterer can get you into the designer showrooms without a decorator. They call ahead and tell them they have a client (you) coming down to buy fabric.

Buying Fabric at Fabric Stores

Up until recently, consumers couldn't find interesting selections of fabric unless they went through a decorator to get access to the design showrooms. Now there are retail fabric stores such as Pierre Deux, Laura Ashley, Ralph Lauren, and many department stores that have a wide variety of fabrics available. And in these more upscale fabric stores, you will find service people who are capable of helping you plan a room.

There are even less expensive retail fabric stores such as Silk Surplus, IKEA, and the ones clustered on and around Grand Street on the Lower East Side.

Some of the exclusive mills that once sold only to designers are now more concerned about the volume of their sales and are willing to sell much less expensive, nonexclusive, unlabeled fabrics in bulk to huge discount fabric stores such as the Rag Shop in Secaucus, New Jersey. So, if labels and exclusivity aren't that important to you, you can get great fabrics for much less.

For the Intrepid picks of good decorating-fabric stores, see page 223.

Buying Fabric at the D & D Building

The Decorator and Design Building at 979 Third Avenue between 58th and 59th Streets sells fabric wholesale to the trade. That's about 30 percent off the retail price. If you want to try to access it yourself, it will be up to the discretion of the individual showroom whether to let you in. Some will at least let you browse. Some might even let you buy the fabric too, especially when the design market is soft. It's worth a try. These design showrooms do not post prices. If they agree to sell to you at all, make sure you ask them if they are selling to you at the wholesale or retail price.

> There is a reason why you can go to two different fabric showrooms and see almost the same fabric for wildly different prices. Fabric companies contract with mills to have fabrics made and depending on where the fabric is made, the quality of the fabric (colors and materials), the detail of the design, and the exclusivity of the label, the price can vary tremendously. Be advised that the durability of a fabric is not necessarily dependent on the price, but on how much wear and tear the fabric is going to get, how well it is upholstered, and how well you maintain it.

> Many times your upholsterer will have excess designer fabric that might work for you. Ask her!

If your upholsterer is the one who sends you, he might charge you 15 percent for getting you in, but you still save 15 percent, so it's worth it.

Buying Furniture

Furniture is very expensive, and there is no wholesale furniture district per se that is accessible to the public. There are so many styles and types of furniture to choose from that if you don't know what you are looking for, you have to do some homework. Do you want antiques? From what period? Do you want contemporary? From which country? Do you want designer or architectural pieces? What about art deco? How about today's mass-marketed items?

INTREPID APPROACH
Before buying furniture, consider the following:

1. *Try to avoid paying retail prices.* Furniture is so expensive that we recommend that unless you are in a tremendous hurry, wait until the furniture you want goes on sale. It almost always does. Call your favorite furniture stores and ask them when their sales are coming up.

2. *Consult Corky Pollan's book: Shopping Manhattan* (Penguin, 1989). She has devoted sixty-four pages to every type, style, and price of furniture available in New York City and where to buy it.

3. *Consider buying at auction.* Many auction houses specialize in furniture sales. For many it is the preferred way to furnish their homes at discount prices. Yes, it is hit or miss but the deals on one-of-a-kind, beautifully made pieces or just plain good, functional furniture can be outstanding. Even if a piece has to be reupholstered, it still might be an excellent deal. There are exhibit days prior to any auction to look at and actually touch the goods and the experts in charge of the auction will tell you exactly what condition the furniture is in. See Chapter Three, Street-Smart Shopping, for in-depth information about auctions. See also page 150 for the Intrepid Pages of Auctions.

4. *Don't count out mass-market furniture.* Mass-produced furniture comes in many forms and styles, and frankly we're impressed. We have seen furniture mass marketing at its best right here in New York City, so consult our Intrepid Pages of Home Renovating/Redecorating Stores, page 216, and go see for yourself.

> Furniture designers that sell to the trade only hold their own samples sales once a year. We suggest you call your favorite designer and ask when their sale is coming up or subscribe to the **S & B Report.** You will be paying wholesale prices or less. Just be aware that this is leftover inventory so you will have fewer pieces to choose from, and make sure you check the furniture for any possible flaws.

TIPS FOR DECORATING ON A SHOESTRING

☞ Rearranging your furniture doesn't cost anything and if you have no money to spend, it can really change how you feel about a room. You can buy a floor-plan kit or a simple template at an art supply store to help you visualize different arrangements. If you don't think you have a good eye, invite a friend over who does.

☞ Declutter your space. Do you really need everything you have? Every mantel, bookcase, and corner doesn't have to be a shrine. We believe that less is much more. Try it. It will really open up your living spaces. (See Chapter Six for decluttering tips.)

☞ In the bedroom, just changing your duvet cover and pillows can transform the whole look of the room. Your bedspread is the major item in the bedroom that draws one's eye.

☞ For the living room try slipcovering your couch. It might run you $450 but just that and adding pillows can completely alter the look in this room. You don't want to spend the money to upholster your couch if you have small children—it will just get ruined.

☞ If you have wood floors and don't want to cover them but want a new look, change the wood stain or bleach them.

☞ If you want to alter your wall-to-wall carpeting, either get an entirely different color, or a beautiful throw rug to put over it. That one small piece (like an oriental) will change the overall look of the room. If you have nice wood floors underneath, you might decide to get rid of the wall-to-wall carpeting completely and have throw rugs, or no rugs at all. No rugs on nice wood floors can look great and open up a room, making it look much larger.

☞ For a change in the kitchen, put in new countertops. Install new handles on the cabinets. Put down a different floor—tiles if you can afford it or choose from different styles of vinyl and linoleum. You can also "reface" your cabinets; take off the doors and the sides and have new ones put on. There are shops that specialize in refacing. It is a great way to give your kitchen a bright face-lift without spending a lot of money.

☞ On the walls, just putting a wallpaper border around a room can make a big difference. If you haven't washed your wallpaper in a long time, you can't believe the difference a little cleanser and water can make.

☞ For the windows, just buying an attractive rod and draping beautiful fabric over it can make a big change. Also, wash your windows! Dirty windows can make an entire room look drab.

☛ For a new look in the bathroom, you can get your porcelain bathtub, tiles, and sink resprayed in any color. You can change the faucets. You can add a vanity to the sink or take it away. You can add or take away shower doors. A new shower curtain, bath rug, and towels can change a bathroom.

☛ Painting can turn a drab room to a sparkling room, but never make the mistake of hiring a painter because he's cheap. An improperly done job can create thousands in damage later on. Get a painter who knows what he is doing who can spot trouble areas and can determine if sanding, scraping, spackling, and the like are necessary first. If you live in a rental, ask the landlord if he is willing to give you an allowance toward the paint job.

☛ The feel of a room can be altered dramatically by changing how it is lit. Track lighting, spot lighting, low lighting can soften, warm up, cool down, or highlight areas of a room.

THE KITCHEN RENOVATION CHECKLIST

☐ Are the pipes in good working order? Sometimes a landlord is planning a plumbing renovation for the whole building, so before you start spending money on yours, check with him.

☐ Do you have enough power (circuit breakers) to accommodate your new appliances?

☐ Do you know exactly where you want the electrical outlets placed in your new kitchen?

☐ Where do you want your new lighting fixtures?

☐ What kinds of hinges do you want to use in your cabinets? We recommend the kind that allow the door to fully open (European hinges).

☐ What handles do you want on the cabinets?

☐ Do you want your cabinets to extend all the way up to the ceiling? You may want them to if you're short on storage space. Some people don't like ceiling-height cabinets because it means they have to use a footstool to get items down from the top shelves.

☐ How deep do your cabinets have to be to accommodate your dishes? Some dishes such as large platters may require deeper cabinets than others.

☐ How many silverware drawers will you be needing?

☐ Are you thinking about putting in pullout shelves? Know that you will lose width—one inch on either side.

☐ Do you want to put in a utility closet?

☐ What color and materials do you want your cabinets to be?

- [ ] Do you want your countertops to be Formica, wood, Corian, or granite?
- [ ] Is your sink big enough? Do you want a water filter? Do you want instant hot water? Do you want a spray nozzle? Do you want your sink to be stainless steel or porcelain?
- [ ] Is your dishwasher next to your sink? It should be.
- [ ] Do you want your oven to be gas or electric? How big? One or two ovens? How many burners? Do you want it to be vented out the window? If you have kids you may want to avoid island burners.
- [ ] What side do you want your refrigerator door to open on? Leave some empty space above your refrigerator so that it can "breathe." Also, it is not electrically efficient to place your refrigerator next to your stove.
- [ ] Do you want a microwave?
- [ ] Do you want a washer and dryer?
- [ ] Do you want ceramic tile floors, vinyl, or linoleum? Ceramic tile is very nice but is expensive and can be hard on your feet.

THE INTREPID PAGES
OF
HOME RENOVATING SOURCES AND SERVICES

$ = inexpensive $$ = moderate $$$ = expensive

ARCHITECTS, INTERIOR DESIGNERS, AND DECORATORS
The following should be called during regular office hours.

ASID: AMERICAN SOCIETY OF INTERIOR DESIGNERS ★ (212) 685-3480
They are the credential-granting agency to which many degreed architects and designers belong. You specify your needs, taste, and budget on an application form. They will then recommend three choices. Most of these designers will not accept a job under $15,000. There is a $10 handling fee.

DON CLAY ★ Space Room Planner ★ (212) 228-9533
Don has many credits to his name, and having taught at Parsons for six years is one of them. He firmly believes that space planning is the backbone of any renovation work. He has the capability to tackle any aspect of your project from conception through to completion. He charges an initial $200 to visit the site. If you proceed with the job, that fee is deducted from the bill.

FASHION INSTITUTE OF TECHNOLOGY ★ (212) 760-7654
The free-lance bureau handles all inquiries for advanced students or graduates. Call April Kinser; she will recommend students who have graduated within the last five years. No fee.

PAGE GOOLRICK, ARCHITECT ★ (212) 794-4700
Page, a talented, young architect, has her own company and usually does not accept jobs under $100,000. She charges an hourly fee, which is typically not to exceed 20 percent of the cost of construction. However, she is available for hourly consultations at $100 per hour.

PETER MOORE, INTERIOR DESIGNER ★ (212) 861-5544

A talented, Columbia School of Architecture graduate, Peter prefers to handle the entire job from architecture plans to furnishings. He usually charges 15 percent of the cost of construction. Minimum job: $25,000. He is also available for hourly consultation at $65 per hour.

DESIGNER PREVIEWS ★ (212) 777-2966

Karen Fisher matches the right architect or designer to the client. She shows you slides of their work. Most of her designers won't do a job for under $10,000. Her fee is $100.

NEW YORK SCHOOL OF INTERIOR DESIGN ★ (212) 753-5365

Speak to Sheila Chapline in the placement office. Over the phone she is more than happy to recommend professors and graduates who might be right for your job. There is no fee for this service.

PARSONS SCHOOL OF DESIGN ★ (212) 229-8937

Speak to the placement office. Students and graduates put up notices when they are looking for work. The office might be able to match you up. No fee.

CARPENTERS AND MORE

There are all different types of carpenters. We have discovered some who truly are craftsmen and artisans.

PETER RONDASH ★ (516) 997-5326 ★ $-$$ ★ No Insurance

Peter is a more-than-capable carpenter who holds down a regular job but is always looking for side work (he'll work evenings). He knows his own limitations and will tell you what he honestly cannot do. He is great for small jobs.

ALAN LAX STUDIO INC. ★ (718) 389-6097 ★ $$ ★ Insured

Alan can handle all types of woodwork jobs. He has expertise in lacquer, custom cabinet work, and more. His shop is located in Brooklyn. Estimates are free and his emphasis is on quality craftsmanship.

CARPISTRY ★ (212) 595-0028 ★ $$-$$$ ★ Insured

Robert Bennish is a designer and craftsman. He prefers to design his own pieces that suit your needs, but he is more than capable of following other people's plans. He has designed and built art deco bedroom sets, entertainment units, and more.

JOHN FOWLER ★ (212) 686-2277 ★ $$-$$$ ★ Insured

John has been working in New York City for twenty years and is known both as a contractor and interior renovation expert. Talented

---

as a carpenter and designer, he's an overall craftsperson. He has worked on everything from rooftop decks to kitchens to bathrooms.

RESTORATIONS BY PETER SCHICHTEL ★ (201) 605-8818 ★ $$$ ★ Insured
Although the bread-and-butter business at RPS is the restoration and preservation of all types of antiques, they are woodworkers at heart, and jump at any excuse to pursue their craft.

CARPET INSTALLATION AND REPAIRS
KEVIN BISHOP ★ (718) 935-1672 ★ $ ★ Not Insured
A free-lance carpet installer and repairer who will work evenings. A pleasant man who knows how to use the tools of his trade. Cash only.

HUDSON CARPET ★ (212) 548-1400 ★ $$–$$$ ★ Insured
They mostly do carpet installation and repairs for the trade. Their prices might be slightly higher but you are paying for superb and timely workmanship.

DEMOLITION AND CARTING
Finding good people who will do demolition and/or carting away of debris is tough in this city.

PIERRE COBB ★ (212) 491-6970 ★ $ ★ Not Insured
Pierre is one of a kind. He can tackle any job that requires muscle, from helping you move your furniture around to breaking down cement walls. And best of all, he carts anything and everything away. He even works evenings. His only fault may be his timeliness; leave yourself some leeway when you make an appointment.

DECORATING DEPARTMENTS IN MAJOR STORES
Big department stores often have in-store decorating services. It is a wonderful way for them to guarantee they will sell some of their furniture. Customers beware: This is only a good way to go if you like their furniture!

BLOOMINGDALE'S ★ 1000 Third Avenue (at 59th Street) ★ (212) 705-2590
They have a staff of interior designers who all have had at least four years of work experience. This is full service—they supply painters, wallpaper hangers, plumbers, etc. The fee is based on a sliding scale depending on how many rooms are being renovated. For one or two rooms the minimum you must spend is $7,500 (half of which must be spent at Bloomingdale's). First you make an appointment in the store with a designer at no fee. If you choose to continue, the designer comes to your home and creates a floor plan. There is a $650 fee for

that. If you go ahead with the job a $500 refund of the floor-plan fee is applied to your final bill.

MACY'S ★ 151 West 34th Street ★ (212) 560-4154

They do not get involved with construction. They are more of a decorating service whose primary interests are finding you the right furniture, carpeting, upholstery, and fabrics. There is a $250 fee for drawing plans, which is reimbursed after you spend $1,500 at Macy's.

ELECTRICAL AND LIGHTING PEOPLE

This is one area in which you don't want to take any chances with hiring low-end noninsured workers.

SPIELER AND RICCA ★ (718) 392-4100 ★ $$–$$$ ★ Insured

Ask for Frank or Ronnie. This is one of the best companies in the City. Reliable and professional.

STANLEY RUTH COMPANY ★ (212) 993-4000 ★ $$ ★ Insured

Experts in recommending and installing all types of air-conditioning and heating units.

KAREN WENDEROFF ★ (718) 788-1629 ★ $–$$ ★ Not Insured

Karen is a lighting consultant for any apartment in New York City. She is great at creating a lighting plan and then can facilitate the purchase of all your fixtures.

EXPEDITERS

New York is a jungle when trying to get renovation plans approved by the building department. Even most architects and designers don't attempt to process the plans themselves; they hire experts to do this. The experts are called expediters. If you want to file plans, you will need one too.

DAVID MANDEL ASSOCIATES ★ (212) 242-2233

David's company is great to know about. Aside from being expediters they are licensed architects and do construction management. The beauty of this firm is that they will do *any* portion of the job. So if you only need a licensed architect to draw up plans and file them, he will accommodate you.

DAVID TRACHTENBERG ★ (212) 643-1797

David is an expert in filing architectural plans and pushing them through the buildings department.

FLOOR FINISHERS

Making a wood floor beautiful can be a tricky job but these people can handle it.

ABE BRENTLY FLOORS ★ (212) 292-8436 ★ $–$$ ★ Insured
Abe is a pro. You can count on him to make your floors as beautiful as they can possibly be. He has a good eye and state-of-the-art equipment.

LARRY CONDELL FLOORING ★ (718) 723-6720 ★ $–$$ ★ Insured
Larry has expertise in both refinishing old floors and laying new wood over. He has a good eye for color and will work very hard to give you just what you want while explaining the possible pitfalls. He is also available for small repair work.

PEISER FLOORS ★ (212) 289-2220 ★ $$ ★ Insured
Ask for Matty—he will make an appointment for an estimate. They do clean and professional work.

FURNITURE REFINISHERS

Don't despair if you think your wood furniture is chipped, stained, or looks simply dismal. New York has some of the top refinishers. They can make your pieces look beautiful and even change their color. If you are worried about your furniture when it is out of the home, don't despair—many times your home owner's policy will cover you, so check.

JOSEPH BIUNNO COMPANY ★ (212) 629-5630 ★ $$ ★ No Insurance
Joseph Biunno is the fourth generation of his family to work his magic on restoring, repairing, and refinishing antique to contemporary furniture. One of his specialties is making skeleton and barrel keys for antique pieces and furniture doors, and he makes house calls. Don't forget—an antique piece of furniture is worth more if it has an original working lock.

RELIABLE FURNITURE ★ (718) 387-7308 ★ $$ ★ No Insurance
Sam Garachi is one of the best, an artisan from way back. We haven't run across any piece of furniture that Sam can't make look wonderful. He can either work in your home or bring your item to his studio. He works with a great cabinetmaker.

GENERAL CONTRACTORS

Be careful when hiring a contractor. Do your homework well or call our picks.

BARRY FISHELBERG INC. ★ (718) 658-0192 ★ $$ ★ Insured

Barry Fishelberg Inc. is a family who's been in business for over twenty-five years. Now his two sons have joined him. Their expertise lies in total and complete apartment renovations. Barry has a custom cabinet shop on the premises as well as a staff of laborers, tile people, electrician, Formica specialists, painters, and wallpaper hangers.

POINT WAY GROUP INC. ★ (212) 371-0236 ★ $$ ★ Insured

A contracting company that is run by "Ivy League" graduates. They have been in business for over five years. They have the capability to handle large jobs; however, they are unique in that they have an expertise in "cleaning up other contractor's messes." Their interpersonal skills combined with their knowledge and expertise make them a good company to call.

KITCHEN/BATHROOM STOREFRONT CONTRACTORS

ELGOT ★ 937 Lextington Avenue (68th and 69th Streets) ★ $$–$$$ ★ (212) 879-1200 ★ Insured

Walk in off the street and take a look. They can do partial or total kitchen renovations. They have on staff two kitchen designers. There is no fee for their initial consultation. If you want to go ahead they will create a floor plan for $375 which becomes your property. If you continue, that fee is deducted off the price of the job.

HASTINGS ★ 30 Park Avenue South (at 19th Street) ★ $$–$$$ ★ (212) 674-9700 ★ Insured

Works the same way as Elgot and has been around for years.

ST. CHARLES KITCHENS ★ 150 East 58th Street ★ $$–$$$ ★ (212) 838-2812 ★ Insured

St. Charles has been doing business for years and operates along the same lines as Elgot.

PAINTERS

New York is full of all types of painters—rental painters, co-op painters, artist painters—from which we provide a sampling. Be wary of the painter who says he can paint your two-bedroom apartment in one day.

ARTISTIC FINISHERS ★ (718) 392-3750 ★ $$$ ★ Insured

As the name implies, Rudy specializes in all types of artistic wall and furniture painting. His company gives the "Royal Treatment" in sponge, strié, and other technique painting. He can arrange for an expert in trompe-l'oeil to fly here from Turkey. Their work is fantastic but don't call unless you plan to spend a lot.

BAUER PAINTING ★ (201) 964-4942 ★ $–$$ ★ Insured

William Bauer is a find. A house painter, he usually works in New Jersey but you may be lucky enough to get him to come to New York City. He works with a couple of talented painters and he can also do some light carpentry work. Wallpapering services available.

GREGORY CRAMER ★ (914) 636-4393 ★ $–$$ ★ No Insurance

Gregory has a BFA from Carnegie-Mellon and specializes in painting murals and furniture. His enchanting Peter Rabbit and Alice in Wonderland wall murals are simply the best and can often cost less than wallpaper.

DEL PILAR DESIGN ★ (212) 518-0062 ★ $$ ★ Insured

Victor Del Pilar owns this wonderfully run house-painting company. He is a fabulous painter who works with a small skilled crew. He has a great eye for color and detail. Best of all, he can handle many types of renovation work: tile, kitchen remolding, appliance installation, and more. Wallpapering services are also available.

SUSAN JOHNSON ★ $ ★ No Insurance

Susan is proficient in many artistic paint finishes. She will provide you with samples of her techniques so you can make an informed choice.

VICKI LEVITES ★ (212) 260-3838 ★ $–$$ ★ No Insurance

Decorative painting for furniture, interiors, and objects. She even custom-paints guitars. Techniques include sponge, glazing, faux marble, stenciling, strié, and murals. Charges by job and free estimates. All rooms must first be prepared by a painter.

JOSEPH LUKSICH ★ (718) 746-0597 ★ $–$$ ★ No Insurance

A warm, talented, and friendly house painter. Joe works mostly solo and his strength lies in clean, simple paint jobs.

JEANNE MANZELLI ★ (203) 673-9514 ★ $–$$ ★ No Insurance

Jeanne is a fine artist painter and designer. She specializes in trompe-l'oeil and mural painting for any type of apartment. Exceptionally talented in landscapes, animals, and whimsical designs, she also works on furniture. Jeanne usually charges by the day.

PERFECTIONAL PAINTING ★ (516) 485-3110 ★ $ ★ No Insurance

Doug Walrath specializes in multicolor, textured, and airless spray applications. A relatively inexpensive but durable process.

STONE SPRAYER ★ (212) 292-6000 ★ $ ★ Insured

If you need to have your walls, furniture, or file cabinets spray painted these are the people to call. They can produce a Zolatone or stucco type finish, to name a few. Free estimates.

PLUMBERS

Plumbing problems in New York can be a nightmare. These two companies have a good reputation and have the ability to respond quickly.

J. BARONE & CO. INC. ★ 414 East 116th Street ★ (212) 722-4666 ★ $$–$$$ ★ Insured
They have been serving New York for thirty years and do a good job.

FRED SMITH ★ (212) 744-1300 ★ $$–$$$ ★ Insured
A reputable and large plumbing company, they handle the plumbing needs of many condos and co-ops in New York.

PORCELAIN BATHROOM REFINISHER

One of the charms of New York is our prewar buildings with all their wonderful architectural detail and those fabulous old bathrooms. Well, sometimes those bathrooms need some sprucing up and it can be done simply and rather inexpensively.

DURA-GLOSS ★ (516) 225-5037 ★ $$ ★ Insured
Tom Peck started his company three years ago. His reglazing process includes a chemical cleansing, acid wash, any minor repairs, three coats of primer, three coats of color, and two coats of clear finish. He gives a two-year unconditional guarantee.

KELKOTE ★ (800) 698-8271 ★ $–$$ ★ Licensed, Bonded, and Insured
Michael Rogers knows his craft. He specializes in refinishing your tub ($285), your pedestal sink ($175), tiles on the wall (half way up) with tub ($825), and you can pick from a variety of colors. He stays away from toilets and floors (simply because they can scratch easily). His work comes with a three-year guarantee and he says that the process lasts ten to fifteen years. They have a showroom in Westbury, Long Island.

REFACING KITCHEN CABINETS

BARRY FISCSHELBERG ★ (718) 658-0192 ★ $$ ★ Insured

POINT WAY GROUP INC. ★ (212) 371-0236 ★ $$ ★ Insured

TILE AND MARBLE WORK

JOHN ARTIMIDO ★ (718) 531-8119 ★ $$ ★ Insured
Works on ceramic tile, marble, and granite. He does excellent work.

Laying stone is quite difficult and if it is done poorly, it really looks bad. So hire John.

TINO'S MARBLE ★ (201) 348-4785 ★ $$ ★ Insured
An expert marble installer who also works with granite and tile. No stone is too tough for him. He has a good sense of design.

UPHOLSTERY AND WINDOW TREATMENTS

BRIDGETTE POOLE ★ (212) 674-5189 ★ $-$$ ★ Not Insured
Bridgette has a background in textile design and has started her own business. She helps you shop for material, and then makes unstructured chair covers, pillows, draperies, and roman shades. Her prices are reasonable, her work is exceptional, and she is a good source for finding other talented people in the field of renovating.

STUDIO M ★ (212) 532-4540 ★ $$-$$$ ★ Insured
Studio M works on everything but upholstered furniture. They specialize in draperies, balloon shades, bedspreads, and other kinds of window treatments.

VERSAILLES DRAPERY AND UPHOLSTERY ★ (212) 533-2059 ★ $$-$$$ ★ Insured
A family-run business for over thirty years. The finest custom upholstery work that we have seen in New York City. They have a wonderful eye for material, color, design, and fit. This expertise does not come cheap but when you have spent money on fabric you want the job to be done right and to last. They specialize in restoring eighteenth-century original furniture, as well as making any new piece of upholstered furniture you might want; and it does not cost as much as you might think.

For Other Upholsterers See Intrepid Page 223.

WALLPAPER HANGER

Most good painters work in conjunction with a wallpaper hanger.

ANGEL ★ (718) 848-0204 ★ $$ ★ No Insurance
A great paper hanger who knows just how much paper you will need and knows which paper will last the longest. You can't go wrong.

WINDOWS

When walking down the street it seems that scaffolding is always over our heads, being set up for new window installation. New windows can dramatically cut down on the noise of the City.

PANORAMA WINDOW ★ (212) 292-9882 ★ $$ ★ Insured

Doug Simpson is a reliable, hardworking man who deals with the installation of one new window with the same diligence as he does for an entire building. He tells you all your realistic options, explaining the possible mess and repair work that you will encounter. He is also extremely aware if your new windows will not accommodate your existing window treatment.

WINDOW GLASS

ABALONE SHADE & GLASS ★ (212) 744-0556 ★ $ ★ Insured

Call them to replace any window glass in Manhattan.

THE INTREPID PAGES
OF
HOME
RENOVATING/REDECORATING
STORES

APPLIANCES, MAJOR

It is possible to buy large appliances in the New York area for a discount, but it is not always a pleasant experience. So be sure that you know exactly what you want and that you get everything in writing. You can get an idea of what you want by looking at the more expensive stores.

DEMBITZER BROTHERS ★ 5 Essex Street ★ (212) 254-1370
A great discount shop that sells all major brand-name appliances. They do not install but will recommend a company that does.

HOME SALES DIAL-A-DISCOUNT ★ (212) 513-1513
All you have to do for this service is make a phone call. You need to know the exact make and model number of your item. You certainly should check the price here before you go elsewhere. They sell air conditioners, major kitchen appliances, trash compactors, TVs, and VCRs.

TOPS APPLIANCE ★ Secaucus, New Jersey ★ (201) 902-6900
A clean, large store that sells everything from calculators to stereo systems to high-tech oven ranges. The more you purchase the better the deal they give you. The managers have a good work ethic. They deliver to Manhattan and they can arrange for installation. And the best part is that they discard your old, disconnected appliances at no extra cost.

ARCHITECTURAL DETAIL SHOPS

Even if you are renovating a modern apartment, you still have the option to add some old-world detail.

ARCHITECTURAL SALVAGE WAREHOUSE ★ 337 Berry Street, Brooklyn
★ (718) 388-4527
The New York City Landmarks Preservation Commission retrieves items from City-owned buildings that are marked for demolition and sells them here. You can find: shutters, windows, fixtures, doors, and more. Prices begin at $40.

URBAN ARCHAEOLOGY ★ 285 LaFayette Street ★ (212) 431-6969
In this 50,000-square-foot shop you will find items that date back 150 years. Because of the large space they have set up entire rooms filled with bookcases, fireplace mantels, pool tables, and even brick facing.

DECORATIVE HARDWARE

When renovating we find it can be the little "things" that are hard to find but that ultimately make a big aesthetic difference. You can find just the right doorknob, furniture handles, or closet pull if you know where to go.

KRAFT HARDWARE ★ 306 East 61st Street ★ (212) 838-2214
A wonderfully stocked, decorative supply store that deals mostly with the trade. They do accept cash or checks. They have an extensive selection of doorknobs, hinges, hooks, and handles and don't forget to look at their display of faucets, shower heads, vanities, sinks, tubs, etc.

SIMON'S HARDWARE ★ 421 Third Avenue (29th and 30th Streets) ★ (212) 532-9220
They have a complete selection of decorative hardware such as door-knobs, handles, switch plates, house numbers, closet pulls, and deco-rative trim, as well as a commercial department that sells industrial hardware and equipment. Best of all, you will find many types of professional laborers who buy at Simon's. Don't be shy—get their card and check them out.

M. WOLDHONOK & SON ★ 155 East 52nd Street ★ (212) 755-0895
If you can imagine doing one-stop shopping for all your decorative hardware needs this is the place. All types of pulls, surface mount knobs, reproduction hardware, towel rods, and more. Their drapery hardware section can't be beat.

FLOOR COVERING

ABC CARPET AND HOME ★ 881 Broadway (at 19th Street) ★ (212) 473-3000
We have looked around and when all is said and done, you really can't go wrong with ABC. Their prices and choices are good and if you

appeal to their human side you can even get good service and samples. Remember: Some buildings in New York City require you to carpet a portion of your apartment.

A REFINED SELECTION ★ 42 West 15th Street ★ (212) 255-4450
Here you will probably find the largest selection of ceramic tile in New York City. They carry everything from plain, ordinary four-by-four-inch white tile to hand-painted tile from Europe. You can commission them to create any design you want.

COLOR TILE SUPERMARKET INC. ★ 903–907 Broadway (at 20th Street) ★ (212) 979-8788
A chain that carries a reasonable selection of linoleum, vinyl, and ceramic tiles as well as the equipment you need to do the installation. If you can't install, they are happy to arrange it for you.

COUNTRY FLOORS ★ 15 East 16th Street ★ (212) 627-8300
Here you will find a gorgeous selection of ceramic and terra-cotta tiles from all over the world. Their prices are high, but their selection is great. If you bring them a floor plan they can help you arrange a design. They don't install but they do provide you with a list of installers.

DESIGNED WOOD FLOORING CENTER ★ 281 Lafayette Street (Houston and Prince Streets) ★ (212) 925-6633
It's great to know a storefront that specializes in putting down wood floors. You can choose from all different colors and styles.

EINSTEIN MOOMJY ★ 150 East 58th Street ★ (212) 758-0900
Before you go to this location call to make an appointment with Mark. He is one of the best salespeople in New York. Mark has a good understanding of which carpet is appropriate for what spaces. He does not try to oversell you or promise you something that they cannot deliver.

FURNITURE

There are few things you buy in life that can outlive you, but furniture is one of them. It is no secret that furniture can be expensive, especially fine pieces; so know what you want and what you can spend. Remember: Most furniture takes eight to twelve weeks to arrive so start early. For expensive or period pieces we suggest Corky Pollan's book, *Shopping Manhattan* (Penguin, 1989). For contemporary (which often tends to be the least expensive), the department stores Bloomingdale's and Macy's have a good selection, but also try:

APARTMENT LIVING ★ 12 West 21st Street ★ (212) 260-5050

They stock the catalogues of all the major American furniture makers and encourage you to spend time looking through them. After that you should spend time in the major department stores looking at similar furniture. Once you see what you like go back to Apartment Living. They usually can beat any price you have seen. They say they are not in the business of helping you decide, but our experience is that they are very helpful.

THE BOMBAY COMPANY ★ Locations Throughout the City ★ (800) 829-7789

If you are in search of furnishings that reflect your appreciation for the finer things in life, rather than your ability to spend money, go to The Bombay Company. There you will discover elegant furniture and accessories that are not expensive. They make wonderful reproductions and sell them at more than reasonable prices. Their furniture is shipped in a compact package and is easily assembled.

IKEA ★ Elizabeth, New Jersey ★ (908) 289-4488 ★ Hicksville, Long Island ★ (516) 681-4532
★ Call for directions

We can't say enough about IKEA, the Swedish-owned chain. Not only have we used it in our office but also in our home. A "clean," inexpensive, and when not crowded a fairly painless approach to furnishings and cabinetry. The staff tries hard to be accommodating but they are not supposed to hold your hand every step of the way. They sell furniture and other merchandise such as fabric, dishes, sheets, flooring, and more. Be prepared to walk around with a pen, paper, and measuring tape because it is up to you to write down the order number, color, and measurements of each item that you want to buy. Delivery is available (to Manhattan the cost is $45) and you can choose the day that you want (but of course not the time). They are equipped with a full restaurant, play area for children, and rest rooms. There are only two drawbacks: (1) locations—you must either go by car, by bus to New Jersey (leaves from the Port Authority), or by train to Long Island (leaves from Penn Station); and (2) assembly—if you really aren't good with your hands you will have to find someone to assemble your purchases. For help, look in our carpentry section. Be aware that IKEA doesn't accept American Express.

FURNITURE RENTAL

CHURCHILL FURNITURE ★ 44 East 32nd Street ★ (212) 686-0444

If you need to rent some furniture, Churchill is the place to go. All short-term renters are given used furniture, for long-term rentals you

---

are given new pieces. Mattresses are always new. For a small, one-bedroom apartment a three-month rental will run $99 per month. Delivery within forty-eight hours.

FURNITURE TOO BIG TO MOVE

Moving large pieces into an apartment with narrow hallways and doors can be a real problem. We have found some sources to help you.

P. NATHAN ★ 304 East 94th Street ★ (212) 722-3643
P. Nathan can make you a couch and best of all they might be able to cut yours in half to get it through the door.

TELESCA-HEYMAN ★ 304 East 94th Street ★ (212) 534-3442
If you have a piece of wooden furniture that is too large to fit either in the elevator or through your door call these people. They might be able to cut the piece and then reassemble it once it is inside your apartment.

LAMINATION

Sometimes it is a good idea to Scotchgard or laminate your fabric, especially if you have children.

CUSTOM LAMINATION ★ 932 Market Street, Paterson, New Jersey ★ (201) 279-9174
They can laminate most types of fabric and it can all be done by mail.

LAMP SHADES

We found that a lamp shade can make all the difference in bringing out the beauty in a lamp.

JUST SHADES ★ 21 Spring Street (at Elizabeth Street) ★ (212) 966-2757
A great selection of ready-made shades and if you can't find what you want they will make it for you.

UNIQUE LAMPSHADES ★ 247 East 77th Street ★ (212) 472-1140
Ron has the best eye in New York for deciding what shade works with what lamp. Don't be surprised when sometimes a custom-made shade doesn't cost more than a ready-made one. For a small fee he will come to your home to inspect your lamps and shades.

LIGHTS AND LIGHT BULBS

Your best bet for both antique and contemporary fixtures is the lighting district on the Bowery. You won't be disappointed by the trip downtown because the selection is tremendous. Don't buy in the first place you visit and always bargain.

LIGHTING BY GREGORY ★ 158 Bowery (Delancey and Broome Streets) ★ (212) 226-1276
One of our favorites.

JUST BULBS ★ 938 Broadway (at 22nd Street) ★ (212) 228-7820
For the best selection of light bulbs.

LUMBERYARDS

Many people seem surprised to find out that New York City has a number of lumberyards. If you're "handy" you can certainly save a bundle by doing any carpentry yourself. The best part about these yards is that they not only sell raw wood, but they can also get you all types of doors, shutters, and premade cabinets. Many can make tables and even do custom kitchen cabinets. By going straight to the yard you may be able to save money by cutting out the middleman. It's worth a try.

BROADWAY LUMBER ★ 517 West 42nd Street ★ (212) 695-0380 ★ Other Locations Throughout the City
Knowledgeable and friendly, they seem to know exactly what you need and the tools that will help you. A well-stocked yard with a delivery service.

CANAL LUMBER ★ 18 Wooster Street (at Canal Street) ★ (212) 226-5987
More lumber, doors, shutters, etc. Another excellent source for your "wood" needs. Delivery available.

DYKES LUMBER ★ 348 West 44th Street ★ (212) 246-6480
Dykes carries a wide range of decorative lumber supplies. If you are a novice in picking out the "right molding" they are quite helpful and will give you samples to take home. Their delivery service is prompt.

METAL PLATING

You would be surprised at how much better your hinges and door-knobs look when they have been treated and polished.

HYGRADE POLISHING & PLATING COMPANY ★ (718) 392-4082

MIRRORS, WINDOW SHADES, SHOWER DOORS

CENTURY MIRROR AND GLASS CORP. ★ 213 Fordham Street, City Island ★ (212) 885-1666
This shop deals mostly with the trade, but sometimes they do work for the individual. They do incredible work with glass and mirrors. They can make everything from tables to countertops.

NORTH AMERICAN ENCLOSURES, INC. ★ 85 Jetson Lane, Long Island ★ (800) 645-9209

They have a large selection of shower door enclosures at reasonable prices. They deliver but they do not install.

STANLEY SCHOEN ★ 1651 Third Avenue (92nd and 93rd Streets) ★ (212) 369-0320
You can find cheaper places in town but certainly not better workmanship. They are reliable and accommodating. Mirrors installed, glass tabletops, or protective glass for your tables, tub enclosures, window shade treatments, picture framing, and more. Free estimates.

NATURAL STONE YARD

New York does have everything—even a marble yard. If you are in the market to buy any natural stone you should always see the entire slab and not just one small piece. Stone varies widely in color, shade, and grain.

FORDHAM MARBLE ★ 1931 West Farms Road, the Bronx ★ (212) 893-3380
It is a great place to go if you are buying stone. They show you all the slabs that are currently available and if you like one they reserve it for you. A full-service operation in that they give you advice, arrange for the floor plan, and do the installation.

PAINT STORES

Paint brands do differ so beware. We happen to like Benjamin Moore. Be careful when choosing a finish—make sure you understand what it will look like when it has dried.

DELMO PAINTS ★ 1641 York Avenue (at 87th Street) ★ (212) 722-7797
A great small supplier of Benjamin Moore and Paragon paints. They have a good attitude and a great sense of color if you ask their opinion. Their computer seems to do a very accurate color mix. Same-day delivery up to 3:00 P.M.

JANOVIC ★ Third Avenue at 67th Street ★ (212) 772-1400 ★ Other Locations Throughout the City
They carry a wide selection of name brands as well as their own, and have a great selection of equipment that you will need if you are doing the painting. Next-day delivery.

PEARL PAINT ★ 308 Canal Street (Broadway and Church Streets) ★ (212) 431-7932
A large selection of paints and equipment. Delivery of an order can take a few days and there is a $40 minimum on deliveries.

PICTURE FRAMING

FILM AND FRAME CITY ★ 1222 Lexington Avenue (82nd and 83rd Streets) ★ (212) 472-2781
Larry is one of the best shopkeepers in New York. He never forgets a

face or a frame. He always finds just what you need and has a good supply of stock frames. He specializes in custom work.

SIMON SHERMAN ★ By Appointment: (212) 348-9557
Replacing an old frame can make a world of difference. Simon does framing for some of the major galleries and dealers. His specialty is graphic art, photographs, lithographs, and oriental art.

PICTURE HANGING

FINE ART INSTALLATION ★ 143 West 20th Street ★ (212) 242-3106
If you have an art collection of any worth, you should consider hiring these professionals to hang them. They are trained in choosing the right kind of lighting, hooks, spacial relations, and color.

PLUMBING PARTS

NEW YORK REPLACEMENT PARTS ★ 1464 Lexington Avenue (93rd and 94th Streets) ★ (212) 534-0818
A real find in a city where your plumbing parts can take you back to early 1900's. Best bet is to bring in your old part and see if they can replace it. Also a wonderful source for contemporary fixtures.

UPHOLSTERY FABRIC

Fabrics vary greatly in color, style, quality, and price. Shop around before you make any decisions. You can find fabric for $3.99 a yard and you can find fabric for $399 a yard. We always advise our clients to think about how the furniture will be used. For example, if you have young children you might want to hold off on buying very expensive fabric until the kids are older.

HERMES ★ 45 West 34th Street ★ (212) 947-1153
Leather abounds here! Great for covering walls, sofas, chairs, and more.

INTERCOASTAL TEXTILE CORPORATION ★ 480 Broadway (Broome and Grand Streets) ★ (212) 925-9235
A great place to go for closeouts of designer decorative fabric. Bring your lunch and plan to spend some time looking around.

LAURA ASHLEY ★ 714 Madison Avenue (63rd and 64th Streets) ★ (212) 735-5000
This location is dedicated to home furnishings—wallpapers, lamps, furniture, and fabrics. They do a great job coordinating everything.

LE DECOR FRANCAIS ★ 1006 Lexington Avenue (72nd and 73rd Streets) ★ (212) 734-0032

If you want beautiful European fabrics and trim without going with a decorator you must go to Le Decor Français. This is a full-service store; they will go to your home, look at your furniture, and then recommend fabric choices and design possibilities.

PIERRE DEUX ★ 870 Madison Avenue (at 70th Street) ★ (212) 570-9343
French country fabrics and furniture. The fabrics have wonderful patterns and colors. They also do upholstery.

THE RAG SHOP ★ 200 Mill Creek Place, Secaucus, New Jersey ★ (201) 867-5010
If you are looking for a primary source for first-quality decorative fabrics as well as trims and accessories at better than wholesale prices, this is the place. They sell Waverly, Woodridge, Concord, Covington, and more. Average price per yard is $8.99–$12.99, and when on sale $6.75–$9.75.

RALPH LAUREN ★ 867 Madison Avenue (at 72nd Street) ★ (212) 606-2100
His complete line of fabrics is sold at this main store.

RICHARDS INTERIOR DESIGN ★ 317 Grand Street (Allen and Orchard Streets)
★ (212) 966-3606 ★ 1325 Madison Avenue (93rd and 94th Streets) ★ (212) 831-9000
They sell Robert Allen, Kravet, Waverly, and many more designer fabrics at a discount. A full-service store that can handle all your upholstery needs at a good price. The uptown shop carries some different fabrics and the upholstery work is done by different laborers. The uptown shop also charges higher prices because you get more service in nicer surroundings.

SILK SURPLUS ★ 235 East 58th Street ★ (212) 753-6511
This store is owned by Scalamandre and sells their discontinued fabrics to the retail customer. A great way to buy excellent-quality goods that the consumer normally could not get himself.

HARRY ZARIN CO. ★ 292 Grand Street (Eldridge and Allen Streets) ★ (212) 925-6112
Great buys on closeouts of designer fabrics. Though the store is well laid out you will have to spend some time looking through the thousands of yards of fabrics. The staff is well informed and helpful.

UPHOLSTERY/WINDOW DRESSING SUPPLIES
BZI DISTRIBUTORS CORP. ★ 105 Eldridge Street (Grand and Broome Streets)
★ (212) 966-6690
Wonderful prices can be found in this friendly and accommodating

store. They have a large selection of drapery hardware, upholstery supplies, trimmings, foam rubber, blinds, and more.

M & J TRIMMING CO. ★ 1008 Avenue of the Americas (37th and 38th Streets) ★ (212) 391-9072

The best source for braid, rope, cord, and other ties that can be used on upholstered furniture and window treatments.

VAN WYCK WINDOW FASHIONS ★ 39 Eldridge Street (Canal and Hester Streets) ★ (212) 925-1300

This is the store for the do-it-yourself person and the prices are great on tie backs, poles, finials, rods, and brackets.

WALLPAPER

Before you begin, don't forget you can be creative and use some floor covering for your walls. When looking for wallpaper, be aware that most of the time it must be ordered and that you need to know the amount of rolls that you need. We suggest you get an extra one or two rolls, just in case you have a leak or a rip. Kitchen paper should always be washable! Also bring any color swatches, fabric samples, etc. that you are trying to work with. At best, you will be able to tear off a small piece to bring home as a sample.

JANOVIC PLAZA ★ 1150 Third Avenue (at 67th Street) ★ (212) 772-1400 ★ 161 Sixth Avenue (at Spring Street) ★ (212) 627-1100 ★ 159 West 72nd Street ★ (212) 595-2500

They have many wallpaper books to look through so be prepared to spend some time browsing. They deal with various designer papers such as Schumacher, Waverly, Kinney, Norman & Baer, Woodson, and more. If the paper is in stock at the manufacturer you should be able to get it in a few days. They do stock a good selection of wallpaper in the store at decent prices.

GRACIOUS HOMES ★ 1217 Third Avenue (70th and 71st Streets) ★ (212) 988-8990

Operates in a similar way to Janovic.

PINTCHIK DECORATING CENTERS ★ 1555 Third Avenue (at 87th Street) ★ (212) 289-6300 ★ 2475 Broadway (at 92nd Street) ★ (212) 769-1440 ★ 278 Third Avenue (at 22nd Street) ★ (212) 777-3030

Follows a procedure similar to that of Janovic.

POST WALLCOVERING: ★ By mail: (800) 521-0650

Call Post to check on the price. You need to know the title of the book, pattern/style number, retail price, and amount you need. They take credit cards over the phone.

S·I·X
ORGANIZING YOUR LIFE

NTREPID PHILOSOPHY

ATTITUDE Free time and enough living space are essential to our sense of well-being, but are in short supply in this city. To improve the quality of your urban life, you must choose to actively preserve, if not increase, both.

APPROACH Organizing your home and how you operate out of it will do a lot to simplify your life and make it more enjoyable. And if you can get out from under the clutter and disorganization, you will have time to burn and room to breathe.

KNOWLEDGE If you realized how much quality time you lose because of your lack of organization, you would clean up your act immediately.

ECONOMICS Disorganization is money down the drain, every day.

Declutter

INTREPID APPROACH
The Intrepid New Yorker believes that except for important documents, anything that you have not looked at, used, or enjoyed in over a year is clutter and should be gotten rid of or, if absolutely necessary, should be stored away from your living space.

Use it or lose it! In New York City we don't have garages, attics, and basements to throw our clutter into, so if we don't use it, we'd better lose it or we'll drown in it.

INTREPID TIP
There are some things you should know about clutter:

◇ You will never use 80 percent of the paper that is currently stored in your home—ever again!

◇ Clutter costs real money. If you rent space for your clutter it can cost hundreds—even thousands—a year. If your monthly home payments are $2,000 and 10 percent of that space goes to clutter, that's $200 a month, or $2,400 a year that you spend for unusable space.

◇ If it often takes you more than sixty seconds to find things you use a lot, if you have quite a few items you haven't looked at, let alone used in a year, if you save things "just in case"; if you have more than you use of any one item; if your clothes are always wrinkled in your closets—you are not nearly as productive as you could be, and you are wasting valuable living space.

INTREPID APPROACH
Follow Intrepid's twelve steps to maintaining a "clutter free" home.

1. You must set limits on space allocated to clutter and never waver from that limit.
2. Clean out your clutter twice a year. A good time to do it is when you switch your seasonal clothes and you have to reorganize your closets anyway.
3. If you have multiples of linens, hardware, plates, pots and pans, utensils, plastic containers, appliances, sporting equipment, etc.—get rid of all unused extras.
4. Do not save any "you never know" or "just in case" items!
5. Make it a rule that if something comes into the house, something goes out. If you buy a new toy for your child, give one away.
6. Keep items as close to where they will actually be used as possible.

The following list suggests how long you have to keep certain documents. For IRS audits, you should keep your tax returns permanently. All other tax documentation and receipts, only three years from date of filing, with the exception of major asset acquisitions, including stocks, bonds, or property. You only have to hold onto dividend information until you get the year-end annual statement. Keep home-improvement costs information as long as you own your home and three years after you've sold it. Keep last year's utility bills for home resale information. Keep car maintenance receipts for as long as you own the car. Keep the receipts for any major purchase for the life of the item.

7. Don't buy furniture unless it is functional as well as decorative.
8. If you absolutely have to keep some articles from all those magazines and newspapers, clip them and put them in a "clip" basket.
9. Get brutal. Part with those books and *National Geographics* that you will never read again.
10. Get rid of those clothes that just don't fit you, that are outdated, threadbare, that you haven't worn in a year.
11. Get rid of all paperwork and documents that you don't absolutely need or are required by the IRS to keep.
12. Go into your medicine cabinets and look for all the expired dates on your medications and throw those bottles and tubes out! And cosmetics should be tossed every three months due to the bacteria that collect on them once the makeup has been opened.

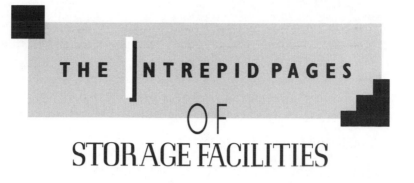

THE INTREPID PAGES

OF STORAGE FACILITIES

MOVING COMPANIES THAT HAVE STORAGE

CIRKERS MOVING AND STORAGE ★ 444 West 55th Street ★ (212) 484-0200

A clean, well-maintained, and well-run storage facility in a relatively convenient location. A first-class operation with more than accommodating personnel. Some of New York's celebrities use this place for storing both documents and excess belongings. You can either have your own bin or wall storage space and of course they pick up and pack. The smallest private space to store your belongings is five by seven feet. One-year rental is $170.

SHLEPPERS MOVING & STORAGE ★ 16 East 79th Street ★ (212) 472-3820

For storing your belongings out of Manhattan, Shleppers runs an efficient operation that is completely full service. (You are not meant to go in and out yourself.) Cost is 330 cubic feet (about seven feet in each direction) for $66 per month.

WAREHOUSE STORAGE

MANHATTAN MINI STORAGE ★ (212) 255-0482 ★ Locations Throughout the City

These facilities are well maintained and offer fairly good quality service. The security is good: computerized card access to automatic elevators and storage floors, closed-circuit TV surveillance, and on-premise management at all times when they are open. You bring your belongings and move them yourself. Smallest room space is five feet by five feet; cost is $64 a month. Smallest economy unit is a four-by-four-by-four-foot cube. Cost is $34 to $36. There are some twenty-four-hour locations.

HOW TO TURN CLUTTER INTO MONEY

INTREPID TIP

You can sell or at least get a tax deduction for all your possessions.

Clothes:

❊ You can get a tax deduction for clothes that go to charities such as the Salvation Army, Goodwill, thrift stores, etc.

❊ You can take them to "consignment" stores, which will try to sell your used clothes for you. If they sell, you will receive a percentage of the profits. They are most likely to take clothes that are in season and in good condition.

Books/magazines/records/tapes:

☛ There are five or six bookstores in New York City that will buy your used books from you. They all have different policies regarding which types of books they will accept or reject—hardcovers, textbooks, fiction, nonfiction—but it is possible to make some decent money.

☛ You can sell your old magazines, records, CDs, and tapes to dealers who specialize in "oldies but goldies."

Furniture:

☛ You can sell your everyday knock-around furniture to used furniture dealers. It's a little like dealing with Sanford and Son, but they will come and appraise the furniture, hand you a check or cash, and cart it off then and there.

☛ You can sell your furniture to an auction house. There are two ways to do it: (1) If you want to play it safe and get cash immediately, a representative from an auction house will come to your home, appraise your furniture, and buy it from you for a set sum. (2) If you want to gamble to see if you can get more than what an auction house will pay for it, you can try to auction your furniture. The auction house will set an official estimate for what they think it will go for at auction. Then you have to sit back and hope for a lot of active bidding.

Garage Sales:

❊ You can also put ads in the local papers and hold a city "garage" sale. Different types of

> •
>
> The Intrepid New Yorker decided to sell all our living room and bedroom furniture. We asked three different auction houses to come take a look. One was only interested in one piece. One offered $3,000 for the lot. The third offered $7,000.
>
> •

> •
>
> If you want to get rid of items too big to cart off yourself, call the New York City Sanitation Department's "bulk pickup" and see if they will pick up what you have and on what day. There are different numbers to call depending on what part of the City you live in. It's up to you to get whatever you are throwing out down to the street. If it's too big to cart down to the street, see page 208 for our favorite demolition expert, who for a fee will take it off your hands.
>
> •

ads have different prices. An ad costs from $50 and up in the major city papers (listed under "'Newspapers" in your yellow pages).

✻ Call your community board (see page 87) to find out the name of your neighborhood's paper or see page 162 for our list. List only your telephone number when you advertise, never your name and address. You want to make sure that the cost of the ads will not exceed what you will actually get for the sale items. But it is a great way to get people in the door.

✻ If you only have a few inexpensive items, we recommend you put up signs on public bulletin boards in your building or at your local grocery store. If you can't be bothered throwing your own garage sale, The Intrepid New Yorker Company will be happy to do it for you. (212) 534-5071.

OF
WHERE TO SELL
(Or Just Get Rid of)
YOUR BELONGINGS

CHARITY AND THRIFT STORES

CALL AGAIN ★ 1735 Second Avenue (89th and 90th Streets) ★ (212) 831-0845
They have the capability to pick up if you have a lot. They list what you donated and you set the deduction.

IRVINGTON HOUSE ★ 1534 Second Avenue (at 80th Street) ★ (212) 879-4555
In Manhattan they pick up if you have at least three large cartons. They send you an appraisal.

MEMORIAL SLOAN-KETTERING THRIFT SHOP ★ 1440 Third Avenue (81st and 82nd Streets) ★ (212) 535-1250
Minimum amount for pick up is *a lot* (furniture, etc.). Items must be in good condition. They set the deduction. If they feel it is under $50 you get nothing.

SALVATION ARMY ★ Locations Throughout the City ★ (212) 757-2311
No minimum amount needed for pick up. You set the deduction. Pick up service: 536 West 46th Street, (212) 757-2311. For store locations see the white pages.

SPENCE CHAPIN ★ 1430 Third Avenue (at 81st Street) ★ (212) 737-8448
They will pick up heavy items, such as furniture. Light items you bring to them. They set the deduction. They send you an appraisal.

CONSIGNMENT CLOTHING SHOPS

Most shops only accept seasonal clothing that is in good condition and you must make an appointment. Each store has their own policy with regard to returning the merchandise to you—so check! Remember: You don't get paid unless the merchandise sells.

DESIGNER RESALE ★ 324 East 81st Street ★ (212) 734-3639

This shop only accepts designer clothing in good condition. You will receive 50 percent of the sale and if it is not sold after three months you can pick up your goods.

ENCORE ★ 1132 Madison Avenue (at 84th Street) ★ (212) 879-2850

Encore has a well-deserved reputation for carrying designer label clothing for women. They give you a three-month contract—if it doesn't sell you have one month to pick it up, beyond which they keep it. You get 50 percent of what it sells for.

EXCHANGE UNLIMITED ★ 563 Second Avenue (at 31st Street) ★ (212) 889-3229

One of the only consignment shops that accepts men's clothing as well as women's. This shop has been in business for fifteen years and has a good quantity and quality of merchandise. Items go on a sales-reduction system up to 75 percent off; you get 50 percent of the sale. If it doesn't sell by the end of the season, you get it back.

MICHAEL'S ★ 1041 Madison Avenue (79th and 80th Streets) ★ (212) 737-7273

A women's resale shop vying with Encore for the quality of its merchandise. You receive 50 percent of the sale, and get unsold items back after three months. Designer labels *only* in good condition. No older than one to two years.

ONCE UPON A TIME ★ 171 East 92nd Street ★ (212) 831-7619

Children's clothing. You get 40 percent of the sale. They keep it for six months or more. Generally they don't give items back unless there's a specific item about which you've made an agreement.

RITZ THRIFT SHOP ★ 107 West 57th Street ★ (212) 265-4559

Ritz deals only in fur coats and they are quite selective in what they accept—and don't expect to get a lot of money. They buy outright and also take items on consignment if you don't like the price they offer.

SECOND ACT ★ 1046 Madison Avenue (79th and 80th Streets) ★ (212) 988-2440

Joan Blake runs this great shop of twenty-six years. They sell children's clothing, toys for young toddlers, books, and occasionally some sporting equipment. All items on consignment only. They do not give back clothing.

SECOND COUSIN ★ 142 Seventh Avenue (10th and Charles Streets) ★ (212) 929-8048

Clothing for children under ten years old, only on consignment. You get items back after three months.

WHERE TO SELL BOOKS

ACADEMY ★ 10 West 1st Street ★ (212) 242-4848
They will not buy textbooks, technical, or paperback books. They will buy art, photography, and rare books.

ARGOSY BOOKS ★ 116 East 59th Street ★ (212) 753-4455
Here you can sell your older, rare books. They will not buy textbooks or, generally, books of this century.

BARNES & NOBLE ★ 105 Fifth Avenue (at 18th Street) ★ (212) 675-5500
They buy current-edition textbooks, fiction, and trade. You must have student I.D. to sell textbooks. They will not buy hardcover fiction.

GRYPHON ★ 2246 Broadway (80th and 81st Streets) ★ (212) 362-0706
They tend to purchase any good literature. They prefer art, history, science, philosophy, and good cookbooks. They will not buy technical books or textbooks.

STRAND ★ 828 Broadway (at 12th Street) ★ (212) 473-1452
They are interested in mostly hardcover, but they do take paperbacks. The books should be in good condition.

WHERE TO SELL CAMERAS

OLDEN ★ 1265 Broadway (31st and 32nd Streets) ★ (212) 725-1234
Bring in your camera and a technician will price it—any day except Thursday and Sunday.

WILLOUGHBYS PEERLESS CAMERA STORE ★ 110 West 32nd Street ★ (212) 564-1600
Bring in your camera and they will give you a price.

WHERE TO SELL FURNITURE

CHRISTIE'S ★ 502 Park Avenue (at 59th Street) ★ (212) 546-1000
Deals with high-quality goods. They only work on consignment, and take commission on an inverse sliding scale—the higher the price, the less they take. You both decide the lowest price you would be willing to accept. If it does not sell you either take it back or put it up for auction again.

CONSIGNMENT SHOWCASE, INC. ★ 434 Atlantic Avenue, Brooklyn ★ (718) 858-1155
They usually will agree to take most of your everyday knock-around furnishings. Bring it in, set a price together, and then they sell on consignment. They will give you some idea over the phone if your items will sell.

LUBIN ★ 30 West 26th Street ★ (212) 924-3777
Deals in solid furniture to antique pieces. Depending on the market, they will either purchase your item outright from you (they bring you a check and take the item away), or you give them your furniture to sell on consignment. In that case, you pay for trucking. They take 20 percent commission or $100, whichever is greater.

SOTHEBY'S ★ 1334 York Avenue (at 72nd Street) ★ (212) 606-7000
Operates in a similar fashion to Christie's.

TEPPER ★ 110 East 25th Street ★ (212) 677-5300
Works the same way as Lubin.

WILLIAM DOYLE GALLERIES, INC. ★ 175 East 87th Street ★ (212) 427-2730
Speak to Gillian Ryan. They occasionally buy outright—depending on what condition the item is in. You must first bring in or send photos of the items that you want to sell. If they are interested, they will send someone to take a look.

WHERE TO SELL MAGAZINES

ABRAHAM'S MAGAZINE SERVICE ★ 56 East 13th Street ★ (212) 777-4700
They buy only the more esoteric literary and artistic magazines.

JAY BEE MAGAZINE STORES, INC. ★ 134 West 26th Street ★ (212) 675-1600
They purchase traditional magazines such as *Time, Life, Newsweek, Vogue, People*, etc. You get about ten cents a magazine.

M&M SANITATION RECYCLING CENTER ★ (212) 255-1544
Here they recycle cans, plastic, cardboard, and newspaper/magazines. No money is given but you'll get it out of your home, and be paid with a good conscience.

WHERE TO SELL RECORDS

SECOND COMING RECORDS, INC. ★ 235 Sullivan Street (Bleecker and West 3rd Streets) ★ (212) 228-1313
Depending on the market, they will purchase any kind of record.

SKYLINE ★ 13 West 18th Street ★ (212) 759-5463
They will buy all kinds of records and books.

Repair

Anything that needs repairing is just another form of clutter. How many items do you have in your home right now that you have not been able to use for months because they need repairing? A blender that can't mix, a calculator that can't add, scissors that can't cut— there are two ways to look at this type of clutter:

1. If you haven't bothered to get it repaired in, say, six months, then come to terms with the fact that you probably don't need it.
2. If you really do need it, but you are still not getting it repaired, consider the following: Take a personal day off from work. Months of weekends have borne no progress so a more deliberate approach is in order. It will feel liberating to get your home in working order once and for all. And you don't have to bother trying to find repair places; The Intrepid New Yorker has already done that for you.

REPAIRING AND MAINTAINING YOUR WARDROBE

The efficiency with which you start your day will set the tone for the rest of it. Having well-maintained outfits that you can slide into effortlessly in the morning will reflect how organized you really are and how efficiently you use your time. Sorting through clothes that are in a constant state of needing ironing, mending, and cleaning will not help you get to that business breakfast on time or put your best professional face on once you're there.

INTREPID APPROACH
Try the following and see what a difference taking these steps will make:

- Decide today that you are going to get all your clothes repaired. Get it all done at once so you are starting out with an entire wardrobe in good working order. After that, it should be easy to stay on top of occasional cleaning and repairs.
- Discard all worn-out, tired clothes, including socks, hose, and underwear. Make sure you have at least seven days worth of these items in very good condition. In the office, women should always have on hand several pairs of hose; men should have on hand one clean shirt and tie.
- As soon as clothes come back from the cleaners, get them off the wire hangers and onto good wooden or plastic ones. Flimsy hangers make clothes crease and lose their shape. And keeping clothes in plastic cleaning bags yellows the fibers, and makes it harder to sort through them daily.

- Organize your clothes in the closet by outfits: hang blouses, suits, jackets, pants, and skirts that go together. Place corresponding sweaters on the shelf above them.
- Don't mix seldom-worn clothes or weekend clothes in with your Monday-through-Friday clothes. Set aside a separate space for those. Put your off-season clothes in garment bags and hang them in a separate space too. If you don't have enough room in your closet for off-season clothes, put them in storage boxes under your bed. Never store your off-season clothes without dry-cleaning them first.
- Don't put sweaters in drawers; they are hard to find, hard to pull out, and they will get wrinkled. Put them on shelves in your closet.
- Special racks and hangers designed for shoes, ties, and belts will keep them in ready-to-wear shape and immediately accessible.
- Wash good lingerie in lingerie bags so they don't get ruined in the washing machine.
- At the end of your day, hang the clothes you've worn in the bathroom to air out and steam *before putting them back in the closet.*

If they do get a little wrinkled in the closet, steam them in the bathroom the night before you plan to wear them. They will be dry and ready to go by morning. Always plan your wardrobe the night before, so you know in advance that the outfit is ready to wear.

Disorganization costs you precious free time—lots of it. Spending extra time trying to find a decent outfit to wear, looking for misplaced keys, balancing your checkbook by hand because your calculator is broken, searching for your bills so you can pay them—all spend valuable time for the wrong reason. If you think you waste an average of fifteen minutes a day due to disorganization, that adds up to four lost days a year. If you think you waste a half hour a day, that's eight lost days. If you think you might actually lose an hour a day, that's fifteen days a year, or a three-week vacation! If that doesn't give you incentive to get your act together, we don't know what will.

THE INTREPID PAGES
OF
REPAIR
AND MAINTENANCE SERVICES

We have never been stumped trying to find a reliable repair person and we have found that many of the better people run family businesses. They pass the trade on from generation to generation. Be precise about what is broken and get everything in writing. Most important, always appeal to someone's human side. Explain to them why you are desperate to have your camera back in one week in time to go on safari, why you need your word processor looked at today because you work out of your home as a free-lance writer, or why you need your dress mended for a big date you have on Saturday. People really do care.

BOOK BINDING

LEO WEITZ/HERBERT E. WEITZ ★ 1377 Lexington Avenue (90th and 91st Streets) ★ (212) 831-2213

Your books will be in good hands here. Old books can be worth a lot, so maintaining the bindings is quite important.

CAMERA REPAIR

PROFESSIONAL CAMERA REPAIR SERVICE ★ 37 West 47th Street ★ (212) 382-0550

This shop appears to be one of the largest repair places in the City. They attempt to do repairs in their shop (and are often successful) but sometimes the camera must be sent back to the manufacturer. They work on still cameras from 35 mm and up as well as video cameras.

MORMENDS ★ 1228 Madison Avenue (88th and 89th Streets) ★ (212) 289-3978

They will send your camera back to the manufacturer and then inform you of the estimate. A trustworthy and timely shop.

CAMPING EQUIPMENT

DOWN EAST ★ 73 Spring Street (Lafayette and Broadway) ★ (212) 925-2632

A great place to get your gear repaired, modified, or customized, as well as a good store to purchase any camping-related item you may need.

CHAIR CANING

VETERAN'S CANING SHOP, INC. ★ 550 West 35th Street ★ (212) 868-3244

Chair caning, rush seating, and split seating—all can be done by this family-owned business (over ninety years in the business).

WEST SIDE CHAIR CANING AND FURNITURE REPAIR ★ 133 West 72nd Street ★ (212) 724-4408

Jeffrey Weiss is an expert in caning and keeps very busy. His prices are reasonable but he does have limited hours.

CLOCK AND WATCH REPAIR

HENNOR JEWELERS AND CLOCK MAKERS ★ 966 Lexington Avenue (70th and 71st Streets) ★ (212) 744-1058

Norman Hennor's shop has been in the same location for more than fifty years. It is wonderful to observe him work. He can work on $1,000 clocks as well as Timex watches. Only in New York!

DOLL REPAIR

NEW YORK DOLL HOSPITAL ★ 787 Lexington Avenue (61st and 62nd Streets) ★ (212) 838-7527

A family business that was started ninety years ago, they can repair, clean, and spruce up any doll. They don't take on any project that they can't do a good job on. Deposit required.

DOWN REPAIR

I. ITZKOWITZ ★ 174 Ludlow Street (Stanton and Houston Streets) ★ (212) 477-1788

Only in New York can you walk by a hole-in-the-wall store and see feathers flying around and know that it is a place to bring your down to get repaired and reconditioned. They also make new comforters, pillows, mattress covers, and percales, and patch quilts.

J. SCHACHTER ★ 85 Ludlow Street (Delancey and Broome) ★ (212) 533-1150

Schachter is the place to go if your down pillows and comforters are looking less than plump and fluffy. Reconditioning entails dusting the inside free of decomposed down, sterilizing the remaining down, adding new down, and changing the fabric cover. Although this sounds like a lot of work, it can be cheaper than buying a new one.

FURNITURE REPAIR

For everyday pieces of furniture that need repair call a carpenter (see page 207, or consult the yellow pages).

ANTIQUE FURNITURE WORKROOM ★ 225 East 24th Street ★ (212) 683-0551
Keep in mind that this is mostly for repair of good-quality antiques and that a repair to keep the value of the piece does not come cheap. Their work as well as their attitude is beyond reproach.

JEWELRY REPAIR

For hooks, loose catches, and small problems.

ALEX'S JEWELRY ★ 1230 Lexington Avenue (83rd and 84th Streets) ★ (212) 734-5787
Fairly prompt. Good attention to detail when doing repairs.

ALEX'S REPAIR ★ 1157 Madison Avenue (85th and 86th Streets) ★ (212) 988-5135
Any repair; prompt, reliable, and honest.

MURREY'S JEWELERS ★ 1395 Third Avenue (79th and 80th Streets) ★ (212) 879-3690
This is a gem of a store; honest, trustworthy, and efficient.

KNIVES AND SCISSORS SHARPENED

FRED DECARLO ★ (201) 945-7609
He will come to your home.

LAMP REPAIR

Depending on the problem, you should first try your local hardware store. After that:

LEE'S LIGHTING STUDIO ★ 1755 Broadway (at 56th Street) ★ (212) 581-4400
★ 1069 Third Avenue (at 63rd Street) ★ (212) 371-1122

LUGGAGE REPAIR

JOHN R. GERADO, INC. ★ 30 West 31st Street ★ (212) 695-6955
This is the authorized repair service for Louis Vuitton and Gucci. Need we say more? Believe it or not, you can even take your Samsonite, because they repair everything—even your soft luggage.

LEXINGTON LUGGAGE ★ 793 Lexington Avenue (61st and 62nd Streets) ★ (212) 223-0698
They can repair Hartman, American Tourister, Samsonite, and more. A repair takes usually less than a week and they always stand by their work.

CLOTHES REPAIR

For additional names and numbers, see page 16.

MAGIC MENDERS ★ 118 East 59th Street ★ (212) 759-6453

Experts in immediate repairs. Reliable and friendly. They can fix zippers, weave tears and pulls, fix straps on bags.

MEDA ★ 2 West 45th Street, 15th Floor ★ (212) 840-7657

The mender of the impossible. She has been mending anything and everything for over twenty-five years. If it can be fixed, she can do it.

PEN REPAIR

FOUNTAIN PEN HOSPITAL ★ 10 Warren Street (Church Street and Broadway) ★ (212) 964-0580

A family business started in 1946. Not only can they repair any broken pen, but they are experts in advising you as to what pen is right for you.

PIANO TUNER

To find a tuner we suggest you call:

JUILLIARD SCHOOL OF MUSIC ★ (212) 799-5000

TURTLE BAY SCHOOL OF MUSIC ★ (212) 753-8811

POCKETBOOK REPAIR

A dingy, dirty, broken bag just isn't worth having.

ARTBAG CREATIONS ★ 735 Madison Avenue (64th and 65th Streets) ★ (212) 744-2720

Bring your better bags here to be fixed and maintained. We have never heard the words "can't be done" when we have brought in a repair. With the high cost of pocketbooks, it makes sense to repair the old. They also carry a great selection of new bags.

MODERN LEATHER GOODS REPAIR SHOP ★ 2 West 32nd Street ★ (212) 279-3263

Another fabulous source for bag repair. Whether you need a needle-point mounting, a good cleaning (suede, leather, or canvas), or just a repair, you can get it done here.

RESTORATION

Repair and maintenance of porcelain, ceramics, lacquer, enamel, stone, glass, wood, and silver.

CENTER ART STUDIO ★ 250 West 54th Street ★ (212) 247-3881

Lancing Moore runs an impeccable repair and restoration shop. He concentrates on museum-quality pieces but that should not discourage you from making a phone call to see if he can accommodate you. This expertise does not come cheap but buying new pieces is much more.

GEM MONOGRAMS ★ 628 Broadway (Bleecker and Houston Streets) ★ (212) 674-8960
Don't despair. You can get your Steuben and Baccarat pieces repaired. Gem carries a large stock of crystal pieces that hang on chandeliers.

HESS RESTORATIONS ★ 200 Park Avenue (at 17th Street) ★ (212) 260-2255
Hess works on ceramics, silver, ivory, lacquer, and more. Remember, restoration can be expensive but here you have two options: commercial-invisible restoration or museum-quality restoration. Commercial can run twice as much so be sure you know what you want.

THOME SILVERSMITHS ★ 49 West 37th Street ★ (212) 764-5426
This family business was started in 1931 and it is the place to go to restore, replate, and repair all your silver.

RETINNING AND COPPER REPAIR

RETINNING AND COPPER REPAIR, INC. ★ 525 West 26th Street ★ (212) 244-4896
This is old New York. After you climb the four rickety flights (yes, they do have an industrial elevator) you enter New York of the early 1900s. Here you will find the art of retinning in action. So don't throw out your worn pots—they can be made to look like new. They can also clean up any brass or copper hardware.

SEWING MACHINE REPAIR

CROWN MACHINE SERVICE ★ 2792 Broadway (107th and 108th Streets) ★ (212) 663-8968
Crown is the authorized service center for over fifty companies. Don't despair if you have an antique or computerized machine, because this is the place to repair those too. Best of all, house calls are provided.

MILTON KESSLER ★ (718) 763-7897
A truly personalized service—this is Milton's home so do not call late at night. You are lucky to have him to repair your machine. He will tell you just what is wrong and how you can prevent it from happening again.

SHOE REPAIR

For shoe repair shops, see page 16.

SMALL APPLIANCE REPAIR

For phones, VCRs, toasters, TVs, etc. call the 800 number of the company manufacturing the product you want repaired. The customer service department will give you the authorized repair location closest to you. Anything and everything can be repaired in this city. *Keep in mind:* If the product is no longer covered under warranty, it might be more economical to buy a new one. Always get an estimate first.

ADVISORY REPAIR ★ 175 Seventh Avenue (at 20th Street) ★ (212) 243-0786
★ 1425 Lexington Avenue (at 93rd Street) ★ (212) 534-3800

They repair all leading brand names, except Sony. Included are products under warranty. Their estimates of time and price are quite accurate.

BORGERS ★ 1409 Second Avenue (73rd and 74th Streets) ★ (212) 873-2013

Thank goodness for Borgers because they make house calls! Has your VCR been unhooked for ages? Is your TV still on the blink? All because of lack of time and energy? Well, fret no longer.

ELECTRA-CRAFT ★ 348 West 42nd Street ★ (212) 563-2885

An efficient, good repair place for most major brand names.

TYPEWRITER, WORD PROCESSOR, AND CALCULATOR REPAIR

LINCOLN TYPEWRITERS AND COPY CENTER ★ 100 West 67th Street
★ (212) 787-9397

A congenial store that has a free pickup and delivery service. It's a good bet that they can not only detect the problem, but can fix it as well.

UMBRELLA REPAIR

Depending on how much your umbrella cost it might make sense to get it repaired.

GLORIA UMBRELLA MANUFACTURING CO. ★ 39 Essex Street (Grand and Hester Streets) ★ (212) 475-7388

For those located downtown this is a good bet for repair of those inside-out umbrellas.

UNCLE SAM UMBRELLA SHOP ★ 161 West 57th Street ★ (212) 582-1977

The largest seller of umbrellas in New York. They also make it their business to repair.

VACUUM REPAIR

ACME VACUUM CLEANER COMPANY ★ 1236 Lexington Avenue (83rd and 84th Streets)
★ (212) 879-1980

Here's a company that picks up and repairs your vacuum for a fair price when you know it is broken and you are just about to throw it out—what more needs to be said?

ACTIVE VACUUM CLEANER COMPANY ★ 735 Amsterdam Avenue (95th and 96th Streets)
★ (212) 362-8477

Another great choice and they also pick up and deliver.

ORGANIZING YOUR SPACE

Living in New York City teaches us to work with limited space and get the most out of it. Here are some ways to get the most out of every square foot in your home.

❢ INTREPID APPROACH
You can acquire floor space you never dreamed of by "thinking vertically."

❑ *Make wall space functional:* In New York City, wall space shouldn't just be used to hang pictures. Make it functional. It is valuable square footage that can be built upon attractively to store your personal belongings.

❑ *Build vertically:* When building wall units and shelving, build "up." Take advantage of the vertical spaces you have.

❑ *Think vertically when buying furniture too.* Buying an armoire is a lot more economical in terms of space than buying a horizontal chest of drawers that eats up floor space.

❑ *Build loft space:* If you have very high ceilings, consider making a small loft space for storage and/or as an office. The Intrepid New Yorker has seen many a city space doubled by adding a loft area.

ORGANIZING YOUR KITCHEN

☛ **Hanging appliances:** You can double your counter space by buying appliances such as microwaves, coffeemakers, and toaster ovens that are designed to hang from your cabinets.

☛ **Lazy Susans:** You can double your cabinet space with double- or triple-tiered "lazy susans" to store everything from spices to cups and saucers to pots and pans.

☛ **Pegboards:** If you have any wall space in your kitchen, you can hang pots and pans, pot holders, and utensils from a pegboard that attaches to the wall and can go all the way from floor to ceiling if you want it to. Another option is to buy wrought-iron pot hangers. The effect either way is a "country kitchen" look.

☛ **Holders for utensils:** You can stand a lot of your kitchen utensils in nice-looking contemporary or old-fashioned jars or vases and put them on your countertops. They are actually more accessible this way and it frees up your drawer space. Your good kitchen knives can be hung on knife holders on the wall or put in holders that sit on the countertop.

☞ Cabinet tops: If you have space on top of your cabinets, you can put anything from cookbooks to a wine rack there.

ORGANIZING YOUR LIVING ROOM/BEDROOMS

☞ Furniture that stores: As we stated earlier, you can buy decorative furniture, but make sure it is functional as well. See if you can't find a great looking bed that also has storage space, for example, or a bedside table that has extra drawers, or a beautiful chest or trunk to use as a coffee table. And again, think vertically. Consider buying that armoire over a chest of drawers.

ORGANIZING YOUR UTILITY CLOSET

☞ Pegboards: You can double this space by hanging pegboards floor to ceiling on the back wall. You can attach as many hooks as you need to hang buckets, mops, vacuum hoses, dusting clothes, ironing board, etc. One Intrepid New Yorker has so much extra space in her utility closet now that she's even added her skis, tennis rackets, and kites!

> One of the biggest mistakes people make when trying to stretch their closet space is breaking a wall down between closets to make a walk-in closet. You can actually get much more out of two, well-constructed closets.
> —New York Closet Company

ORGANIZING YOUR BATHROOM

☞ Open shelving: Nice shelves in your bathroom can accommodate your extra towels. And it makes them immediately accessible.

ORGANIZING YOUR CLOTHES CLOSETS

You can triple your closet space if you are willing to hire a closet organizer for about $1,000. If you are planning to stay in your home for a long time, it is a valuable one-time-only expense. They will gut your closet and rebuild it with their space-saving materials.

You can double your closet space just by using some inexpensive space-saving techniques.

> If you need a "work room" but your apartment is too small for one, Manhattan Mini Storage is now renting inexpensive, private work spaces in the SoHo area. They are open twenty-four hours a day and have electrical outlets, air-conditioning, free shelving, and total enclosure for privacy. In addition to storing your property in them, you can also conduct business activities or even personal hobbies. Call (212) S-T-O-R-A-G-E.

1. Make one-half of your closet hanging space for all your "long" clothes, such as suits and dresses; install another hanging rod at waist level in the other half so that you can hang your shirts and jackets in the top half, and slacks and skirts in the bottom half.
2. Use layered hangers for skirts and pants.
3. Your hangers should all face the same direction. Believe it or not, this is a big space saver.
4. Put wire standing racks for shoes on the floor. These racks hold your shoes vertically so you can double your floor space. You can also hang a shoe rack on the back of your closet door.
5. Buy special belt hangers and tie hangers for your closets. Again, it will save you space and also keep your belts and ties neat and easy to find.
6. You can buy special bags for your socks and lingerie that hang from hooks in your closet.
7. Put partitions between your sweaters that are stacked on shelves in your closet. That way they will stack better and higher, and stay in place.

THE INTREPID PAGES

OF
SPACE-ORGANIZING COMPANIES AND SUPPLIERS

BETTER YOUR HOME ★ 103 West 96th Street ★ (212) 866-8700
Home furnishings! Housewares for your bathroom and kitchen, frames, racks, shades, and stools. You name it and they carry it.

CALIFORNIA CLOSETS ★ 1625 York Avenue (85th and 86th Streets) ★ (212) 517-7877
A well-known closet company that knows what it is doing. Their work is clean and efficient and they have a good sense of design. They charge about $100 per linear foot when they organize your closet. They sell a small assortment of do-it-yourself merchandise.

GRACIOUS HOMES ★ 1220 Third Avenue (70th and 71st Streets) ★ (212) 517-6300
Once again a great place for hooks, hangers, shelves, brackets, pegboards, lazy susans, and the like. If you need something that they don't carry we will be surprised—but just in case they don't have it, they will tell you where to get it.

HOLD EVERYTHING ★ 1311 Second Avenue (at 69th Street) ★ (212) 535-9446
Although they sell all over the United States, we are sure that the need for this store is greatest in New York City. Every conceivable device for storing and organizing your entire apartment. Sock dividers, shoe organizers, one-stop shopping for your desk-supply holders, bathroom shelving, hat boxes, and more.

NEW YORK CLOSET COMPANY ★ 1458 Third Avenue (at 83rd Street) ★ (212) 439-9500
The wonderful thing about this company is that they are owned and operated by a Manhattan couple who have to contend with space problems themselves. They have a good eye, excellent materials, and more than fair prices for this kind of work. Their shop is filled with do-it-yourself organizing merchandise.

WOOLWORTH ★ Locations Throughout the City
For a good assortment of plastic containers.

Maintain your paperwork

TAKING CHARGE OF BOOKKEEPING AND PAPERFLOW

How many of you can locate within sixty seconds your Con Ed bill, insurance records, any IRS receipt, or your family's social security numbers? Inefficient bookkeeping can be a black hole into which time and money can disappear. There are specific ways to get control of it.

Work Station

You have to create an efficient work station and place where your paperwork is kept. It's okay if you have to store your papers separately from where you work on them, just as long as they have a designated place. Your work station should include pens, pencils, stapler, calculator, paper, stationery, Rolodex, and phone. And they should all be in good working order. Make your work station whatever you want it to be. If you don't have room for a desk, keep your work supplies in a drawer or cupboard near the phone.

Files

Set up a filing system that works for you. You should have labels that read "To Do," "To Pay," "To Read," "To File." If you usually have a lot of tickets to events and social invitations, you could also keep an "Invitation/Tickets" file. They could come in the form of attractive baskets or office-style file boxes, or folders that go in a file drawer. The most urgent tasks, however, must be put in an active file that is placed in the most visible area of your work station so you can't miss it. We recommend accordian files or Pendaflex hanging files for important documents that you store, such as bank and insurance statements and policies, warranties, and school records.

> For those of you who hate bookkeeping of any kind, we recommend you plan to get it done while watching a favorite television show or a rented movie you've been dying to see. Or, if you commute, keep duplicate file folders in your briefcase so you can take your paperwork with you and get it done on the train.

Your Mail

Open up all your mail the minute you get it and separate the bills, the junk mail, the personal mail and put them in their appropriate files. This way you will never forget to pay your Con Ed bill or lose important documents because they were mixed in with your mail-order catalogs that got tossed out.

Vital Information

It takes so much time fumbling through phone books and accordian files trying to pull out information you use on a fairly regular basis. We recommend you put all your "vital" information in a Rolodex for easy access: your family's social security numbers and clothing sizes, the security number for your alarm, bank account numbers, license plate numbers, critical telephone numbers such as twenty-four-hour plumbers and locksmiths, and any services you use regularly such as phone, cable, Con Ed, insurance, post office, and credit card company.

> " At the beginning of the calendar year, make a list of all the major expenses you expect to incur over the course of the year and their due dates, so that you don't come up seriously short of cash because you forgot about one. This would include everything from club and union dues to school tuition and car payments.
> —Judy Paine, Bookkeeper "

Safe Deposit Boxes

You should put all valuable documents in a safety deposit box: original birth certificates, citizenship papers, wills, household inventories and appraisals, contracts, passports, stock and bond certificates, important insurance papers, property titles and deeds. People who have had these papers destroyed or stolen and gone through the protracted replacement process will tell you how important it is to get them out of your home.

Monthly Bills

As stated earlier, open your bills as soon as they come in the mail so you know what they are. Then, put them in your "To Pay" file. If you don't have it automatically, make sure you apply for the twenty-four-hour banking service your bank has. It allows you to call up any time day or night to find out what you have in your account and what checks and deposits have cleared. When you sit down to write your bills you'll know precisely what you can pay and what you can't.

IRS Receipts

The Intrepid New Yorker has a foolproof and effortless way of filing the dozens if not hundreds of receipts you save every year to document tax deductible expenses. A small effort now means no effort at tax time. Lost receipts and undocumented expenses could cost you hundreds if not thousands of dollars in deductions. And should you get audited, the IRS will disallow any deductions with no documentation. We devised the following system after a painful audit in which we had to return $1,000 to the IRS.

★ Buy an inexpensive day-on-a-page date book.

★ At the end of each day, or once a week—whichever you prefer—staple every receipt that you know is deductible to the day it corresponds to. Write in on that page as well as on the receipt itself what the expense was for,

---

whether it was the books you had to buy for research purposes, a business lunch and with whom, taxis to an interview, etc.

★ It's the end of the year and—presto!—you now have a documented and organized book of tax information, receipts and coordinating appointment calendar all in one. Any IRS auditor would be impressed by this. All deductible expenses are accounted for and all you have to do is add up the deductions by category on a calculator. Period. It is foolhardy to be careless about keeping track of your receipts and deductible expenses; it is cash down the drain.

Wallets and Purses

Never carry a lot of credit cards or a checkbook in your wallet. Only take the one or two credit cards or checks you need for that day. A few years ago, an Intrepid New Yorker had a purse stolen. She had three credit cards and a checkbook in it. Even though she had the checks and credit cards cancelled right away, the thief managed to spend over $20,000 with them in a few hours. It took almost a year to unravel the mess and clear her name with creditors and the bank. This story is quite common. It's a nightmare you don't ever want to go through in this city or anywhere else.

STAYING ON TOP OF YOUR SCHEDULE

How many meetings have you been late for? How many parties have you missed? How many birthdays have you forgotten? How many projects have been put off—primarily because you don't have one organized location for all your need-to-know information?

Your Date Book

Get a daily planner date book that travels with you at all times. The best ones are the complete planning systems that companies such as Filofax put out. They should include:

● A day-at-a-glance calendar in which to make note of all meetings, appointments, special occasions, holidays, etc. At the beginning of each calendar year write in on the appropriate day all the important events you want to remember. Add a separate page in your book that precedes each upcoming month and list all that month's events on it. At a glance you can see everything that is coming up and you can plan for it—such as buying a birthday present before the date is upon you and it's too late. As you receive invitations or buy tickets to events, put the information in your date book immediately so you can file the tickets and invitations away in a safe place until you need them.

● An active "to do" list that you can refer to and add to daily.

- A long-term-project list so you can stay on top of your goals.
- A list of your favorite restaurants by neighborhood so you don't always have to rack your brain for a place to meet someone.
- Important vital information such as social security numbers, clothing sizes, bank account numbers, etc.
- A pocket to put receipts into.
- All your important telephone numbers. One way to break down your telephone numbers is by white and "yellow pages": one section for friends, relatives and business associates; the other for services, stores, schools, organizations, etc. Another way to make your telephone list more user-friendly is to highlight the numbers you use most frequently with transparent magic markers.

Wall Calendars

We also think wall calendars are a great tool. As a backup to your datebook, keep a wall calendar at home. It will show you at a glance what is happening in any given month and can also be the calendar that your spouse and the rest of your family can refer to for information.

Bulletin Boards

We also believe in bulletin boards that you place (if you can) right by the front door or in your kitchen. This bulletin board can hold your wall calendar, receipts for cleaning and repairs, tickets to shows, a list of deliveries you are expecting, etc.

OF
OFFICE SUPPLIES

LEE'S ART SHOP ★ 220 West 57th Street ★ (212) 247-0110
A good supply of wall calendars and other organizational tools that you might need.

STAPLES ★ 1075 Avenue of the Americas (40th and 41st Streets) ★ (212) 944-6744
We can't say enough good things about this very well stocked store with fabulously low prices. A great selection of folders, pens, calendars, and more. And if you buy enough, they do deliver.

VENTURE STATIONERY ★ 1156 Madison Avenue (84th and 85th Street) ★ (212) 288-7235
A good selection of attractive organizers, Filofaxes, Dayrunners, and the inserts.

VIKING DISCOUNT OFFICE PRODUCTS ★ By Mail: (800-421-1222)

> •
> Judy Paine is a great bookkeeper. She charges $50 per hour. You can hire her on a onetime basis to show you how to keep your own books or you can hire her to maintain your records. You can call her at (212) 369-4006.
> •

A mail-order supplier with great, great, great prices on pens, pads, calendars, envelopes, tape, and even file cabinets and calculators. You must get on their mailing list.

USED AND NEW FILE CABINETS
★ on West 23rd Street
On West 23rd Street between Eighth and Ninth Avenues there are a myriad of stores that sell used file cabinets.

S·E·V·E·N
PARENTING
IN THE
BIG CITY

Raising a child in the city is more complex than raising a child in a small town. First, it can be much more expensive.... Second, there are many more types of family life-styles and social philosophies living side by side.... Third, there are negatives inherent in big-city life you want to protect your child from, but there are also a lot of stimulating possibilities you want to expose your child to. Wading through all the information and making in-

INTREPID PHILOSOPHY

ATTITUDE As demanding and informed parents, you can create a quality of life here in which your children can flourish.

APPROACH You must decide how you want to provide for your child and what kind of life-style suits your family best in terms of your financial means and your social philosophy.

KNOWLEDGE In New York City there are so many options for kids and the family that it would be shortsighted to make a choice before you know exactly what you are choosing from. There are scores of dedicated professionals who care and will help you sort through all the possibilities.

ECONOMICS Money can buy the best of everything for your child here, but don't limit yourself by thinking you can't provide a wonderfully enriched life for your child on a conservative budget.

formed decisions can be overwhelming. As a result, we have decided to zero in on two critical areas that create the most angst and indecision among NYC parents—making child-care choices and school choices. What type of school atmosphere is suitable for your child and should you choose public or private institutions? What type of child care is most appropriate not only for your child but for your lifestyle? You want the best for your child, but how do you know what *is* the best? We are going to cut out at least some of that indecision for you, and give you the information that is vital to making an informed choice.

❢ INTREPID APPROACH
The most important thing you should know is that you can create a small town network of advocates for your child in every critical area. The Intrepid New Yorker has found dozens of dedicated professionals in New York that only want the best for your kids. We will tell you who they are. Because we are not going to cover any other child-related issues in this chapter, we are going to start you off with an extensive list of resources that will more than get you started in any area of parenting in this city.

THE INTREPID PAGES
OF
INVALUABLE INFORMATION SOURCES FOR NYC PARENTS

Here are some resources that will more than get you started. These sources will not only help guide you through child care and school options, they will also give you a good knowledge base for many other areas of child-rearing that this chapter does not discuss.

THE PARENTS LEAGUE OF NEW YORK ★ 115 East 82nd Street ★ (212) 737-7385

Yearly membership is $35. In the Intrepid New Yorker's opinion, every parent should become a member of the Parents League. We challenge you to find a better way to put $35 to use. The league is a nonprofit organization of dedicated parents and independent schools providing current information and consultation on education, entertainment, and enrichment opportunities for families in New York City. It has been helping parents since 1913, and is a gold mine of resources. Just walk into their well-staffed, friendly office with file cabinets up to the ceiling and see for yourself. Or call Patricia Girardi, the extremely knowledgeable executive director of the Parents League who has been assisting parents from that office for seven years.

You can use the Parents League to:

- ☛ Choose a school
- ☛ Locate a summer camp
- ☛ Find a baby-sitter, young helper, or tutor
- ☛ Discuss and select toddler activities
- ☛ Find after-school programs
- ☛ Organize a birthday party
- ☛ Plan a family vacation

You will automatically receive these publications yearly:

- ☛ *Parents League Calendar and Guide*—to children's activities, baby-sitting services, after-school programs, party services, parent resource centers, workshops, etc.

- *Parents League News*
- *Parents League Review*
- *Toddler Activities Book*—on all types of toddler programs available in New York City, what they are, and what they cost.

THE 92ND STREET Y PARENTING CENTER ★ 1395 Lexington Avenue ★ (212) 415-5609 ★ Main Y number: (212) 427-6000

The Parenting Center at the 92nd Street Y is a nurturing and educational haven for parents and their children. It offers a wide selection of programs and activities for parents and kids, newborn to three years old. In addition, parents can participate in discussion groups and workshops that focus on children of all ages from toddler to teen. If you want to feel instantly at home and in good hands, call director Fretta Reitzes. She has been dedicated to offering assistance, support, and resources to parents who use the Y for more than a decade. You can pick up a copy of the 92nd Street Y catalog in their lobby. It will tell you virtually everything they have available.

BANK STREET BOOKSTORE ★ 2875 Broadway (at 112th Street) ★ (212) 678-1654

Owned and operated by The Bank Street College of Education, this bookstore is an excellent resource of educational books for parents, teachers, and children. Parents can bone up on everything from what is being taught to children in schools today to what to look for in a quality day-care center.

PARENTS AND KIDS DIRECTORY ★ P.O. Box 1717, Dover, New Jersey ★ (212) 473-3348

A publication focusing on ages birth through thirteen years. A subscription is six issues a year for $16.95. What it offers:

✳ A comprehensive list of events coming up at museums, children's theaters, libraries, and parks
✳ Local, current information on what's happening in education, health, and entertainment

NEW YORK FAMILY MAGAZINE ★ (914) 381-7474

A magazine focusing on ages birth through thirteen years. A subscription is $30 for eleven issues a year. What it offers:

✳ A daily calendar of all events happening for kids
✳ Articles on issues pertinent to parents living in New York

THE BIG APPLE PARENTS' PAPER ★ 928 Broadway, Suite 709 ★ (212) 533-2277

A monthly newspaper that focuses on ages birth through ten years. A subscription is $18 for one year. You can also find it free in schools, pediatricians' offices, libraries, children's stores, and maternity wards at hospitals. What it offers:

* News and feature articles pertinent to New York City families
* Centerfold calendar of upcoming events

FROMMER'S THE CANDY APPLE: NEW YORK WITH KIDS
★ (PRENTICE HALL)
Written by Bubbles Fisher, you can find this wonderful book in most New York City bookstores. Just some of the areas covered in the book:

* An extensive list of parent resources, support groups, and information centers
* What to do for fun in the city with kids
* Holidays, parades, street fairs, special events
* Shopping for clothes, shoes, books, and toys
* Restaurants for kids
* Haircuts for kids
* How kids can avail themselves of the arts
* After-school programs, classes, and summer camps

FAMILY PUBLICATIONS ★ 333 West 52nd Street, Suite 1008 ★ (212) 595-4569
You can find their pamphlets free at pediatricians' offices, boutiques, and schools. What they offer:

* Family Entertainment Guide
* Child Care Guide
* Expectant Parent's Guide
* Teachers' Guide

CHILD CARE CHOICES

CHOICES FOR MOTHERS AT HOME WITH NEWBORNS

As first-time parents you remember all too well what it felt like when you first got home from the hospital with your brand-new baby. You're in shock, you're elated, you're exhausted. How do you assess what kind of help you need, if any, when you haven't been through this extraordinary situation before? In this city, there are many options available to you.

BABY NURSES

Baby nurses are a great luxury and relief to many first-time parents. It is important, however, to understand that you are getting a very specific type of care:

Pros:

☆ They will guide and teach jittery, inexperienced parents.
☆ They are trained nurses capable of handling an emergency.
☆ They will take the middle-of-the-night feedings if you want them to. For some parents, sleep deprivation is so overwhelming that getting needed rest is the best part about hiring a baby nurse.
☆ They will actually stay twenty-four hours a day, and they don't mind sleeping on a cot in the baby's room.

Cons:

★ They are extremely expensive. For professional expertise and twenty-four hour duty you will probably be paying $125 a day.
★ They consider themselves nurses, not housekeepers. They will take care of all the baby's needs from laundry to boiling bottles, and they might make a light meal for you, but don't expect to be indulged beyond that. Most aren't going to do any extras when the baby is asleep. Those parents who delude

themselves into thinking they are hiring a professional "mom" often feel uncomfortable and resentful having a stranger around the house who isn't mom and who won't help out more. Make no mistake about what you will get when you hire a baby nurse.

INTREPID TIP

There are specific ways to find the right baby nurse. Call one of the respected employment agencies that specialize in placing nannies, baby nurses, and baby-sitters that The Intrepid New Yorker has listed for you in our Intrepid Pages of Child Care/ Housekeeping Sources, page 267. Because there are a lot of different types of caregivers, it is important that you spell out exactly what you are looking for. You will find none who will work less than a minimum of eight, twelve, or in some cases twenty-four hours a day.

We suggest you interview a few different baby nurses before settling on one. If you don't, the agency will simply make a choice for you. You are looking for someone you think you will feel comfortable with in your home for extended periods. Make sure you do your interviewing at least a month in advance of your due date so you can choose someone you are compatible with. Understand, however, that if you deliver early, you might not be guaranteed to get the person you interviewed.

"DOULAS"

"Doula" is a relatively new term in America for a professional, nurturing "mom" for hire. There are fewer and fewer nuclear families left intact and living in close proximity, therefore, fewer grandmas and moms to help out with the new baby. Doulas attempt to fill that void. They will do whatever the new mother is in need of most that moment. It could be laundry, helping the older kids get to bed, feeding the newborn, or maybe just sitting and talking to the new mom. Some are registered nurses with mothering skills. Some are laypersons with parenting and mothering skills. Some you can hire for a minimum of four hours a day, some have a minimum of about fifteen hours, but you can use those fifteen hours in any configuration you want.

> " We substitute for what 'Mom' would have automatically done years ago in this country if she were still living next door. We mother you. In fact, I won't hire anyone to work as a doula in my organization unless they know how to mother the mother.
> —Alice Gilgoff, President, Mother Nurture "

Pros:

☆ You are not getting any one type of help. They are willing to fill any need to the best of their ability.

☆ They are more "motherly" in their approach.

Cons:

★ They are quite expensive—probably $15 to $20 an hour.

★ They are unlikely to stay twenty-four hours a day to take the middle-of-the-night feedings.

CREATIVE ALTERNATIVES

❚ INTREPID APPROACH
There are creative, less expensive alternatives to doulas and baby nurses for hire. For those parents who don't have the money to spend on professionals, or for those more seasoned parents who are having their second or third child, you *can* find other ways of hiring help.

✔ Hire a student through one of the dozens of colleges in the area whose schedule is compatible with yours and can give you a few hours every day to run errands, clean, and prepare a meal. Every school has a temporary employment office, because a good many students are looking for work. One approach might be tapping into the nursing school employment offices. See The Intrepid Pages of Professional Schools, page 45.

✔ Consider finding an able-bodied grandmother who would love to keep herself busy for a few hours a day. You could place a notice at the local senior citizen center, or at the churches and synagogues in your area.

CHOICES FOR WORKING PARENTS

There are so many working families in this city that the need for child care is great. As a result, there are many child care options to choose from and just as many applicants. No hire will ever be as important to you as this one. Our aim is to explain your options and help you make a careful choice.

⏺ INTREPID APPROACH
Consider the following before choosing a type of care:

- *No one type of care is necessarily better than another.* Whether you choose in-home care or group care, the primary issue you need to worry about is whether your child is getting quality care.
- *What is best for your child?* Is he getting to an age where he would thrive in the company of peers in an environment that has plenty of stimulating activities, materials, and staff members? Or is he so young that you would prefer he be nurtured one-on-one? Some school-age children like after-school activities; others do better at home.
- *Philosophical choices.* Do you prefer one person taking care of your child in a home environment? Good caregivers can provide a stimulating environment for your child right at home, creating age-appropriate activities and play groups. Or do you prefer group care in which your child is always exposed to other children and is stimulated daily by several caregivers in a constantly active, busy environment?
- *Practical choices.* What are your financial considerations? Day-care centers are usually less expensive than in-home care. However, if you have numerous home-related responsibilities, it might be cost effective to hire an in-home caregiver who will also do housekeeping and errands, pick up the kids from school, etc. Do you have access to good day-care centers right in your own neighborhood or is traveling a good distance every day going to be a hardship for you?

AT HOME CAREGIVERS

Live-in or Live-out: That Is the Question
There are definite pros and cons to hiring a live-in:

Pros:

☐ You get twenty-four-hour coverage with the exception of their designated nights or days off, so you have less worry about finding a baby-sitter for an evening out and you won't experience the continual stress of trying to get to and from work on time. For some women in demanding jobs, this can make all the difference.

☐ Live-ins can be considerably less expensive because you are providing them with room and board.

☐ Live-ins usually have a less active life apart from your family and therefore may be much more willing to go on vacations with you when you go, more flexible about work hours, etc.

Cons:

■ You have very little real privacy, especially in small, New York City apartment spaces. There's no downstairs "family room" or third floor bedroom to escape to.

■ The tendency, when you have a live-in, is to spend more time away from your child simply because it is so convenient to do so. You can stay a little later at work or say yes to another cocktail party invitation so much more easily knowing you have someone there to watch your child.

What Type of Baby-sitter Do You Want?

INTREPID APPROACH
Define your expectations. What is important to you in a baby-sitter? Ask yourself:

Understandably, some parents fall so in love with their baby nurses that they want to hire them as full-time baby-sitters. This can be a mistake. The infants they are so good at nurturing outgrow them when they start becoming active and in need of constant stimulation and exposure to life outside the home. Many baby nurses are not geared toward or interested in becoming energetic educators and companions for growing boys and girls. Make sure the person you hire is, before making that hire.

✴ *Do you want a trained nanny?* Some parents, especially career parents, want a professionally trained and fully educated caregiver who comes with child care degrees and strong opinions. Their salaries will range from $400 to $800 a week depending on the amount of training they have had.

✴ *Do you want someone who has had prior child care experience who is also willing to do housework?* This is most likely not a degreed nanny, but someone who is great with children and is also more than willing to help around the house. In New York, salaries will range from $250 to $400 for a live-out, $225 to $400 for a live-in.

✴ *Do you want an au pair?* An au pair lives with a family as part of the family. For anywhere from $100 to $300 a week, the au pair provides help with light housework and child care. Be aware that because they are young, you will have to supervise them much more than you would a mature, career caregiver. Make sure you spell out exactly what you expect—the hours, time off including holidays, ability to entertain in your home, ability to drive, housework responsibilities, etc. Don't count on them to stay more than a year.

How Do You Find Your Full-time Baby-sitter?

♪ INTREPID APPROACH
Word of mouth is the number one best way to find a baby-sitter. Volume is the key—if you make one or two inquiries, don't expect to get anywhere. Call all the parents you know who have baby-sitters. Ask around at the playground. Get the word out that you are looking. There is nobody who knows more about which baby-sitters are looking for a job and who the best baby-sitters are than other parents and baby-sitters.

Before you hire your baby-sitter, find out exactly what your legal obligations are to her. Whether she is American or foreign born, there are a variety of payroll tax, insurance, and possible immigration issues you need to address to avoid possible fines and penalties. In an off-the-books arrangement, you can run into problems if the caregiver decides to file for Social Security benefits at a later date. If she can prove prior earnings, you could be liable for years of unpaid taxes and interest, plus fees for late payment and late filing. To find out what you need to know, call: Unemployment Insurance—(518) 457-9000; Social Security—(800-772-1213); Workman's Compensation—(718) 802-6954.

♪ INTREPID APPROACH
Look for ads in the paper or put your own ad in the paper. *The Irish Echo, The New York Times,* and *The Village Voice* are the best papers in which to look for a qualified nanny. If you place your own ad, make sure you state clearly what you are looking for so you don't get calls from inappropriate candidates. Then, as calls come in, we recommend you let your answering machine take the messages. It's another way to weed out applicants who don't sound right to you.

♪ INTREPID APPROACH
You can go through agencies that specialize in placing baby-sitters and household help. Reputable agencies are the most luxurious way to go. You tell them exactly what you are looking for, and they conduct the search, check the references,

and send you only those candidates they think fit the bill. The drawback is that you have to pay a commission that is usually equal to one month of your baby-sitter's salary. If within the first month of employment you are not happy with the choice you made, the agency will most likely send you more candidates at no extra charge.

How to Interview Your Candidates for Baby-sitter

❢ INTREPID APPROACH
Screen applicants by telephone. Telephone screening will help you eliminate most unsuitable applicants. Find out immediately if the applicant is interested in the specific duties you have in mind. If she is, here are five basic questions to ask her on the phone:

1. Have you worked with kids before? What ages? For how long?
2. Have you other kinds of work experience?
3. What do you like about working with children?
4. Why did you leave your last job(s)?
5. May I have the names and phone numbers of two references, including your last employer?

❢ INTREPID APPROACH
Check references. Call at least two references. Listen to a per son's tone of voice as well as what is actually said. Does he sound completely positive and forthcoming? You might want to ask him:

1. What were this person's strongest qualities?
2. What were her shortcomings?
3. How dependable and on time was she in general?
4. Why is she no longer working for you?
5. Would you hire her again?

❢ INTREPID APPROACH
Interview applicants in your home. Have a candidate come for an

> Before hiring a caretaker for your child, you must talk to references, and always meet and talk to your candidates in person. Listen very carefully to what you are being asked. If the primary concerns are 'When is my vacation? How many sick days do I get? Do I have to do any cleaning?' that will tell you a lot about the person. But an interview doesn't always paint the correct picture, so don't commit to anybody until you have given them a one- to two-week trial run. A good agency will let you do that before requesting their fee.
> —Fran Stewart, Owner, Fran Stewart Agency

hour or two so you can see how she interacts with your child. See how comfortable you feel with her. Talk to her about your child-rearing philosophy—everything from how and when to discipline to what types of daily activities you think should be organized for your child. Get her opinions. Do you sense she has the interest and ability to grow with your child and help him develop? Ask specific questions:

1. Tell me about yourself (training, education, background, interests, green card). Any personal issues that might prevent you from being committed to the job for a year or more?
2. How do you envision your role as a caregiver?
3. Describe your previous child care experience (hours worked, daily responsibilities).
4. What do you see as your strengths and weaknesses?
5. My child is —— years old. What do you think is important to plan in an average day for him? How would you stimulate him and help him develop?
6. How do you feel about structure in a child's life (regular meals, play dates, activities, naps, etc.)?
7. How do you feel about discipline and handling upsets? If my child cries when I leave for work, how would you handle it (or other example)?
8. Do you have any training to handle an emergency? Do you know how and when to use the Heimlich maneuver and CPR?

If you need part-time baby-sitters you can call any one of the baby-sitting agencies in Manhattan but you will have to pay from $7 to $10 an hour for a minimum of four hours. For much less money and no minimum, call any Manhattan college employment office for student baby-sitters (Barnard has a very good baby-sitting service), or if you are a member of The Parents League, you can comb through their lists of teenage baby-sitters who live in your area.

If your children are school age and you really don't need baby-sitting help until three or four in the afternoon, consider bartering for any extra hours of help you need with a college student. If a student is looking for free room and board, perhaps you could offer her/him that in return for baby-sitting duty in the late afternoons and a certain amount of evenings and weekend time.

Setting up a Good Relationship with Your Baby-sitter

INTREPID APPROACH
Have your baby-sitter start a few days before you go back to work. Your child can adjust to her in your presence,

and at the same time you can get her acquainted with your house, the neighborhood, and how to manage your child's routines.

Assess the situation in those first weeks. Does the caregiver:

☞ Respond to your child with affection, warmth, and good humor? Conversely, does your child appear comfortable and happy with her?

☞ Handle your child's upsets in a loving, calm, and supportive manner?

☞ Act in a manner that complements your child-rearing methods?

☞ Enjoy talking with you about your child's development?

☞ Encourage curiosity and confidence by helping your child to learn by exploring and experimenting?

☞ Create the appropriate daily activities and stimulation for the age of your child?

☞ Appear to feel good about herself and the work she is doing?

INTREPID TIP
Here are some tips for maintaining a good relationship:

❦ Mutual respect is critical.

❦ Communicate regularly about how your child is doing and how you expect her to handle certain situations.

❦ If you are concerned about anything, bring it to her attention promptly. Conversely, pay attention to her concerns too.

❦ Don't expect your caregiver to do more in a given day than you could reasonably expect from yourself.

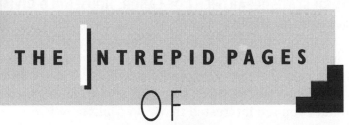

THE INTREPID PAGES
OF
NYC CHILD CARE/HOUSEKEEPING SOURCES

CHILD CARE/HOUSEKEEPER AGENCIES

AVALON NURSES REGISTRY ★ 250 West 57th Street ★ (212) 245-0250

Avalon has been in business for over forty-five years. We find them efficient and reliable, and as long as you explain your needs they will try hard to match you up. Their hours are 8:30 A.M. to 10:00 P.M.

Newborn Nurse: speak to Roz	$125 per twenty-four-hour day (fee included); $12 per hour, eight hours minimum; $3 car fare
Child Care:	$300–$400 per week; fee: five weeks salary; thirty-day trial period
Baby-sitter: speak to Marylou speak to Pat	$9 per hour (4 hours minimum), newborn to six months $7 per hour (4 hours minimum), seven months and up

FRAN STEWART ★ 1220 Lexington Avenue ★ (212) 439-9222

Fran has had her own agency for five years. She is quite responsive to your needs and will go the extra mile to be sure that you are happy. Office hours are 9:00 A.M. to 4:00 P.M. After that leave a message on her machine and she will return your call.

Newborn Nurse:	$120 per twenty-four-hour day (fee included); $12 per hour, 8 hours minimum
Child care:	$250 to $400 per week; fee: one month salary, thirty-day trial period
Baby-sitter:	$10 per hour (4 hours minimum), two months or younger $8 per hour (4 hours minimum), two months or older $1 per extra hour, per child.

NEW YORK STATE DEPARTMENT OF LABOR, HOUSEHOLD DIVISION
★ Mr. Birnbaum ★ (212) 621-0741

They accept job orders for caregivers/housekeepers for private households in Manhattan. Applicants must have been employed for six months during the last year and have a current reference that is checked by the agency. Make sure you get two more references from a candidate you are interested in. Best of all, there is *no fee*. We have tried it and it works.

RESOURCES ★ 109-19 72nd Street, Forest Hills, NY ★ (718) 575-0992

Resources has been in existence since 1987. Manuel owns this agency that deals only with Filipinos. Manuel and Emmelda try very hard to make the right placement.

> *Child Care:* $300 and up per week; fee: three weeks salary, half due on placement, remainder at end of month

DOULAS

IN A FAMILY WAY ★ 124 West 79th Street ★ (212) 877-8112

Christine Kealy, Beverley Small, and Teresa Goetz run a full-service doula company. They offer a one-year package that begins at conception and continues through postpartum. The package includes consultation about the type of delivery you want, wardrobe consultation, fitness programs, discussion groups, a lending library, nutritional advice, and a certain amount of doula hours. For the yearly fee of this package please call, or you can use their doula service—$395 for fifteen hours spread over a two-week period. They are a wonderful source of information for new mothers.

MOTHER NURTURE ★ (718) 631-BABY

Mother Nurture usually works with about six doulas, so call early if you think you might want to go this way. There is a $25 registration fee that includes interviewing the doula in your home. Doulas make around $15 per hour.

NANNIES

BEACON HILL NANNIES ★ Boston, Massachusetts ★ (617) 227-5592

Beacon Hill can provide au pairs eighteen and over, and nannies twenty-one and over. All are American.

Au Pairs: Require their own room, and medical coverage. They will work about a forty-five-hour work week. Their duties include child care and light housekeeping, "not the family housekeeper." Approximately $275 to $300 per week. The fee is $1,700, plus $125 for a criminal record check, with up to two replacements during the year.

Nannies: College-educated with Early Childhood or Child Development courses. They receive about $300 to $500 per week. Placement fee is $2,600 plus $275 application fee, which includes a videotaped interview of all candidates. Up to two replacements during the year. They also have a payroll system where you pay the agency and then they pay the nanny every two weeks.

KNIGHTSBRIDGE NANNY ★ London, England ★ 011-44-71-584-9323
Call Christine who will be able to walk you through the British version of nannying. This agency prides itself "on placing the right girl in the right job." They have nannies or governesses available for hire. Live-in nannies with no training begin at $200 per week. Trained nannies who hold NNEB degrees (two-year child care program) begin at $375 per week. Governesses receive about $600 per week.

The fee is 20 percent of the annual salary. Refund is given up to the first ten weeks. However, it is decreased by 10 percent each week. You or someone you know in England must interview the girls in person and fill out an application.

MORAINE PARK TECHNICAL COLLEGE ★ (414) 922-8611, Ext. 324
Speak to Donna Dixon who heads up the program. They offer a very serious two-year program that encompasses all areas of child care. The graduates see themselves as professionals in the field of child care. There is *no placement fee* because it is a community college. The placement office does an excellent job in working with their graduates to be sure that they not only have a job but one that is appropriate for them. Their graduates usually get paid between $250 to $550 per week.

NATIONAL ACADEMY OF NANNIES ★ (800) 222-NANI
Call Martine Bailey in the placement office. She will guide you through the process of choosing the right nanny for your family. The academy offers a one-year training program where students live with a sponsor family and go to school at night. They are all U.S. citizens and the average age is twenty-two. The courses they take include nutrition, safety, and child care. One advantage of hiring a nanny from the academy is that they have already lived with a family and therefore they know what to expect. You are expected to cover them for major medical, workman's compensation, two weeks paid vacation, six paid sick days, and five to six holidays. Most nannies begin at $300 per week. The placement fee is $1,200.

SULLIVAN COUNTY COMMUNITY COLLEGE ★ (914) 434-5750

Call Mary Wilson who is the chairperson for Early Childhood Nursery Education. They just began to offer a one-year certificate or a two-year associate degree in their child care nanny program. Their courses are comprehensive and cover all areas of child care and child rearing. Their first class will graduate in June 1993. Because this is a community college, there is *no fee for placement*. Both men and women attend this program. Job fee is negotiated between you and the nanny.

AU PAIRS

AU PAIRS ONLY ★ (212) 725-7444 ★ Contact: Judy and Crystal

This company has been in business for five years. They arrange for men and women from the Midwest and West Coast ages eighteen to twenty-five to be au pairs. They make a one-year commitment. They must have their own room and TV, and a plane ticket home. Average work schedule is eight hours per day, five days a week. Their duties include child care and light housekeeping. Their salary is approximately $175 per week. There is a $50 application fee; $950 fee payable when the au pair arrives, with a two-month guarantee.

AU PAIR IN AMERICA ★ (203) 869-9090 ★ Contact: Lauren Kratovil

The American Institute for Foreign Study Scholarship foundation developed this program to promote international exchange between European youth and American families: "Au pairs are welcomed as full-fledged family members." Au pairs are between the ages of eighteen and twenty-five. They make a one-year commitment. They require private room and board. They work no more than forty-five hours per week spread over five and a half days, and duties include child care and very light housekeeping. The salary is $100 per week pocket money (fifty-one weeks). There is a $200 application fee; $3,250 program fee payable one month before arrival and transportation to the host community. In addition, "The host family includes the au pair on family outings and some special events and vacations and helps the au pair enroll in educational and/or cultural enrichment courses that are offered by the local adult community education program. The host family is responsible for up to $300 in tuition fees per year."

GROUP CARE

More middle class families should look at group care as a practical and philosophical choice, not just a budgetary one. It is shortsighted to think group care is just for people who can't afford to do anything else. There are excellent day-care programs available to parents in

New York City, right in your own community, and they are utilized by families just like you. Many choose group care because it fits their child-rearing philosophy as well as their schedule. And yes, it does happen to be less expensive than in-home care.

Finding Quality Care

The critical objective is to find quality care, and there are organizations in New York dedicated to the task of helping you do just that. If you are considering day care for your child, the first thing to do is call them.

★ Parents take note: The organizations below will give you referrals, *not* recommendations. They will give you comprehensive guidelines for ferreting out a quality program, but it is up to you to assess a program and decide which type of care works best for you and your family.

★ In addition, be assured that the standards for licensing are high in New York City, and are based on "minimum standards" set by the New York City Health Code. The New York City Department of Health, Bureau of Day Care, regulates the care of children up to six years of age in group and family centers in order to protect their health, safety, and well-being. Parents may request pamphlets on precisely what those standards are through their office. They are comprehensive and easy to read.

CHILD CARE INC. ★ (212) 929-4999

This is a not-for-profit membership organization that not only helps parents find quality, affordable child care, but provides training and support services to those who work with young children, and serves as an information clearinghouse on important child care issues. Trained counselors will help you find the right type of child care program from over 4,500 licensed programs including infant/toddler centers, family day-care networks, Head Start centers, early childhood programs, after-school centers, and summer day camps.

DAY CARE COUNCIL OF NY, INC. ★ (212) 398-0380

Functions much the way Child Care Inc. does. They too will help you review your options for care and provide you with guidelines for choosing a quality program. There are five knowledgeable counselors there to whom you can talk. If your particular issue does not have an easy answer, the counselors will put their heads together with the director of the program to come up with the appropriate solution for your needs.

THE BUREAU OF DAY CARE, THE NEW YORK CITY DEPARTMENT OF HEALTH
★ (212) 334-7813

This is the licensing agency for child care services (public and private) operating within New York City. It also offers consultation, education, information, and technical assistance to individual groups, organizations, and networks involved in child care. They have an intimate knowledge about each center because they have to monitor them regularly to determine their eligibility for retaining their licenses and certificates. The Intrepid New Yorker encountered two high-level staff members there who made us feel extremely secure about the professionals behind the day-care licensing system. They really know their stuff. Contact Virginia Lee, Training Coordinator, Bureau of Day Care; or Harriet Yarmolinsky, Coordinator, Family Day Care.

> The Agency for Child Development (ACD) administers all publicly funded day care in New York City. For parents who need financial assistance for day care, the information and referral unit of ACD can give you information about your eligibility for publicly funded day care. Call (212) FOR-KIDS.

Gwen Wellington ★ Bureau of Day Care Borough Manager for Manhattan ★ (212) 280-9273

Here is another person you should know about. The Bureau of Day Care has "hands-on" field managers in each borough. They can provide you with intimate knowledge of the day-care facilities in your borough.

Family Day Care

Family day care is the oldest form of day care in this country. Your child will spend the day with a small group of children in the home of a provider who lives in your community. Family day-care homes must meet certification regulations of the New York City Health Code. No family day-care service in New York City can provide care to more than two children under two years of age or to more than six children all together. Some may have an assistant. Many parents of infants and very young children prefer this environment for their child because it provides daily stimulation and socialization with other children, while at the same time remaining small, nurturing, and homey.

INTREPID TIP
There are both pluses and minuses to family care. You really have to examine it from the perspective of your own particular needs and wants. What is good for one parent isn't necessarily good for another.

Pros:

✔ There is one caregiver who will look after your child every day.

✔ A family care provider can be flexible about the hours and days of operation to allow for varying schedules of the parents, as well as the schedules and daily activities of the kids.

✔ Your child is in a stimulating, active, but homey atmosphere that includes socializing with other children of varying ages.

✔ Parents with similar backgrounds and needs can develop a support system for each other.

✔ Family day care can be less expensive because overhead costs are low. The cost in New York City averages about $150 a week.

Parents take note: The day-care system is in the process of being updated. Specifically, the system for certifying family day care will change in 1992. As of this writing, family centers will only have to register in order to put up a shingle. Check with the New York State Department of Social Services Metropolitan Regional Office at (212) 804-1157 to find out how these centers will be registered and monitored for quality.

Cons:

♦ Family care providers usually have less training in child development than day-care center staff members.

♦ There may not be the variety of activities and materials or as much structured learning as is found in more formal programs. You have to make sure that there are interesting and stimulating things for your child to do.

♦ The caregiver has to focus on up to six children, not just yours.

INTREPID TIP

There are organizations called Family Day-Care Networks that are located in many different neighborhoods in New York City. Their role is to be the local link to family day-care centers in a particular community. They help supervise and monitor the centers, and they are happy to assist parents in finding programs in that neighborhood. If there is no network covering your neighborhood, the organizations we've just mentioned will help you.

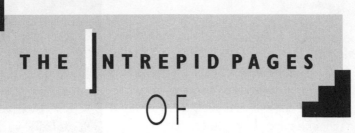

THE INTREPID PAGES

OF INDEPENDENT FAMILY DAY-CARE NETWORKS

BOROUGH OF MANHATTAN COMMUNITY COLLEGE
199 Chambers Street
New York, NY 10007
(212) 618-1123
Arline Garcia, Coordinator

FAMILY RESOURCE CENTER FAMILY DAY CARE NETWORK
137 East 2nd Street
New York, NY 10009
(212) 677-6602
Olga Villa, Contact

HACER CHILD CARE NETWORK
611 West 177th Street
New York, NY 10033
(212) 927-2800
Marie Sexerin, Coordinator

LIVING HOPE FAMILY DAY CARE
161 East 104th Street
New York, NY 10029
(212) 427-2431
Beatrice Oritz, Contact

Early Childhood Programs/Group-Care Centers
Any center or school caring for seven or more children under the age of six must have a license issued by the New York City Department of Health. That license is renewed every one or two years and must be prominently displayed. They must comply with specific requirements for facilities, health, safety, staffing, and education programs. Parents who prefer this environment for their kids like the fact that

there are qualified educators, daily enriching activities for their children, and a more schoollike atmosphere. For parents trying to choose the right day-care facility for their needs, they should consider the following:

1. The high end for a day-care facility for a nine-hour day, five days a week is about $250 a week.
2. Day-care facilities in New York City average about fifty-five kids in each. But they can have as few as eight kids or as many as three hundred. Every center must be run by an educational director. There must be a certified teacher for each age group of children. There are regulated ratios of teacher to child. For example, for two months to twelve months the ratio is four to one with a maximum group size of eight. For groups twelve months to two years and two years to three years, the ratio is five to one with a maximum group size of ten.
3. Centers can be called day care, nursery, child care, preschool, or prekindergarten. Child care is often thought of as "custodial" and nursery school as "educational." Not so. Many schools have "extended" hours so that your child can be cared for after school is over, and child care centers have educational programs. The main difference is sponsorship—they might be private, nonprofit, for-profit chains, schools, or religious institutions.
4. Program hours range from two hours to all day. If you are a working parent, you might want an all-day day-care center for your child. You might find ones that operate from 6:00 A.M. to 6:00 P.M., 7:00 A.M. to 7:00 P.M., 8:00 A.M. to 6:00 P.M., etc. Or you may just want to leave your child for a few hours.

Pros:

✔ In a quality center you are placing your child in a more formal program that helps develop your child in many stimulating ways.
✔ He's being cared for and taught by a variety of teachers who have been trained in early childhood development.
✔ He's learning socialization skills by sharing his day with many other children.

Cons:

♦ Your child will not receive the same, focused attention that he would if he were at home with a baby-sitter or in a smaller, family-care setting.

> There are many different child care options for parents. One option is not necessarily better than another and every option has its benefits. Most importantly, parents need to feel secure and comfortable with their choice. And their choice must meet their family's emotional, financial, and logistical needs. You must not let yourself feel threatened or insecure about another parent who says, 'I would only want my child to ...'
>
> —Fretta Reitzes, Director, Parenting Center at 92nd Street Y

- You as a parent have to establish relationships with more than one caregiver in order to stay on top of your child's well-being and development.
- There is less flexibility in the hours, structure, and the program designed by a particular center.

How Do You Determine Quality Group Care?

INTREPID TIP

There are professionally agreed upon standards and industry-wide statements on what constitutes quality care. The following is a checklist of some of the most important things you should examine in depth when looking for care outside your home:

☐ Make sure they are properly certified or licensed and meet all required standards for New York City and/or New York State.
☐ Find out about the education, experience, and leadership skills of the caregiver(s) and their own ongoing development and learning.
☐ Look at the type of interaction among the caregivers and the children; it is the single most important determinant of quality.
☐ Know the child care and rearing philosophy of the caregiver or center.
☐ Analyze the program for the following: age-appropriate activities, materials, and equipment; daily structure of meals, naps, excursions, and play; proper stimulation planned for intellectual, emotional, and social development.
☐ Determine how open they are to parent involvement and caregiver-parent interaction and cooperation.
☐ Look at the morale and treatment of the staff.
☐ Examine the amount of space allocated per child, the structure of that space, and the atmosphere inside that space.

INTREPID TIP

There are professionally compiled "checklists" for parents to help them find a quality program. Child Care Inc., The Day Care Council of New York, and The Bureau of Day Care all have prepared checklists for parents with an inexperienced eye to use to help find a quality program. Just call and ask for one. They are free.

The National Association for the Education of Young Children can also help parents zero in on quality care. No group-care center can be certified or licensed without meeting the "minimum standards" required. However, the NAEYC has created a strict accrediting system for "maximum standards" for which day-care programs can volunteer to be evaluated. It is based on years of study and research on what constitutes quality care. Because it is voluntary, if a center has not been accredited, it doesn't mean they aren't good. As a parent you can write for a list of programs that have been accredited in New York State. You can also write for brochures, checklists, and catalogues the NAEYC provides on how to determine quality care that are, again, based on their high, maximum standards. Send a self-addressed, stamped, business-size envelope to:

NAEYC
National Academy of
Early Childhood Programs
1834 Connecticut Avenue, N.W.
Washington, DC 20009

The NAEYC recommends that the adult/child ratio for two-year-olds should be one to four or one to six with no more than twelve children in the group. For three- and four-year-olds, the ratio should be one to eight or one to ten with no more than twenty children in the group. They also recommend that there be thirty-five square feet of indoor play space per child. Parents worry about the effect of leaving young children for long days in group care and the institutionalized feeling of the care. The solution to this problem, the NAEYC says, is dividing spaces into soft and cozy interest centers so children can be alone or in small groups. A good program should feel less like a school and more like a busy family.

If you want their brochures on how to choose a quality program, or one of NAEYC's resource guides relating to your children, you may request a free catalogue of what is available by writing to NAEYC.

GOING TO SCHOOL

The Intrepid New Yorker has found something very interesting going on in New York City. In researching how to access the independent schools and public schools in Manhattan, we found out that many parents wouldn't consider sending their kids to public schools. In fact, they knew little or nothing about New York City public schools, but they made the assumption that public schools in Manhattan are so bad that they would have to move to the suburbs to find good ones. Well, we have found some excellent public schools in this city, and it's high time this myth was debunked so that parents don't cheat themselves out of sending their kids to them, if that's what they choose. We will tell you the basics about what you need to know about private schools first, but we have found that they are pretty much a known entity to parents, they are easy to access, and you can get as much information as you need about them. That is not true of the public schools in this city. So we are going to devote the bulk of this chapter to explaining how the public school system works in New York, how to access it, and what its schools really do offer.

Expensive toddler classes are a new fancy concept that parents have managed to live without for centuries. You can stimulate your child for a lot less by taking advantage of the many cultural institutions for kids in Manhattan. A $50 yearly membership will gain you unlimited access to the West 83rd Street Children's Museum, which has floors of creative activities for kids. Even if you had to take a taxi there regularly, it would still cost you a fraction of the cost of a toddler class.

Nursery schools

The Myths

There are a few myths about nursery schools that a Parents League Forum recently took the time to dispel:

1. Contrary to public opinion, there *are* enough places to include *every* three-year-old who wants to attend a regular nursery school.

2. Contrary to public opinion, three-year-old children *are not penalized* in the admissions process if they have not previously attended a "traditional" toddler school program in which the parents leave their child for two or three hours a day, a couple of days a week. In truth, many children under three aren't even ready for this type of program. And some educators feel that creation of toddler programs in the early seventies was tied to economic need, not scholastic need.

3. Contrary to public opinion, *there are many more good nursery schools* in New York City than the handful that all the parents know about and think they have to try to get their child into. Look to your own neighborhood first. You may be surprised at the quality of programs you find.

> The best-kept secret in New York City is that if you have to, you can get your child into nursery school in May or June for that fall. We've never heard of a child who hasn't gotten into school. Openings occur during this time due to last-minute cancellations. In fact, The Parents League functions also as a clearinghouse for late-coming families.

How to Find a Good Nursery School

❗ INTREPID APPROACH
Talk to friends and neighbors about what schools are in your area. Your church or synagogue may have a good nursery school. If you are a member, The Parents League will gladly help you find a nursery school. Also, the NAEYC can provide you with a list of accredited programs in your area (see page 276).

1. Look at a wide variety of schools so you can feel confident in your final selection.

2. Send for applications to the schools you have picked. This should be done one year prior to enrollment. In fact, you should request applications no later than two weeks after Labor Day, because many nursery schools won't hand out applications after that. At that point you will go in for a consultation and find out the procedure for orientation, interviews, and visits.

Nancy Schulman, Director of the 92nd Street Y Nursery School, gave The Intrepid New Yorker the following sound advice about how to look at a nursery school:

☐ *Trust your instincts about a program.* Is it a place where you and your child feel comfortable? Are the interactions between children and teachers warm, respectful, and attentive?

☐ *Classrooms should be clean, spacious, and well organized.* They should have a wide variety of toys and materials that can be used creatively and constructively. Outdoor space need not be expensive, but should be well supervised with equipment that is durable and safe.

☐ *An early childhood program should have a high adult/child ratio with well-trained teachers.* There should be time for large and small group activities that are both teacher initiated and child initiated.

☐ *Look for a nurturing environment that is creative and child centered.* Routines and activities need to be well organized yet flexible to meet the needs of the individual child.

INDEPENDENT (PRIVATE) SCHOOLS

Many of the independent schools in New York City are very good. They are also very expensive. Kindergarten will run you about $9,000 just for starters. It would be hard to find another city anywhere in the world that has as large a number and as wide a range of private schools as New York does.

INTREPID TIP
The choices of private schools can be overwhelming. You can get additional consultation outside your child's current school from the following services:

EDUCATIONAL RECORDS BUREAU ★ (212) 535-0307
Since 1969, ERB has served as the central testing agency for the Independent Schools Admissions Association of Greater New York. Children test with ERB to gain admission into any private school. For a fee, ERB also offers a consultation service to assist parents in selecting an appropriate school. A staff psychologist can help you identify a suitable school for your child, based on the test results and what type of environment you are looking for.

THE PARENTS LEAGUE ★ (212) 737-7385
If you are a member (surely by now you can see how far your $35 membership goes!), The Parents League will also help you in your search. For $10 The Parents League will sell you the "New York Independent Schools Directory," which is published by The Independent Schools Admissions Association of Greater New York in cooperation with the Parents League.

PUBLIC SCHOOLS OPTION:
THE BEST-KEPT SECRET IN TOWN

The Intrepid New Yorker is here to tell you that you do not have to move out of New York City to find good to excellent public schools for your kids. With kids of our own, we too started out as disbelievers and are now, after a great deal of homework and research, enlightened converts. One of the reasons so many of us have been disbelievers is that public officials and the press understandably dwell on the serious problems that do exist. So you rarely hear the good news. The other reason is that it requires a lot of work on the part of parents to figure out how to access the public school system and get the information and answers they need. But we've done that work for you: The Intrepid New Yorker has spelled it out in the following pages. But first, we want to whet your appetite with the following quote from one proud superintendent talking about his district (Two), who answers the question "Is it possible to choose public school and still feel that we are being good parents?"

"My answer, both as a District Two parent and as the District Two Superintendent is an unequivocal yes! . . . My confidence is founded in the vision and commitment of our principals, who are in the forefront of educational leadership, shaping schools that are centers of vital intellectual activity constructed around interests, talents, and needs of children. It is founded in the knowledge, creativity, and expertise of our teachers whose classrooms and curriculum are as much renowned for their rigor as their compassion, and whose practice is informed by both the most current research on teaching and learning as well as the well-honed wisdom of their experience. It is founded in my knowledge of the extensive enrichment programs made possible by our unique location . . . , which places us in immediate proximity to world-class arts, cultural, and educational institutions so many of which we collaborate with. . . . Finally, my confidence is founded in my knowledge of District Two parents and their involvement in and with their children's schools—this most important partnership has always made a difference. I urge you to visit our schools. I have no doubt that you will be delighted. And I would not be surprised if you conclude your exploration of our schools by asking yourself how you could afford not to send your child to a District Two public school."
—Anthony Alvarado, Superintendent, Community School District Two

☛ **"Choice":** In recent years a new public school philosophy was born, called "Choice." It means:

ஃ In most districts, families are no longer forced to send their child to the zoned school in their neighborhood.

ஃ Families can "shop" for a school and pick the program that best suits their child inside or outside their district.

ஃ Schools have to compete by creating innovative, imaginative teaching methods to attract good students.

ஃ Teachers who elect to be in a certain program want to see it work.

ஃ Parents who work to learn about the better choices they can make are much more actively involved and committed to the ongoing success of a particular school.

☛ **Community cultural "enrichment":** There is irony in the fact that because public schools don't have the money to have the kind of enrichment programs that private schools take for granted, they access some of the best enrichment opportunities of all—through arts, cultural, and educational collaboration with well-known institutions and corporations in and around New York City. As a result, learning centers like The Lincoln Center Institute, The New York University School of Medicine, The American Museum of Natural History, The Massachusetts Institute of Technology, and the Alvin Ailey theater, to name just a few, pair up with public schools to create ongoing rigorous programs for their students. You can find the top lawyers, architects, doctors, scientists, performers, bankers, and artists in New York offering their expertise to public school classrooms.

☛ **Parent involvement:** Because public schools are always in need of assistance, the good public schools have very active parent associations. As a result, they not only contribute to the success of a school, but give life to a strong sense of support between the school and the community around it.

> Parents who can't afford all twelve years of private school tuition, or who don't want their child only learning about life from within the isolated world of privilege, could, if they so choose, combine both. There is no reason why a child couldn't enroll in public school for the beginning years and private school for the later years, or the other way around. If you are uncertain, just call the admissions office of some of the well-known independent schools in New York City and they will tell you that public schools kids do get accepted to their schools.

A dose of real life: The kids and the families in the public school system come from a wide variety of socioeconomic backgrounds so you are exposing your child to life as it exists on many different levels.

Educational Approaches in Public Schools

INTREPID TIP
The good public schools in New York City are not only ambitious but very diverse in educational philosophies and methods. School District Two has provided the following educational guidelines under which different programs can be designed.

Traditional Classroom: Refers to a learning environment in which whole-class instruction is the dominant mode of teaching and learning. All the kids work on the same material at the same time. This is probably the style of education most parents experienced when they went to school.

Informal Classroom: Refers to a learning environment in which children work in small groups or independently in centers of interest. The centers teach all the basic subject areas (reading, math, writing, science, etc.) but with a thematic content.

Option Schools: Refers to what is currently known as "schools of choice" and represents the forefront of the educational reform movement. They are small, teacher-managed schools with a clear guiding vision and specific philosophical, thematic, and curricular commitments. They have names (rather than numbers). Although they are located in regular school buildings, they are autonomous. Staff, parents, and students elect to be at these schools. They are magnet schools with a mandate for an ethnically, socioeconomically, and gender-balanced population. Admission is by application, which can be obtained at the school. Your child may or may not have to take a test depending on the program.

Gifted and Talented Programs: There are gifted and talented programs for homogeneously grouped classes of children who are identified as gifted. Admission is by application, and your child will have to be tested.

How the Public School System Works

Governance: The school districts of New York City are each governed by the nine members of their locally elected school board. The local school board hires the superintendent who is the chief administrator of the district. The superintendent is responsible for the supervision and administration of all elementary and junior high schools within their districts as well as the educational programs and financial obligations of the district.

☞ **Zoning:** Every residence in New York City is zoned for a neighborhood elementary, junior high, and high school. Each district has jurisdiction over the (elementary and junior high) schools within the zone. Students who reside in the zone of a school are automatically entitled to enroll in it.

☞ **Enrollment in a school outside of your zone:** In most districts in Manhattan, parents who are interested in a school outside of the zone in which they reside may apply for a variance to permit their child to attend that school. If, however, you want to send your child to a school in another district altogether, you have to get your own district's and that other district's permission as well. Districts are not inclined to hold a child back from the program of his choice. Understand, though, that a school is obligated to take the children from their own zone and district first, so you aren't guaranteed of getting in.

> " Parents are always telling me that their friends are shocked when they are considering public school for their children. 'How can you send your child to a school that has no money and isn't safe?' My answer to those parents is, 'How can you make such an important decision based on rumor and innuendo, especially when the alternative cost is in excess of $10,000?' You should want the best for your child and unless you look at all your options, and investigate the public schools the same way you investigated your real estate options when you bought your apartment, you are limiting your ability to give your child the best.
> —Jackie Ancess, Independent Counselor, Public Schools "

How to Access Information about Public Schools

⫸ INTREPID APPROACH
Through trial and error and a great deal of research, we have figured out that the following steps are necessary to take if you want to successfully access the public school system and find out everything you as a parent need to know:

☞ **I. The 92nd Street Y public school forums for parents:** Every fall the 92nd Street Y has a series of lectures on the public school option for parents. Those are followed by a public school convention at the Y in which each public school sets up a booth, dispenses literature, and answers questions. It is by far the best way for parents to get an overview of what is offered in all the New York City public schools in Districts Two and Three, which cover most of the Upper West Side, Upper East Side, and Lower West Side of Manhattan. Just call Fretta Reitzes, director of the Parenting Center at (212) 996-1100, to find out the dates for the next public forum.

☛ **2. Go talk to your school district.** Find out what school district you reside in. Make an appointment to go in to your district headquarters, look at their map of the district, and get a list of all schools in it. Make sure you talk to a knowledgeable person who can tell you what each school offers in terms of traditional schooling, magnet, gifted programs, etc.

Some districts are easy to access and have complete brochures on all the schools in that district. Others might have out-of-date or incomplete information or might be harder to get on the phone. Often this is due to budget cuts, some understaffing, and a very busy work load. *Be Persistent.* You will find very qualified and dedicated educators who want to answer your questions thoroughly and want your child to go to their schools.

Don't get turned off when you walk into a particular district's headquarters. You will be stopped by a security guard who will want some I.D. and you will be entering a somewhat dreary, institutionalized setting. That does not stop those professionals inside from creating wonderful programs for kids. It shouldn't stop you.

☛ **What to ask your school district:**

△ What is your philosophy toward education?

△ How often do you apply for grants and where does that money go? How successful are you in getting grants? (This will tell you a lot about how ambitious the district is in terms of trying to get money for excellent educational programs within their schools.)

△ Are there any special school board policies in place in your district that I as a parent should be aware of? (Example: District Three requires a teacher's aide in every kindergarten class.)

△ What community projects is the district involved in? What projects is the district involved in with parents? What projects is the district involved in with corporations?

△ How does the district access the corporate, educational, and cultural institutions in its district?

△ What percentage of kids read or do math at or above grade level? Which schools have the highest reading and math scores?

☛ **3. Talk to independent groups outside the school system.** It is always a good idea to get some independent opinions outside the school system for a differently biased perspective. The following four are very knowledgeable and helpful:

The Public Education Association
39 West 32nd Street
New York, New York 10001
(212) 868-1640
This is one of New York City's most highly respected advocacy groups and the second oldest in the nation. It was set up to promote public education, study it, and make it better, and the bias is toward parent advocacy. It recently launched the Good Schools Exchange to promote innovative change in elementary and secondary schools. The PEA is also set up to answer your questions about schools. The person you want to talk to is Judy Baum, a dedicated parent herself and fifteen-year veteran of the PEA and Director of Information Services.

National Training and Evaluation Center, Inc.
15 West 84th Street
New York, New York 10024
(212) 877-4480
Victor Toledo owns and operates this testing center that administers the tests for admission into public schools. As a tester and consultant to the Board of Education, he has an excellent grasp on public schools in New York City. He offers consultation to parents who want to find the right public school for their child based on the test scores and the type of programs they are interested in.

The Fund for NYC Public Education
96 Morton Street
(212) 645-5110
Was founded to mobilize private sector support for lasting improvements in New York's public schools. Beth Leif is the Executive Director and is the person you want to talk to about your district or any specific school.

Jackie Ancess
"Consulting for public school choices"
(212) 662-0862
Ms. Ancess spent twenty-three years in the public school system

in positions ranging from Founding Director of the Manhattan East School in District Four to being on the Superintendent's staff in Districts Two and Three. She has also been the coordinator between the public and private schools, the public school liaison to the Parents League, and has spoken at many nursery schools about how to find the right public school. She is now pursuing independent avenues, one of which is as a consultant to parents looking for the appropriate public school for their children.

> "
> The City of New York offers a wide variety of school programs for children of many varied abilities. If parents would put in the time and effort, they can find suitable programs for their children. With the considerable savings they've made by not paying for private school, they would be able to offer their children enrichment possibilities outside of school that other children might never get.
> —Victor Toldeo, President, National Training and Evaluation Center, Inc.
> "

☞ **4. Zero in on an educational philosophy.** Find the one that best suits your child and find out which schools provide it. The Intrepid Pages of NYC Public Schools (page 291) show you the variety of teaching methods that exist.

☞ **5. Tour those schools.** Schools have monthly tours for parents. Call and make an appointment to take one. The two most important people you want to talk to are:

- *The Principal:* The principal is the leader of the school, and you want to know exactly what his/her goals are, long-range vision for the school, overall philosophy, and how he/she is carrying them out. If you can't get in to see the principal right away, *keep trying.* They are there to run the school and are extremely busy. Sometimes the best of schools won't treat you as well as you would like. You will eventually get an appointment.
- *The head of the PTA,* or any active parents in the PTA can tell you what they think of the school from their perspective. Their own kids are in the school and they can tell you what they as parents are happy with and are not happy with. The PTA usually helps run the tours. It is a very valuable resource.

How to Evaluate a Public School

INTREPID TIP
Don't be thrown by the fact that your senses will be slightly assaulted when you first walk in the door of any public school. First, you will encounter a somewhat humorless security guard who will demand I.D. This does not feel welcoming. Second, institutional-green walls will envelop you. We tell par-

ents that they have to look past their first visceral response to see what is going on inside. It in no way reflects the atmosphere or learning going on.

The Intrepid New Yorker provides you with a checklist of some basic guidelines that we have culled from the top professionals in the City public school system to help you size up a good public school:

- ☐ Is the school safe? Education does not go on in schools that are not. Trust your instincts. A school is safe if you feel safe.
- ☐ Are there lots of compositions, art, and other exercises displayed on the hallway walls?
- ☐ Observe the basics: How do the teachers put the kids on the bus? Observe the atmosphere during class changes, lunchtime, and dismissal. Watch the learning going on. What do the classrooms feel like?
- ☐ Look at the instructional programs. How do the teachers instruct? What are they doing in the classroom? Are they engaging a class? Are the kids enthusiastic? Are the kids focused on the teacher and what they are supposed to be doing?
- ☐ Look at the children's work. Is there a balance between product and process?
- ☐ Does the program fit your child? A "traditional" school will probably feel quieter and more tranquil. An "open classroom" school will probably feel livelier and noisier. The traditional school shouldn't feel overly regimented and the open classroom school shouldn't feel overly stimulating. For some kids, a high level of activity is too chaotic; (They need structure.) but some kids are self-starters, and will do better in an "open classroom." What suits your child better?
- ☐ Does your child fit into the demographics of the school? The purpose of public schooling is to expose children to other kids who are different from him, but you want to make sure that there are enough kids who are similar to him as well so that he doesn't feel totally separate.
- ☐ Is the principal a "hands-on" leader who is out of the office observing what is going on in the hallways and in the classrooms?
- ☐ Does the principal have a strong vision and philosophy for the school and is what he/she saying actually being carried out in the classroom?
- ☐ What does the school do when a child has a problem or is a problem? Does it use the bureaucratic approach? A psychological approach? A punitive approach?

- [ ] Is the school a community? What does it stand for? What are its values? How does it demonstrate that?
- [ ] How does the school use the community and local institutions to enrich the programs?
- [ ] How active is the PTA? Does it have a good working relationship with the principal? Do you agree with what their priorities are? Is fund-raising a major focus of their activities and if so what does the PTA pay for?
- [ ] Can a parent have a constructive dialogue with a teacher if their child is not learning? You have to have the feeling that the school is on top of your child's education.

THE INTREPID PAGES
OF
NYC PUBLIC SCHOOLS

What follows is information about the six public school districts in Manhattan. We provide you with the names, numbers and positions of all essential people you will need to access in all districts, but we have chosen to offer in-depth descriptions of eight schools that are located in districts Two and Three because they encompass such a vast area of Manhattan. These schools are a representative sampling of different educational approaches, to give you an idea of what you will find when you explore the public school option. We hope this will whet your appetite to continue the search for finding the right school for you and your child.

COMMUNITY SCHOOL DISTRICT ONE ★ 80 Montgomery Street ★ (212) 349-9120
Area covered: Most of the Lower East Side
Community School Board President: Reverend Leo Lawrence
Community Superintendent: Mr. William E. Ubinas
Deputy Superintendent for Administration and Supervision:
Dr. Anthony Cavana
Deputy Superintendent for Curriculum and Instruction:
Ms. Irma Zardoya
Director of Elementary Education: Ms. Celenia Chévere
Director of Parent Programs: Mr. Ray Rivera
Director of Pupil Personnel: Mr. Fidel Robledo

COMMUNITY SCHOOL DISTRICT TWO ★ 330 West 18th Street ★ (212) 337-8700
Area covered: All of Manhattan below 96th Street on the East Side and below 59th Street on the West Side excepting the part of the Lower East Side in District One.
Community School Board President: Ms. Po Ling Ng
Community Superintendent: Mr. Anthony J. Alvarado
Director of Pupil Personnel: Ms. Marjorie Robbins
Variances: Michael Dance
Director of Curriculum and Instruction: Ms. Shelly Cohen
Director of The Option Program: Ms. Ilene Friedman

District Two cuts a huge swath across New York City neighborhoods and reflects an extraordinarily diverse parent and student body who come from all walks of life and financial means. Tony Alvarado, the superintendent, is quite responsive to parents who are seeking the very best for their children.

Beware and take note: Due to the district's size and the problem of being understaffed it is not easy to obtain information. *Do not just walk in*—it is a waste of time. Call Marjorie Robbins or Michael Dance and make an appointment. There is printed information available on the schools; make sure you tell them you want to have it. If you have trouble getting through to them, call Tony Alvarado's office and explain your problem. No matter what, do not take their lack of responsiveness as a sign that they do not want you in their schools—they do. They simply have not figured out a way to effectively handle initial parent inquiries.

Below are descriptions of six District Two schools that take very different approaches to educating your child that we have included to give you a peek at the variety being offered in our public school system.

LILLIE DEVEREUX BLAKE SCHOOL, P.S. 6 ★ 45 East 81st Street ★ (212) 737-9774
Principal: Ms. Carmen Farina
Grades: K–6
Enrollment: 850

- P.S. 6 is known for its gifted and talented program, which is the largest in the district.
- The instructional program is rigorously academic, interdisciplinary, and centered around the study of novels. Science, math, social studies, and writing activities and projects emerge from the particular novels children read.
- The arts are also an integral component of the children's projects; puppetry, murals, and original playwriting are a sampling.
- The writing program is based on a teaching technique called "The Writing Process." Among other teaching tools it challenges children to publish their own books, complete with illustrations.
- P.S. 6 has a science lab, an art history department, an art studio, music classes, second language classes, and physical education.
- P.S. 6 also has a very active and involved parent body.

BAYARD TAYLOR SCHOOL, P.S. 158 ★ 1458 York Avenue ★ between 77th and 78th Streets ★ (212) 744-6562
Interim Acting Principal: Mr. Howard Schechter
Grades: K–6
Enrollment: 600

- P.S. 158 has heterogeneous group classes. The school is committed to a whole-language approach to literacy so that children learn to read through children's literature.
- Writing, math, science, art, music, and drama are woven into the units of study as students explore the historical time and context of the novel and its author.
- A collaboration with the Teachers College Writing Project has supported P.S. 158's teachers in their development as whole-language teachers.
- A Renzulli Enrichment Program is offered to students who are identified as gifted.
- The special features of P.S. 158 include: a hands-on science laboratory, music classes, a well-equipped art studio, computers, and French classes. Each year the P.S. 158 French language students travel to France to visit their sister class and experience French life and culture.
- It has a very supportive parents' association.

ROBERT LOUIS STEVENSON SCHOOL, P.S. 183 ★ 419 East 66th Street ★ (212) 734-7719
Principal: Ms. Tanya Kaufman
Grades: K–6
Enrollment: 400

- P.S. 183 is a small and intimate school by choice.
- This school offers a child-centered approach to teaching in which creative learning activities build on children's interests, talents, and abilities.
- Reading and writing skills evolve out of a need and desire to communicate ideas using quality children's literature; this approach is at the core of all curriculum studies.
- P.S. 183 is one of ten schools in New York City to be selected for the Bank Street College Math Leadership Program. Recently the school received a Christa McAuliffe Fellowship to implement innovative programs.

MIDTOWN WEST SCHOOL ★ 328 West 48th Street ★ (212) 247-0208
Director: Ms. Saudhi Vargas
Grades: K–3. School will add a grade each year until it reaches 6th grade.
Current Enrollment: 150

- The Midtown West School is a District Two collaboration with the Bank Street College of Education.
- Children are encouraged to grow at their own rate and are taught how to interact with the environment and people through block building, dramatic play, science, mathematics, literacy, music, movement, and the creative arts —all of which are designed to help children make sense of their world.
- Midtown West is one of three schools in the nation to be awarded a three-year grant for a project called Excellent Beginnings. The grant provides for the development of a "Learning for Life" Center for teachers and parents, classroom interns, and the community.
- For parents and children who request it, Midtown West offers parents the option of a flexible day beginning at 8 A.M. and ending at 5:30 P.M. Fees for the extended day option are determined on a sliding scale.

THE MANHATTAN NEW SCHOOL ★ 311 East 82nd Street ★ (212) 734-7127
Director: Ms. Shelley Harwayne
Grades: K–3. School will add one grade each year until it reaches 6th grade.
Current Enrollment: 125

- The Manhattan New School is a collaboration between District Two and the Teachers College Writing Project. All of the Manhattan New School's staff have both studied and taught at Teachers College and are master teachers in the whole-language/process approach.
- The Manhattan New School has been established as a national demonstration site for the whole-language/process approach to teaching.
- Children work in interage groupings in classrooms.
- Parents take an active role in the life of the school.

THE INDEPENDENCE SCHOOL, P.S. 234 ★ 292 Greenwich Street ★ corner of Chambers Street ★ (212) 233-6034
Interim Acting Principal: Ms. Anna Switzer
Grades: K–6
Enrollment: 350

- Education at the Independence School is as progressive and imaginative as the design of its building, which has won awards and recognition for its architecture.
- In each classroom, you will find students of mixed ages working in centers of interest on projects that emerge from themes developed by them and their teachers.
- Students remain with their teachers for two years so that teachers can develop children's potential in depth and so that children can develop their leadership skills within a cooperative, collaborative, noncompetitive environ-

ment. All members of the school community call each other by their first names.

- P.S. 234 has an art studio, a music program, a hands-on science lab program, computers in every classroom in addition to a computer lab, a modern gymnasium, and a well-stocked library, which is the centerpiece of its whole-language, literature-based reading program.
- The school is strongly supported by its parents association and is actively involved in the community.

COMMUNITY SCHOOL DISTRICT THREE ★ 300 West 96th Street ★ (212) 678-2800
Area covered: West Side from 59th Street to 122nd Street

Community School Board President: Ms. Lillian Castro
Community Superintendent: Mr. Anton Klein
Deputy Superintendent: Mr. James Mazza
Director of Alternative Schools: Mr. John Elwell
Director of Curriculum and Instruction: Mrs. Pat Romandetto
Director of Parent Involvement Program: Ms. Caroline Onley

This district's theme "in pursuit of excellence" is indicative of its ongoing commitment to quality education and improved academic achievement. District Three encourages parents to choose a school that is appropriate for both parent and child on the elementary and junior high school levels. They have many magnet schools as well as gifted and talented programs.

Walk right in or call and make an appointment. You will find the district office to be quite organized and accommodating. Pat Romandetto is the person you want to talk to. She has a hands-on knowledge of all the schools in District Three and is good at assessing what your particular needs might be. If you are very interested in the alternative schools in District Three, you should make an appointment with John Elwell. In any case, they are equipped with brochures explaining all their schools including their magnet and gifted programs.

Below are two more examples of interesting, out-of-the-ordinary public schools that can be found in District Three and elsewhere in New York.

THE STRAUS MAGNET SCHOOL OF SCIENCE, P.S. 199 ★ 270 West 70th Street ★ (212) 678-2833
Principal: Mr. Richard Boccadoro
Grades: K–5
Enrollment: 467

- This school stresses learning about the world through inquiry and hands-on experiences. Science, mathematics, and technology themes are integrated with all other subject areas. Upper and lower grades are separated into "small cooperative neighborhoods." Each classroom is the focus of an active learning environment in which the teacher is encouraged to emphasize his or her own unique talents and strengths.

- The Straus School has enrichment partnerships with the Children's Museum of Manhattan, Goddard Riverside Community Center Environmental Program, Learning through an Expanded Arts Program (L.E.A.P.), The American Museum of Natural History, The Metropolitan Museum of Art, and Lincoln Center.

PUBLIC SCHOOL 87 ★ 160 West 78th Street ★ (212) 678-2826
Principal: Ms. Jane Hand
Grades: K–5
Enrollment: 1,100

- P.S. 87 has been compared to a "Mini U.N." A variety of teaching strategies range from informal classrooms to more traditionally structured learning environments.
- P.S. 87 is a training site for city and district mentor programs and seven metropolitan colleges. The active involvement and spirit of the Parents Association demonstrates to all that P.S. 87 is a community of adults working together on behalf of its children.
- Gifted children are stimulated by outside city projects and through programs in science, math, and the arts.
- Enrichment programs include partnership with: The Children's Museum, The Metropolitan Opera Guild, Feld Ballet, and Museum of Natural History.

COMMUNITY SCHOOL DISTRICT FOUR ★ 319 East 117th Street ★ (212) 860-5858
Area covered: East 96th Street to East 128th Street
Community School Board: Dr. Mee Ling Eng
Community Superintendent: Mr. Marcelino Rodriguez
Deputy Superintendent: Ms. Shirley Walker
Deputy Superintendent: Ms. Juana Dianis
Director of Alternate Schools: Mrs. John Falco

COMMUNITY SCHOOL DISTRICT FIVE ★ 433 West 123rd Street ★ (212) 769-7500
Area covered: Most of central Harlem up to 151st Street and Adam Clayton Powell Blvd.
Community School Board President: Ms. Wynola Glenn
Community Superintendent: Dr. Bertrand Brown
Deputy Superintendent: Mr. Samuel Williams
Deputy Superintendent: Ms. Constance Wingate
Director of Curriculum and Instruction: Dr. Sheldon Shuck
Parent Coordinator: Ms. Narcissia Robinson

COMMUNITY SCHOOL DISTRICT SIX ★ 665 West 182nd Street ★ (212) 927-7777
Area covered: From Convent Avenue and 131st Street to 212th Street and Broadway
Community School Board President: Mr. Robert Jackson
Superintendent: Mr. Anthony Arnato
Executive Assistant to Superintendent: Ms. Helen Santiago
Deputy Superintendent: Mr. Leonard Clark
Deputy Superintendent: Dr. Martin Miller
Pupil Personnel Services: Mr. Roy Ferendez
Note: District Six is heavily zoned due to the dense population.

E·I·G·H·T
BEING SAFE AND SECURE IN YOUR NEIGHBORHOOD

C rime in New York is a serious problem that is not going to go away any time soon. It is one of the reasons some New Yorkers are leaving town. They feel helpless and see the crime problem as hopeless. What many New Yorkers don't know, unfortunately, is how effective they could be in reducing crime in their own neighborhoods. It requires considerable citizen effort, but the results are well documented and dramatic. It's time to change our status from crime victims to crime activists.

CITIZEN ACTION DOES WORK!

The best way to explain what can be done is by recounting a true story about one small Manhattan community.

In the summer of 1990, a young advertising executive was murdered while making a phone call from a phone booth right outside his doorman building in the West Village of Manhattan. It shocked the neighborhood to its core. This particular area of the West Village had been having some problems with crack dealers, johns, and prostitutes, but until this frightening event, the community's anticrime efforts had been unfocused and inconsistent. This tragedy changed all that.

Existing block associations got together to agree on what had to be done to take their streets back. They went to their community board leaders and local precinct heads to get help and guidance. They discussed and then implemented the following:

★ *Block patrols:* These were set up to let civilians from each block association take turns patrolling the streets at night, acting as the "eyes and ears" for the

INTREPID PHILOSOPHY

ATTITUDE We can make our homes and communities much safer, but it is up to the citizens of New York to decide they are going to make it happen, building by building, block by block.

APPROACH Hiding behind all ten locks on your front door is not going to solve the crime problem. It's time to come up with a plan to make our streets and community safe, so safe that we won't need all those locks in the first place. And you don't have to do it alone. Your community board and local police precinct will put as much muscle behind the plan as is needed.

KNOWLEDGE You need to know that New York City cannot maintain the quality of living you want without your assistance. The City does work hard, but with increasingly limited resources. Your local police precinct will be the first to admit that they really need community action to make a serious dent in crime in this city.

ECONOMICS Becoming active in your community will cost you little. Not becoming active might cost you your community.

local precinct patrol force. When possible, a foot patrol officer accompanies them.

★ *Patrol vans:* The block associations organized their neighbors to contribute a small monthly donation to pay for private security vans to patrol each block association's area from 8:00 P.M. to 6:00 A.M.

★ *More police officers:* They petitioned for and got police officers added to their local precinct.

Within a matter of a few months, all of these safeguards were in place. In fact, five or six new block associations sprung up around old ones because formerly nonparticipating neighborhoods saw how quickly and successfully others were performing. In no time there was an impressive number of security vans and civilian block patrols on duty every night covering a very large area of the West Village. One block association even took it upon themselves to set up police blockades, which they took turns manning in the evening hours to keep the crack dealers and johns off their streets. The City responded to this extraordinary combined police effort and citizen action by giving this community more officers.

Here is what one officer from the Sixth Precinct had to say about this civilian effort:

Block ASSOCIATIONS: THE KEY TO NEIGHBORHOOD IMPROVEMENT

INTREPID TIP
Block and neighborhood associations have the collective muscle to make your community much safer:

✳ It is an official and organized forum in which neighborhood residents can address the problems in their area on a consistent and ongoing basis.

✳ As a collective and credible voice it can be a powerful tool for getting issues resolved when taking them before local politicians, community boards, and precincts.

✳ Block associations have accomplished everything from getting trees planted to closing crack houses. Use yours to plan and implement the right strategy with your local police precinct for making your neighborhood a safer place to live.

> I've been in the police force for ten years and I have never seen anything like it. This precinct has spent years trying to clean up certain areas of the Village. We would arrest three hundred to four hundred crack dealers, johns, and prostitutes every month, and the next month they'd be back on the same streets. Since the citizens got involved, everything has changed. It can't be done without the community; and when cops see something being done, they work harder themselves—it gives them incentive. I'll give you just one example: In the months since the community started getting involved, robberies decreased by fifty percent.
> —Mike Singer, Community Affairs Officer, Sixth Precinct

HOW TO SET UP A BLOCK ASSOCIATION

The first step toward setting up an effective block association is to call the nonprofit Citizens Committee for New York City (founded by Jacob Javits) at (212) 684-6767. It supports volunteer grass-roots action to improve the quality of life in City neighborhoods. It offers small grants, training publications, and technical assistance to more than 10,000 neighborhood, tenant, and youth associations in the five boroughs. They will help you form new groups and strengthen existing ones. Right off the bat they will send you a free kit called *Tools and Tactics for Neighborhood Organizing* published by their Neighborhood Resource Department. The following is a list of mostly free publications they distribute.

Neighborhood Self-Help Publications

from the Citizens Committee for New York City, Inc.
3 West 29th Street, New York, NY 10001-4501 / (212)684-6767

	Price for NYC Youth and Volunteer Neighborhood Groups	Price for Other (individuals, staffed agencies, government, out-of-town)
Basic Organizing and Fundraising		
Starting a Merchants Association (1980, 26 pp.)	free	$ 2.00 (reduced)
Excerpts from Funding Neighborhood Programs (1983, 15 pp., photocopy only)	$1.00	$ 2.00
Tools and Tactics for Neighborhood Organizing (revised, 1991, 60 pp. organizing kit—forthcoming)	free	$ 5.00
Lend a Hand and Have a Block Party (revised, 1986, 16 pp.)	free	$ 2.50
Lend a Hand in Your Community Board (revised, 1987, 16 pp.)	free	$ 2.50
Lend a Hand to Improve Your Schools (1980, 20 pp., photocopy only)	free	$ 2.50
Starting a Neighborhood Organization (tip sheet) (1990)	free	$ .50
Citizens Report (2-4 issues a year). The newsletter of the Citizens Committee for New York City offering how-to neighborhood guides, stories on New York issues, resources, and Citizens Committee news.	free	$10.00 a year— $ 8.00 for individuals and public libraries
Fighting Drugs and Crime		
Strategies for Drug-Free Communities	free	$ .50
Dealing with Dealing in Your Building—How a Tenant Association Can Fight Drug Problems (1988)	free	$ .50
The Potential for Violence in Anti-Crime Organizing—Ten Tips from the Alliance for a Drug-Free City (also available in Spanish) (1989)	free	$ .50
How to Mobilize to Report Street Crime and Drug Activity (1989)	free	$ .50
Planning a Community Anti-Drug Conference (1990)	free	$ .50
Getting Justice from the Criminal Justice System (1990)	free	$ .50
Starting and Running an Anti-Drug Patrol in Your Community (1990)	free	$ .50
High Risk Youth—Destroying the Myths (1990)	free	$ .50
How to Start a Youth-Run Peer Counseling Project (1990)	free	$ .50
Preventing Drug Abuse in Your Community (1991)	free	$ .50
Neighborhoods United (2-4 issues a year). The newsletter of the Alliance for a Drug-Free City (formerly the Neighborhood Crime Prevention Network), a New York City coalition of community groups engaged in fighting drugs.	free	$ 8.00 a year
Grassroots Anti-Poverty Projects		
Starting a Volunteer Visitor Project (1988)	free	$ .50
Helping the Hungry and Homeless in Your Neighborhood (1988)	free	$ .50
How to Start a Sister Block Project (1988)	free	$ .50
Starting a Homework Help Program (1988)	free	$ .50
Starting a Group for Concerned Fathers (1988)	free	$ .50
Working with Front-Line Professionals to Help People in Crisis (1988)	free	$ .50
Empowering Youth—The Key to Successful Youth Service Projects (1988)	free	$ .50
Improving Intergroup Relations (1988)	free	$ .50
Holding a Jobs Fair (1989)	free	$ .50
Organizing a Jobs Bank (1989)	free	$ .50

For setting up your association the Citizens Committee for New York City recommends the following procedures:

☞ **1. Define the issues.** Some neighborhood groups are organized to bring residents together to resolve a multitude of concerns. Some are formed to deal with a specific crisis. Define the issues and get the history on each issue by talking to your local community board, police precinct if relevant, and community newspapers.

☞ **2. Research the community.** What size area do you want to organize? One building, one block? Several blocks? Who are the likeliest people to join the organization? What groups are going to be the most concerned about the issues? Home owners? Parents? Tenants? Find out what resources your community has—friendly organizations, active local merchants and corporations, city council representative, community board—and solicit their involvement.

☞ **3. Build a core group.** Recruit a handful of people—three or four are enough—to help launch the organization. Find candidates by talking to neighbors and finding out who are the citizens most committed to improving the neighborhood. Leaders of churches, community centers, etc. should know some interested people. The core group will be the temporary steering committee until the general membership meeting is held. The core group should hold an organizing drive, the most common being a block party or a block "clean-up," to get the organization off the ground. Make sure you alert your community board and local precinct that you plan to hold one, and invite them to attend.

☞ **4. Hold the first of regularly scheduled general meetings.** Print flyers about when and where the first general meeting is being held and place them in lobbies, grocery stores, church and school bulletin boards. At the meeting, clarify the issues and goals and the first steps the group will take. A good "agenda" should include:

☞ Decide who's on the steering committee and what their responsibilities are going to be.
☞ Allow everyone who attends the meeting to have a chance to voice opinions and make suggestions.
☞ Prioritize the issues and tasks to be done and decide who will handle what. If the issues are complicated, ask someone to head a committee on each issue.

☞ **5. Agree on a name for the organization.** Having a name is good for morale and also gets uninvolved neighbors familiar with and interested in your group.

☞ **6. Hold regular monthly meetings.** Make sure you have an agenda for every meeting with clear goals and job assignments. Minutes should be taken and issues voted on.

☛ **7. Publish a newsletter.** It's a great way to spread the word about your organization's activities and get other people involved.

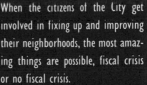

HOW TO KEEP YOUR BLOCK ASSOCIATION ALIVE

Some organizations stay active, some die on the vine. Here are ways to keep yours alive:

- ✔ Go after only those people who have a real investment in the community.
- ✔ Make sure you always have a monthly meeting with a clear agenda.
- ✔ Have at least one representative go to all the community board and police precinct council meetings that occur regularly to stay abreast of what is happening.
- ✔ Make sure your local community, government, and business leaders get a copy of your newsletter.

PLANNING A STRATEGY TO COMBAT CRIME

It is critical that your block association plan the right strategy to effectively combat the particular crime problem that exists in your neighborhood. No two crime problems are the same. One neighborhood might require a block patrol, another a security patrol officer, another a completely different tactic. Use the following experts to help you create an appropriate plan:

◇ The "Anti-Crime Center" of the Citizens Action Committee for New York: This center offers hands-on assistance in fighting drug-related crime by providing in-depth training and technical assistance to neighborhood associations, and by facilitating joint strategy planning between police and communities.

◇ Your local police precinct. Begin to develop a relationship with your precinct. Here are some people you should get to know better:

☞ **Community Affairs Officer:** There is a community affairs officer in every precinct whose job it is to be the liaison between the police precinct and the citizens in the area. No question or problem is too small for him to discuss with you and help resolve. If your block association's neighborhood has a crime problem, he will gladly attend your meetings. He is there at your service. There is also a precinct council meeting monthly in which the community is invited to voice their concerns to the community affairs officer and commanding officer.

☞ **Community Patrol Officer:** Recently, Police Commissioner Lee P. Brown instituted the old-fashioned idea of the community patrol officer, otherwise known as the "beat cop." Every precinct now operates under this new philosophy, which assigns a foot patrol officer to work with residents to resolve immediate social problems that may lie at the root of crime in a neighborhood. Your community affairs officer can tell you who he/she is.

> The New York City Police Department has adopted Community Policing as its dominant mode of police service, and this office heartily agrees with the philosophy. As a point of fact, there are about ten million people in the City on any given business day, and about thirty-thousand police officers to serve them, every day, every week, every year. It is clearly impossible for the police to do the entire job of keeping the City safe, secure and peaceful without the help of the City's residents, business-people and visitors. The only way these goals will be attained is if we—the Police Department—and the people of the City work together. It is up to the ordinary New Yorker to work with us for everyone's benefit and safety.
> —Deputy Police Commissioner Wilhelmina E. Holiday, Community Affairs, New York City Police Department

☛ **Crime Prevention Officer:** There is a crime prevention officer in every precinct whose job it is to help the community make their streets, buildings, and apartments safer. If you request it, they will look at your streets, your building, even your apartment free of charge, and advise you as to what steps to take to make them secure and safe. Your community affairs officer can also tell you who your crime prevention officer is.

> " You pay taxes in your neighborhood too! Make yourself known to your community leaders and elected officials. Don't ask...**demand** that your rights in your community are met. And don't give up. Citizen action works!
> —Reggie Fitzgerald, veteran community activist "

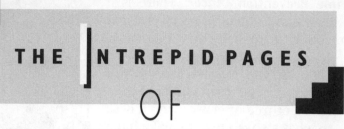

THE INTREPID PAGES
OF
POLICE PRECINCTS AND THEIR COMMUNITY AFFAIRS OFFICERS

PRECINCT 1 ★ 16 Ericsson Place ★ (212) 334-0611
Boundaries—South Ferry to West Houston Street, Broadway to Worth Street
 CAO—Officer Nassella

PRECINCT 5 ★ 19 Elizabeth Street ★ (212) 334-0711
Boundaries—Allen Street to Broadway, East Houston to Brooklyn Bridge
 CAO—Detective Grahame

PRECINCT 6 ★ 233 West 10th Street ★ (212) 741-4811
Boundaries—West Houston to Broadway, South Side of 14th Street to West Side Highway
 CAO—Detective McLaughlin; Officer Singer

PRECINCT 7 ★ 19½ Pitt Street ★ (212) 477-7311
Boundaries—Water Street to Allen Street, East Houston to South Street
 CAO—Officer Torres; Officer Itzkin; Officer Goon

PRECINCT 9 ★ 321 East 5th Street ★ (212) 477-7811
Boundaries—East Houston to East 14th Streets, Broadway to East River
 CAO—Detective Johnson; Officer Tyler

PRECINCT 10 ★ 230 West 20th Street ★ (212) 741-8211
Boundaries—14th Street to 29th Street, Seventh Avenue to Hudson Street; 29th Street to 43rd Street, West of Ninth Avenue to Hudson River
 CAO—Officer Cusicek; Officer Galasso

PRECINCT 13 ★ 230 East 21st Street ★ (212) 477-7411
Boundaries—14th Street to 29th Street, East River to Seventh Avenue
    CAO—Detective Hughes

MIDTOWN SOUTH PRECINCT ★ 357 West 35th Street ★ (212) 239-9811
Boundaries—29th Street to 45th Street, Lexington Avenue to Ninth Avenue
    CAO—Officer Kelley; Officer Hennessey

PRECINCT 17 ★ 167 East 51st Street ★ (212) 826-3211
Boundaries—31st Street to 59th Street, East River to Lexington Avenue
    CAO—Officer Boqucki

MIDTOWN NORTH PRECINCT ★ 306 West 54th Street ★ (212) 767-8400
Boundaries—West of Lexington Avenue to Hudson River, South of 60th Street to 45th Street
    CAO—Officer Burns; Detective Tumelty

PRECINCT 19 ★ 153 East 67th Street ★ (212) 452-0600
Boundaries—59th Street to 96th Street, Fifth Avenue to East River
    CAO—Officer Petrillo

PRECINCT 20 ★ 120 West 82nd Street ★ (212) 580-6411
Boundaries—59th Street to 86th Street, Riverside Park to Central Park
    CAO—Officer Pinachi

CENTRAL PARK PRECINCT ★ 86th Street and Transverse Road ★ (212) 570-4820
Boundaries—Entire Park
    CAO—Officer Sieffert

PRECINCT 23 ★ 164 East 102nd Street ★ (212) 860-6411
Boundaries—96th Street to 115th Street, Fifth Avenue to East River

PRECINCT 24 ★ 151 West 100th Street ★ (212) 678-1811
Boundaries—86th Street to 110th Street, Riverside Park to Central Park West
    CAO—Officer Bonet

PRECINCT 25 ★ 120 East 119th Street ★ (212) 860-6511
Boundaries—Fifth Avenue East to Water Street, 116th Street to 142nd Street
    CAO—Officer Martinez, Officer Patte

PRECINCT 26 ★ 520 West 126th Street ★ (212) 678-1311
Boundaries—110th Street to 133rd Street, Riverside Drive to Central Park West
    CAO—Officer Duke

PRECINCT 28 ★ 2271 Eighth Avenue ★ (212) 678-1611
Boundaries—110th Street to 127th Street, Morningside Avenue to Fifth Avenue
    CAO—Officer Lewis

PRECINCT 30 ★ 451 West 151st Street ★ (212) 690-8811
Boundaries—133rd Street to 155th Street, Riverside Drive to Bradhurst Avenue
    CAO—Officer Mendoza

PRECINCT 32 ★ 250 West 135th Street ★ (212) 690-6311
Boundaries—127th Street to 159th Street, Lenox Avenue to St. Nicholas Avenue
    CAO—Officer Blue

PRECINCT 34 ★ 4295 Broadway ★ (212) 927-9711
Boundaries—155th Street to 220th Street, River to River
    CAO—Officer Delatores

INTREPID TIP

Your neighborhood association can apply for anticrime grants. And there's a real chance you might get them. Grants are given out to those groups that have the best and clearest reason to receive one. So when you apply, make sure you are precise and factual about what the grant would go toward. There are a couple of ways to get grants:

1. The mayor's Stop the Violence Fund is a City grant your association can apply for. You can call the Mayor's Community Assistance Unit at (212) 566-1553 and inquire. Your community board can also tell you the most effective way to apply.

2. You can appeal to any sizeable company doing business in your area for a private grant, such as Texaco, McDonald's, or maybe the parent company of your neighborhood D'Agostino. Many of these companies like the public relations that go along with working with this kind of grass-roots effort. If you choose to go this route, write a clear and factual letter about what your objectives are and precisely why you want the grant. If your block association is applying for the grant, and your association has a newsletter, send your newsletter along with the letter. It legitimizes you even further. It would also be helpful if you could include a letter from your local community board.

CRIME PREVENTION TIPS

The police publish a list of basic safety "dos and don'ts" that you can obtain from your local precinct or by calling The Crime Prevention Division, New York City Police Department in Queens Village, Queens, at (718) 776-6888. There are free brochures on:

✔ Safeguarding men
✔ Safeguarding women
✔ Safety tips for the older person
✔ Crime prevention for children
✔ Safety tips for runners
✔ Safeguarding your auto
✔ Robbery prevention for small businesses and stores
✔ Burglary prevention for your business
✔ Safeguarding your apartment

INTREPID TIPS
Here are recommendations from the New York City Police Department and other security companies on safeguarding your apartment:

Doors

- Check your door and door frame. Do they need to be repaired or replaced?
- All exterior doors should be either metal or solid-core wood (1¾ inches thick).
- Glass or thin wood panels, in or near the door, can be protected by installing polycarbonate glazing and securing with one-way screws.

Locks

- Use a dead-bolt lock with a one-inch throw bolt or a heavy-duty drop-bolt lock.
- Install a highly pick resistant and drill resistant cylinder.
- Protect the cylinder with a guard plate.
- Add a "J" bar to the door frame to prevent crowbarring the lock.
- Any additional locks should be installed eighteen to twenty-four inches above or below the doorknob. Consider children, the elderly, and/or disabled before installing a lock too high.
- Do not use a double-cylinder lock, which is a

> " More robberies occur because of lax security policies in full service buildings where tenants leave keys at the front desk to let maintenance and service people into their apartments than because of break-ins.
> —Mark Lerner, President, Epic Security Corporation "

lock that has a key on both sides. They are prohibited in multiple dwellings and can be deadly if a fire should break out.

Windows

- All accessible windows in an apartment need securing.
- Accessible windows are any within twelve feet of ground level, a building projection, a fire escape, windows near a public hall or route. These should be secured in the open and closed position. In fact, the only absolute security available for windows with easy access is from installation of window gates.
- Skylights should be examined for easy access and secured if necessary.
- Windows below the roof edge may be vulnerable and should be secured using a lock as well as the pinning method. (Note: To secure a window with the pinning method, drill a hole through both sets of window frames where they meet in the closed position. You can now insert a thin nail into the hole to "pin" the windows shut.) Drive a nail into the stationary window frame so that the moveable window will not open more than five inches.

> The best way to secure your fire escape window or any first floor window is with a gate that has been approved by the New York City Board of Standards and Appeals. This gate is commonly known as a "ferry" or "safety" gate, and is operated by a latch and not a padlock or combination lock. The protection afforded by this gate is only as good as the quality of its installation. The screws used for installation of the gate should be long enough so that they anchor the gate to the interior wall stud, or the window frame.
> —New York City Police Department, Crime Prevention Section

- If you have air conditioners, check to see if they are accessible. If so, they may require gates, too.

Alarm Systems

- They are very effective as a deterrent. Epic Security Company says that nine out of ten robbers will head for a home that doesn't have one.
- There are many different types to choose from depending on your needs, so consult a security expert before deciding.
- Most security experts will recommend an alarm that not only rings when there is an intruder, but one that will ring simultaneously at a central command station that in turn will call your home and then the police.
- Security experts don't recommend buying a system off the shelf and trying to install it yourself. You should have it professionally done so that there are no kinks in the system.
- Most commercial operations buy "hard-wired" systems as opposed to wireless systems because they are considered the most reliable.

THE INTREPID PAGES
OF
SECURITY SOURCES

ALARM SECURITY SYSTEMS

All of the companies below give free estimates.

ATLAS ALARM ★ 99 East 34th Street ★ (212) 879-7000

They have the capability to design a system that works for your needs. Systems run anywhere from $600 and up. A central station is signaled when the alarm goes off and then they call the police. There is a monthly fee of $30 associated with this.

SANDS SECURITY ALARM SYSTEMS, INC. ★ 305 West 28th Street ★ (212) 409-9046

The sales representatives here said that unfortunately people come to them to have a system installed after they have been robbed. Depending on the amount of security one needs, a system can cost $600 and up.

WELLS FARGO ★ 53 West 23rd Street ★ (212) 627-2500

Most of their security installations are done on a leasing basis, which they recommend over purchasing because your up-front cost is cut in half. The minimum fee for leasing is $100 a month and there is a $25 per month charge to be hooked up to the central station.

AUTOMOBILE GLASS REPLACERS

Owning a car in New York City gives you a lot of freedom. However, the reality is that a window will probably be broken during a break-in at some point. If that happens, call your insurance agent. Usually you are covered if you repair it through their source. If not, call:

LIBERTY GLASS ★ 546 West 48th Street ★ (212) 265-3052

Open from 8:00 A.M. to 5:00 P.M. Monday through Friday and until noon on Saturday.

MR. GLASS INC. ★ 132 Tenth Avenue (at 18th Street) ★ (212) 989-5550

Open from 8:30 A.M. to 5:00 P.M. Monday through Friday and until 1:00 P.M. on Saturday.

LOCKSMITHS

ABBEY LOCKSMITHS ★ 1558 Second Avenue (at 81st Street) ★ (212) 535-2289
They are available twenty-four hours and service all of Manhattan.
You can make an appointment in advance; we suggest the first appointment of the day. They can work on car locks as well. For emergency calls they accept cash only; during the day they accept checks
and major credit cards.

UNITED LOCK AND SECURITY ★ 2516 Broadway (at 93rd Street) ★ (212) 316-1300
They service all of Manhattan, twenty-four hours a day. In an emergency, the service will dispatch someone immediately, reaching you
within fifteen minutes to one hour. Payment can be cash, checks, or
major credit cards.

VILLAGE LOCKSMITHS ★ 350 Bleecker Street ★ (212) 362-7000
This company runs only a road service business with no storefront.
This is a twenty-four-hour service. They pride themselves on being at
any location within one hour. They can handle car and safe locks.
Cash and major credit cards accepted.

SAFES

Safe store owners say that in today's society, a safe is good insurance.
Many banks are claiming no responsibility for break-ins to their safe
deposit boxes and of course you are a target when you leave a bank
with your valuables.

EMPIRE STATE COMPANY ★ 433 Canal Street (at Varick) ★ (212) 226-2255
A family-owned business operating since 1904. They not only sell new
safes, but are happy to try and repair the old. They have some other
protection devices as well. If possible, they recommend safes that are
bolted to the floor. If you live in a house, they suggest you purchase a
safe that can be hidden in the floor.

REM SECURITY ★ 11 East 20th Street ★ (212) 533-0801
They sell a large amount of safes but do no installations.

SECURITY PATROL COMPANIES

Remember, check with your local precinct to determine what security
patrols you are considering and what measures are legal and appropriate.

EPIC SECURITY ★ 2067 Broadway (71st and 72nd Streets) ★ (212) 580-3434
They have unarmed guards for $9.45 per hour, and radio motor patrol
vehicles at $15.95 per hour. They operate twenty-four hours a day.

Their private city-wide radio system operates within their own fleet of radio motor-patrol vehicles, so they can respond with as many guards as is needed in any situation.

GUARDIAN ANGELS ★ (212) 967-0808

If your neighborhood is experiencing ongoing crime or harassment problems, you should call the Angels and put in a request for a group to come and patrol your territory. There are only 250 Angels in New York City and they must fulfill requests according to priority. In a short period of time, the Angels can make an enormous impact on a neighborhood in distress. However, they cannot do it without the support and involvement of the community.

VGI INC. ★ 420 East 149th Street ★ (212) 665-1515

They have unarmed guards at $12 per hour and armed guards at $16 per hour. They can arrange for vehicles to patrol.

N·I·N·E
LEISURE
NEW YORK
STYLE

f we have accomplished our goal, you now know how to live more efficiently and frugally, and know how to access your community effectively. Presto: You should now have more time and money to spend during your leisure hours. No matter what your passion—sports, pursuing a hobby, volunteering, or simply wanting to be entertained—there is no city that draws more experts in each field as New York does. This chapter will tell you where to find them.

THE INTREPID PAGES
OF
HOBBY CLUBS, SCHOOLS, AND FUN ORGANIZATIONS RUN BY THE PROS

No matter what your passion or hobby, no matter what your level of ability or the amount of time that you have to spend, you can be part of the doing and learning that abounds in New York City, and you can do it in the company of pros.

ACTING

HB STUDIO ★ 120 Bank Street ★ (212) 675-2370

HB offers over 200 different classes to choose from including movement, singing, acting, play writing, speech, and more. They are open seven days a week from 9:30 A.M. to 8:45 P.M. on the weekdays and 10:00 A.M. to 4:00 P.M. on the weekends. The price depends on the particular package that you choose.

NEW YORK FOUNDATION FOR THE ARTS ★ 5 Beekman Street ★ (212) 233-3900

Newsletters, grant information, a job-listing bulletin board, and more can be obtained from this not-for-profit agency that was created to help artists in all disciplines and arts organizations cope in New York.

ADVENTURE

ADVENTURE ON A SHOESTRING ★ 300 West 53rd Street ★ (212) 265-2663

The aim of this organization is to expose its members to the relatively unknown, fascinating people and places that help make New York City the exciting place it is. They arrange everything from walking tours to dining and theater experiences to visits to craft studios. Membership is $40 per year and most events do not exceed a $3 surcharge plus the cost of the event.

SIERRA CLUB ★ 625 Broadway ★ (212) 473-7841

This political action committee has been dedicated to preserving and protecting the environment for one hundred years. The Atlantic Chapter Outing Committee leads hikes, ski trips, backpacking, river touring, bike trips, and City walks every weekend. The cost of these outings is minimal to members. Membership fee is $35 per year and entitles you to the bimonthly magazine and to the national and international outings.

ARCHITECTURE
THE ARCHITECTURAL LEAGUE ★ 457 Madison ★ (212) 753-1722
The membership fee runs $50 per year for those thirty-five and under and $85 for those over thirty-five. You will be invited to more than thirty-five different events throughout the year all relating to architecture issues, problems, and history. You will receive a newsletter, discounts on certain books, and more.

ART
THE ARTS STUDENTS LEAGUE OF NEW YORK ★ 215 West 57th Street
★ (212) 247-4510
They are open seven days a week and offer classes in painting, drawing, sculpture, and graphics. For $115 a month you can take classes five days a week for three and a half hours a day. For $55 a month you can take two classes a week and for $38 a month you can take one evening class a week.

SCULPTOR SUPPLIES ★ 222 East 6th Street ★ (212) 673-3500
They sell sculpting supplies as well as rent fifteen studio spaces in which you can work. The fee per month ranges from $200 to $900.

ASTRONOMY
AMATEUR ASTRONOMERS ASSOCIATION ★ 1010 Park Avenue ★ (212) 535-2922
This organization boasts over four hundred active star-gazing members in the metropolitan area. The basic membership runs $36 per year and entitles you to lecture programs at the Museum of Natural History, twice-monthly evening get-togethers to discuss advanced theories, and of course, actual gazing events.

BILLIARDS
THE BILLIARD CLUB ★ 220 West 19th Street ★ (212) 206-POOL
They have a total of thirty-three pool tables and they can arrange for private lessons. Open seven days a week; the fee ranges from $5 per table per hour and up.

SOCIETY BILLIARDS ★ 10 East 21st Street ★ (212) 529-8600
Here you can play on one of their twenty-five tables seven days a week. The lowest fee is $3 per hour per person.

BIRDWATCHING

NEW YORK AUDUBON SOCIETY ★ 71 West 23rd Street ★ (212) 691-7483

There are always weekend outings to local New York City bird habitats as well as occasional overnight trips to nearby nature centers. You can attend lectures and films throughout the year. Membership fee is $40 and there is a separate fee for the outings.

BRIDGE

BEVERLY BRIDGE CLUB ★ 130 East 57th Street ★ (212) 486-9477

Open daily from 10:30 A.M. to midnight. Admission fee in the evening is $7 and during the day it is $8 (lunch included). They offer classes for all levels of play, including beginners for $35 per class.

BUSINESS AS A PASSION

AMERICAN WOMEN'S ECONOMIC DEVELOPMENT CORPORATION
★ 641 Lexington Avenue ★ (212) 688-1900

AWED was designed to help *only women* who wanted to start their own business or who have their own business. For $65 per year they will send you their monthly calendar of events and for an extra fee they will counsel you on any aspect of your business.

NEW YORK VENTURE GROUP ★ 605 Madison Avenue ★ (212) 832-7300

Founded in 1984, NYVG is a monthly forum created to stimulate interaction among business founders and managers, and representatives of major corporations. They hold monthly breakfast meetings; the fee for most is $30, which includes the meal.

COOKING

JAMES BEARD FOUNDATION ★ 167 West 12th Street ★ (212) 675-4984

Become a member of this famous culinary center and be able to dine with great chefs from all over the world who come here to prepare and share their gastronomic delights.

KAREN LEE ★ 142 West End Avenue ★ (212) 787-2227

Karen Lee is a nationally recognized author, teacher, and caterer for the past seventeen years. Her classes fall into four main categories: nouvelle chinoise; vegetarian cooking; soup, salad and pasta; and classic Chinese. New classes form every four to six weeks, September through May, and are offered both in the morning and the evening.

LAUREN GROVEMAN'S KITCHEN ★ 55 Prospect Avenue, Larchmont, NY ★ (914) 834-1372

Lauren's goal is to teach people to create food that not only looks, smells, and tastes wonderful but that inspires the people who eat it to want to do it themselves. All her recipes are original and there is nothing she cannot prepare; she is considered to be one of the up-and-coming chefs in the country. She has classes for all levels of ability.

PETER KUMP'S NEW YORK COOKING SCHOOL ★ 307 East 92nd Street ★ (212) 410-4601

The New York Cooking School is a small school dedicated to teaching cooking as a fine art in the tradition of European cooking schools. In addition to gaining a thorough background in French techniques, students also study other cuisines from a variety of other countries. This is a place for those who are serious about good food and cooking, whether for a restaurant, catering operation, take-out shop, or personal enjoyment. Classes are offered during the day, evening, and weekends.

DANCE

ARTHUR MURRAY DANCE STUDIO ★ 677 Fifth Avenue ★ (212) 935-7787

Anyone interested in ballroom or freestyle dancing should make an appointment for a half-hour consultation. They have the capability to tailor a program to fit your need in either group or private lessons. There are eight teachers on staff.

NEW YORK SWING DANCE SOCIETY ★ (212) 696-9737

Membership fee per year is $35, which includes a quarterly newsletter and free admission to the Friday night practice sessions held at Musical Theater Works, 400 Lafayette Street, from 6:30 to 8:30 P.M.

ROSELAND BALLROOM ★ 239 West 52nd Street ★ (212) 247-0200

Roseland is open for ballroom dancing on Thursday and Sunday from 2:30 P.M. to 11 P.M. On Thursdays there is a deejay and the admission is $5; on Sundays there is a deejay and a live orchestra for $10. If you are without a partner there are hosts and hostesses for $1 per dance.

FILM

ANTHOLOGY FILM ARCHIVES ★ 32 Second Avenue ★ (212) 505-5181

Here they feature independent and avant-garde films, sometimes with a question and answer period led by the director. The membership fee is $40 a year and the screenings are $4. Certain events are only offered to members and some of them are free.

FOREIGN CULTURES

ALLIANCE FRANÇAISE ★ 22 East 60th Street ★ (212) 355-6100

For the basic membership fee of $55 a year you can attend most events for free such as lectures, dance performances, operas, readings, lectures, films, and have full use of their library. You do not have to be fluent in French to partake but you obviously must have some understanding or at least a strong desire to learn.

THE ASIA SOCIETY ★ 686 Park Avenue ★ (212) 288-6400

For $50 a year you will receive a newsletter three times a year that announces all the upcoming cultural activities and events. Your membership entitles you to free admission to gallery exhibits and discounted tickets for films, performances, and lectures. Every year they pick a different country to focus on. They are a wonderful resource for any questions you may have concerning this part of the world.

THE ENGLISH-SPEAKING UNION ★ 16 East 69th Street ★ (212) 879-6800

This is a not-for-profit educational and cultural organization that is dedicated to strengthening friendship among English-speaking people. A $70 per year membership entitles you to access their library, lectures, films, and their daily tea hour to which you may bring non-members.

FIERI ★ 25 West 43rd Street ★ (212) 772-7518

This is an Italian cultural organization that meets once a month to discuss educational topics, hold lectures, or partake in a cultural event. They also have other events throughout the year. Membership fee is $40 per year.

GOETHE HOUSE ★ 1014 Fifth Avenue ★ (212) 439-8700

There is no fee to belong to this German cultural organization; just put your name on their mailing list. They will send you information on their movies, lectures, and exhibitions. They also have an extensive lending library for you to use.

ITALIAN CULTURAL INSTITUTE ★ 686 Park Avenue ★ (212) 879-4242

This is a government organization that will put you on their mailing list and notify you about film, art, and music events as well as lectures on all aspects of Italian culture. Events are free of charge and held at museums, concert halls, and theaters throughout New York.

THE JAPAN SOCIETY ★ 333 East 47th Street ★ (212) 832-1155

The basic membership fee is $45 for the year. This entitles you to a monthly newsletter filled with articles, upcoming programs, and activities, a calendar of events published three times a year, and discounts on films, performing arts events, language classes, exhibits, and Japan Society publications. An understanding of Japanese is not necessary to enjoy yourself here.

GLASS BLOWING

THE NEW YORK EXPERIMENTAL GLASS WORKSHOP ★ 647 Fulton Street, Brooklyn ★ (718) 625-3685

This the only glass-blowing institute in New York City. You can either make an appointment to blow your own glass ($22 per hour with some supplies and tools provided), or you can attend a twelve-week course. Courses range from beginner through advanced and start at $496 including materials.

HORTICULTURE

HORTICULTURAL SOCIETY OF NEW YORK ★ 128 West 58th Street ★ (212) 757-0915

This is a place where you can pursue garden design, flower arranging vegetable growing, the art of bonsai, and overall plant nurturing. Basic membership fee is $25 and includes a discount on courses, access to the "plant hotline" from noon to 2:00 P.M., discounts on purchasing plants at their shop, a newsletter telling you about upcoming events, and more.

MILITARY

NEW YORK MILITARY AFFAIRS SYMPOSIUM ★ (212) 688-5086

This is an educational organization that offers a series of lectures on military and strategic policies on either historical or current issues. Experts from West Point as well as professionals involved in the defense industry lead these discussions. Membership fee is $30 per year and includes a newsletter.

PHOTOGRAPHY

MY OWN COLOR LAB ★ 18 West 27th Street ★ (212) 696-4107

They rent darkrooms out for developing color film only. All rooms come completely equipped. The rate is $7.99 per hour and $5.99 per hour for students. They do offer assistance to beginners and hold workshops that range from $20 to $50.

PHOTOGRAPHICS UNLIMITED ★ 17 West 17th Street ★ (212) 255-9678

You can develop black and white film here. The cost is $8 per hour with a minimum of two hours. The rooms come fully equipped except for paper. You need to reserve two days in advance.

POETRY AND LITERATURE

BOOKS AND COMPANY ★ 939 Madison Avenue ★ (212) 737-1450

You must stop by their store to pick up a schedule of their readings. Most are held on Tuesday nights throughout the year and there is no charge to attend.

92ND STREET Y ★ 1395 Lexington Avenue ★ (212) 427-6000

This is one of New York City's meccas for all kinds of cultural events, lectures, and classes with the world's best-known authors and experts from every field. A small fee is charged for each event; call for a catalogue.

THE OPEN CENTER ★ 83 Spring Street ★ (212) 219-2527

The center offers wonderful live storytelling throughout the year for a nominal fee. Call to receive their schedule.

THE NYC POETRY CALENDAR ★ 60 East 4th Street ★ Apt. 21 ★ New York, NY 10003

To receive a year's subscription to this monthly calendar send $15 to the address above. This calendar gives you the most comprehensive listing of poetry readings throughout the City.

POETRY SOCIETY OF AMERICA ★ 15 Gramercy Park ★ (212) 254-9628

This society was founded in 1910 and its mission is to completely support the working poet. It holds contests, classes, and workshops as well as one-day intensive courses. Call for rates.

POMANDER BOOKSHOP ★ 955 West End Avenue ★ (212) 866-1777

This store near Columbia University and Barnard College sponsors one reading per month. Just call and add your name to their mailing list.

SHAKESPEARE AND COMPANY BOOKSELLERS ★ 2259 Broadway ★ (212) 580-7800 ★ 716 Broadway ★ (212) 529-1330

Readings are announced in *The Village Voice* and in their own seasonal mailing list.

THE WEST SIDE YMCA ★ 5 West 63rd Street ★ (212) 787-6557

This Y sponsors a tremendous amount of readings by fiction writers, nonfiction writers, and poets. Call to be placed on their mailing list. A small fee is required for each event.

POLITICS

LOCAL ASSEMBLY AND COUNCIL PERSON

Call your local political officials to find out where the nearest political organizational club is located. They should be able to tell you about ones of all affiliations.

SINGING

BRANDY'S PIANO BAR ★ 235 East 84th Street ★ (212) 650-1944

Every night is open mike night at Brandy's from 9:30 P.M. to 4:00 A.M. The accompanist will play any standard but if there is a particular arrangement you like, bring your own music.

DON'T TELL MAMA ★ 343 West 46th Street ★ (212) 757-0788

Ming Phan owns this club, which features an open mike every night at 9:30 P.M.

DUPLEX CABARET ★ 61 Christopher Street ★ (212) 255-5438

Open mike at the downstairs bar begins at 9:00 P.M. every night. On Friday and Saturday nights, the upstairs bar offers an open mike after the regular show is over around 11:30 P.M.

NEW YORK CHORAL SOCIETY ★ 4026 Dyer Avenue ★ (212) 724-6633

During the summer anyone may join their summer sing every Tuesday and Thursday through August. They begin at 7:30 P.M. at CAMI Hall, 165 West 57 Street. Tickets to participate cost $7, payable at the door.

SOMMELIER

INTERNATIONAL WINE CENTER ★ 231 West 29th Street ★ (212) 268-7517

You can become a full member for $400 a year, which entitles you to weekly tastings, or become a limited member for $125 a year and then you pay $20 for each tasting that you attend. There are also special events that run throughout the year to which members attend at a discount. Nonmembers may partake at full price. Call to put your name on their mailing list.

LES AMIS DU VIN ★ 230 West 79th Street ★ (212) 799-6311

This is an international organization that holds sixteen to twenty events each year consisting of wine and food dinners and tastings for everyone from novice to the connoisseur. The Gramercy Park Hotel is the headquarters for the wine tastings and the dinners are held at different restaurants throughout the City. Membership is $30 a year, which entitles you to *Friends of Wine* magazine published six times a year and discounted admission fees to their events.

STAND-UP COMEDY

BOSTON COMEDY CLUB ★ 82 West 3rd Street ★ (212) 477-1000

On Monday nights at 9:30 anyone can sign up for a seven-minute slot to compete in their comedy competition. The winner gets a $300 booking in Boston as well as their tape sent to *Star Search*, MTV, and *An Evening at the Improvisation*. Competitors must bring two customers at a $5 cover and two-drink minimum.

IMPROVISATION ★ 358 West 44th Street ★ (212) 765-8268

About every six weeks the owner of this club, Silver Sanders Friedman, holds auditions for their Monday night showcases.

STAND-UP NEW YORK ★ 236 West 78th Street ★ (212) 595-0850

Every night of the week at 7:30 anyone can stand up at the microphone and perform eight minutes of material as long as they bring three paying customers. If you bring ten or more paying customers, the club will split the cover with you. The cover is $5 and a two-drink minimum.

TABLE GAMES

BACKGAMMON CHESS CLUB ★ 212 West 72nd Street ★ (212) 787-4629

Open seven days a week from 11 A.M. till very late at night, this small space offers the backgammon, chess, Scrabble, and Boggle player a chance to play for either a monetary profit or loss. The initial cost to play is $2 an hour per person.

MANHATTAN CHESS CLUB ★ 154 West 57th Street ★ (212) 333-5888

Open daily from noon to midnight, they offer lectures, seminars, and open exhibition matches. The yearly membership fee is $300 and they offer a newsletter of $8 per year.

THE VILLAGE CHESS SHOP ★ 230 Thompson Street ★ (212) 475-9580

They have fourteen tables set up for chess play from noon to midnight seven days a week. It is $1.50 per hour or $2 with a chess clock. All levels of play are welcome.

TRAVEL

AMERICAN COUPON EXCHANGE ★ (800) 222-9599

They buy people's free miles and sell them to you and usually make the reservation for you in your name on most domestic and international flights. They deal mostly in business and first-class tickets.

COUPON BANK ★ (800) 292-9250

Another coupon broker who sells other people's free miles to you. They book the flight for you on either Delta, Continental, or Northwest airlines. The majority of their tickets are in first and business class.

FAMILY TRAVEL TIMES ★ 80 Eighth Avenue (at 14th Street) ★ (212) 206-0688

The cost is $35 per year and you will receive ten issues. Each issue gives you ideas on the types of vacations you can take with your kids, from a weekend to an extended period of time.

NOW VOYAGER ★ (212) 431-1616

A cheap way to travel is by becoming a courier but you usually give up your luggage space. There are many restrictions and rules to follow but it sure is an inexpensive way to go.

PASSPORT ★ (800) 542-6670

This newsletter covers a broad view of travel throughout the world, with a strong emphasis on Europe. In addition to the basic newsletter you receive two monthly supplements: one focusing on interesting places to travel abroad and the other on fun getaways in the United States. The cost is $65 a year.

VILLAREPORT ★ WIMCO ★ P.O. Box 1641, Newport, RI 02840 ★ (800) 932-3222

A free publication that comes out about four times a year with updates on various events and issues that are happening in the Caribbean. This company can also help you to find a villa to rent in the Caribbean.

THE INTREPID PAGES

OF

THE Y's

There are Y's throughout the City that have wonderful fitness facilities. The atmosphere is relaxed and the emphasis is on having fun and getting in shape. If you are looking for a game of basketball or racquetball, a running mate, or simply a friendly face you will most likely find it at the Y. This is the small-town answer to the problem of working out in the Big Apple and it sure can be a refreshing change from many of the trendy health clubs in the city. The Y's often offer special programs for children, teenagers, and the elderly.

92ND STREET Y ★ 1395 Lexington Avenue ★ (212) 427-6000

Membership Rates:	Men's full membership—$960
	Women's full membership—$860
	They offer more limited hour memberships for less money.
Facilities:	Pool, two gyms, volleyball, basketball, track, aerobics, and exercise classes, yoga, steam, sauna, and massage, towel and laundry service

VANDERBILT YMCA ★ 224 East 47th Street ★ (212) 755-2410

Membership Rates:	Men and Women—$663
Facilities:	Two pools (one for lap, one for lessons), Nautilus, free weights, karate, yoga, StairMaster, Lifecycles, Nordictrack, aerobic and exercise classes, steam, sauna and massage

WESTSIDE YMCA ★ 5 West 63rd Street ★ (212) 787-4400

Membership Rates:	Men and Women—$663
Facilities:	Silex, Nautilus, free weights, aerobics classes all day, pool, indoor track, handball, racquet ball, sauna, massage, StairMaster, and bikes

YMCA ★ 610 Lexington Avenue ★ (212) 755-4500

Membership Rates:	Men and Women—$50 per year, but you must pay extra for use of facilities
Facilities:	Fitness room, pool, weight rooms, StairMaster, bikes, treadmills, indoor track, steam and sauna

MCBURNEY YMCA ★ 215 West 23rd Street ★ (212) 741-9210

Membership Rates:	$663 per year—includes classes
Facilities:	StairMaster, treadmills, Universal equipment, indoor pool, indoor track, paddle ball courts, basketball, sauna, steam, and massage

THE INTREPID PAGES
OF
CITY-FUNDED RECREATION CENTERS

The City-funded recreation centers are clean, organized, and inexpensive.

ASHER LEVY RECREATIONAL CENTER ★ FDR Drive at 23rd Street ★ (212) 447-2020
Membership Fee: $10 per person, per year
Facilities: Aerobics, weights, machines, Universal equipment, rowing machines, indoor and outdoor pools

CARMINE STREET POOL ★ 3 Clarkson Street ★ (212) 397-3107
Membership Fee: $10 per person, per year
Facilities: Indoor pool, weights, volleyball, aerobics

EAST 54TH STREET ★ 348 East 54th Street ★ (212) 397-3154
Membership Fee: $10 per year for adult; $1 per child
Facilities: Indoor pool, Nautilus equipment, running track, basketball

WEST 59TH STREET ★ 533 West 59th Street ★ (212) 397-3166
At the time of this writing, asbestos is being removed and the facility is closed.

THE INTREPID PAGES
OF
SPORTS ON YOUR OWN OR WITH A LEAGUE

You may not realize it, but you do not need to leave the City to find a softball game, shoot hoops with friends, take a dip on a hot summer day, go horseback riding, take a hike, practice archery, or even play eighteen holes of golf. New York is a city of parks in which you can do all of the above and more if you just know where to go. There are 26,000 acres of green space in New York City, including 862 playgrounds, 15 miles of beach, hundreds of tennis courts, 7,000 acres of natural areas, 20 major recreation centers, 13 golf courses, and more. In Manhattan alone, there are 2,614 acres of park land—that's 17 percent of Manhattan.

The first call you need to make is to the New York City Parks and Recreation press office: (212) 360-8141, or try the City Parks Foundation at (212) 360-1399. Ask them to send you a copy of the Green Pages. The latest edition is 1990 but not much changes. This is a sixty-page booklet that lists all the facilities and programs the Department of Parks and Recreation offers with phone numbers, addresses, and facts, from cricket fields to carousels. It's free and you should not be without it.

Now that you know that New York City is not lacking in any recreational facility, we want you to understand that there are hundreds of teams and organizations to join. Whether you are an aspiring or retiring hockey player, baseball enthusiast, or tennis buff, no matter your sport or your level of skill, there is a group out there just waiting for you to join them. Depending on the activity you choose, you may need a permit from the Parks Department and of course there may be a charge to join a league or group.

ARCHERY

WILLOWBROOK PARK, Staten Island ★ (718) 698-2186

A permit is not required and there is no charge, but you must bring your own equipment, including target. Saturday and Sunday mornings are often reserved for teams. Willowbrook Park is open from dawn to dusk.

BADMINTON

All boroughs have Olympic training programs for children aged twelve to eighteen. This is in conjunction with the U.S. Badminton Association.

On Your Own:

SPORTS FITNESS ★ (212) 408-0204

Give them a call and they will tell you where you can find a game.

Leagues:

For serious play there are several badminton clubs you can join. Call Art Murtha of the U.S. Badminton Association at (914) 923-3300 or (914) 238-4947.

MANHATTAN BADMINTON CLUB

★ (212) 794-0147

Speak with Sandy Denton. They play at various schools.

UNITED NATIONS SCHOOL ★ 23rd Street

★ (212) 949-4038

Speak with Vladimin Rayes.

COLUMBIA UNIVERSITY ★ (212) 960-7088

Speak with Penny Jones.

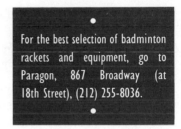

For the best selection of badminton rackets and equipment, go to Paragon, 867 Broadway (at 18th Street), (212) 255-8036.

BASKETBALL

There are hundreds of outdoor basketball courts in New York City.

On Your Own:

Rumor has it that you can find a serious game at 76th Street and Riverside Drive as well as West Fourth Street and Sixth Avenue. You can find a light game on 77th Street between Amsterdam and Columbus Avenues.

Leagues:

NEW YORK URBAN PROFESSIONALS LEAGUE ★ 302 West 79th Street

★ (212) 877-3614

The director is John Bykowsky. There are two seasons: winter and summer. Approximately 240 teams of all different abilities. Players

---

can join as individuals at $124 or teams at $1,240. Games are played on weekday evenings in various high schools throughout Manhattan. The teams are made up of people in professional jobs during the day. Women are welcome.

YORKVILLE SPORTS ASSOCIATION ★ (212) 645-6488
Speak to Al Moralis. Teams or individuals can join. Women's leagues as well.

BICYCLING
On Your Own:
In Central Park the drive is closed to motor vehicles on holidays and on weekends from 7:00 P.M. to 6:00 A.M. On Mondays and on weekdays from April to November, it is closed from 10:00 A.M. to 3:00 P.M. and 7:00 P.M. to 10:00 A.M. You can rent bikes from Loeb Bathhouse (212) 861-4137 at $6 per hour. Pedal carriage rentals (for two adults and two small children) from 67th Street and West Drive (in front of Tavern on the Green) (212) 860-4619 at $15 per hour. Another good ride is Riverside Park promenade from West 72nd Street to 100th Street.

Clubs:
NEW YORK CYCLE CLUB ★ P.O. Box 199, Cooper Station, New York, NY 10276
★ (212) 242-3900
The yearly fee is $17. You receive a monthly bulletin and clinics on how to handle your bike. They hold monthly meetings at a downtown restaurant, which is attended by at least 100 members. This is not a racing club, although those who ride quickly will not be disappointed. They plan weekend rides that can take you up to 120 miles outside the City. Regardless of your ability, there is a ride for you.

THE CENTRAL PARK CYCLING AND SPORTS ASSOCIATION ★ c/o Chiromed
Clinical Associates ★ 825 Seventh Avenue ★ (212) 956-5920
Speak with Errol Toran. The yearly fee is $25. You will receive a bimonthly newsletter. The association welcomes riders of all abilities. They hold bike runs through weekday evenings from March through November.

THE CENTURY ROAD CLUB ASSOCIATION ★ P.O. Box 20412, Greeley Square Station,
New York, NY 10001 ★ (212) 594-6951
Membership dues are $45 for the first year and $15 to renew. You will receive a cycling jersey. This organization concentrates on racing, although they do hold teaching clinics. They hold seventeen races each year in Central Park.

BOATING

On Your Own:
CENTRAL PARK AT THE LOEB BOATHOUSE ★ (212) 517-4723
April through October, $6 per hour for a rowboat (and they will watch your stroller, etc.), $30 per hour for a gondola ride up to five people.

BOCCIE

On Your Own:
In Manhattan you can find boccie courts in the following areas, to name a few: the playground at 96th Street and First Avenue; Houston Street and First Avenue; Randall's and Ward's islands.

BOWLING

On Your Own:
BOWLMOR BOWLING ★ 110 University Place (12th and 13th Streets) ★ (212) 255-8188
Open daily from 10:00 A.M., forty-four lanes.

Leagues:
Call Bowlmor to find a league that fits your ability.

WOMEN ATHLETES OF NY ★ 810 Lexington Avenue ★ (212) 759-4189
Contact Elaine Rosenberg. Individuals or teams are welcome. Women only.

BOXING

GLEASON'S GYM ★ 75 Front Street, Brooklyn ★ (718) 797-2872
Hours are Monday through Friday, 6:30 A.M. to 8:00 P.M.; Saturdays, 9:00 A.M. to 4:00 P.M. This is one of the best facilities. It has a 21,000-square-foot gym with three rings. They offer private lessons. Here you will find professional boxers as well as office workers by day who are boxers by night. Men and women.

CROQUET

On Your Own:
Call (212) 360-8133 to get a City permit. Cost is $30 for the season (May through November). In Manhattan, you can play croquet in Central Park, north of Sheep Meadow at 67th Street near East Drive.

FISHING

For freshwater fishing people who are sixteen years old or over must get a license from the New York State Department of Environmental Conservation (718) 482-4986. Check to see if the fish are edible no matter where you catch them.

On Your Own:
Riverside Park along the Hudson River Esplanade from West 72nd Street to 84th Street, West 91st Street to 100th Street. Also South Cove at the end of Battery Park City Esplanade. For three days during the months of May, July, and October the Battery Park City Park Corporation in conjunction with the Cornell Cooperative Extension offers free fishing lessons. They even provide the equipment. And of course the fish are then set free. Call (212) 248-4990 to find out the exact days.

FRISBEE

On Your Own:
You can pick up a game on any nice day in Central Park on Frisbee Mound just west of Sheep Meadow and at the northern end of the Great Lawn near 86th Street.

Leagues:
FLYING DISC ENTERPRISES ★ 315 West 103rd Street, Suite 8 ★ (212) 662-0391
Speak to Mark Danna.

GOLF

You can even play golf in New York City all year round; and yes, the courses are clean, well organized, challenging, and accessible by subway. You can reserve a tee-off time at seven of the golf courses by calling (718) 225-GOLF about one and one-half weeks in advance. Greens fees are $12 on weekdays, $15.50 on weekends. Motor-cart rental is $21 per eighteen holes. Push-cart rental is $3 per eighteen holes. You can play alone or up to a group of four. Tee times are well adhered to.

HIKING

On Your Own:
In Manhattan there is a nature trail at Inwood Hill Park that is 2.2 miles long. For more information call (212) 304-3629. The Urban Park Rangers also lead guided tours in Central Park. For more information call (212) 397-3080.

Organizations:
ATLANTIC CHAPTER OUTINGS ★ Sierra Club, P.O. Box 800, New York, NY 10024
★ (212) 473-7886
The Sierra Club offers free hiking excursions. To get more information send $3 to the address above or call.

HORSEBACK RIDING

CLAREMONT RIDING ACADEMY ★ 175 West 89th Street ★ (212) 724-5100

English-style riding. You can ride on your own, but you must know how to ride to take a horse to the park. Fee: $30 per hour. They do offer group and private lessons. Hours are daily, Monday through Friday, 6:30 A.M. to 10:00 P.M.; Saturday and Sunday, 6:30 A.M. to 5:00 P.M.

ICE HOCKEY

Leagues:

SKY RINK ADULT HOCKEY LEAGUE ★ 450 West 33rd Street, 16th Floor
★ (212) 695-6557

Open Tuesday through Friday after 3:00 P.M. Eve Stevens is the League Director. Forty-five teams divided into four divisions based on ability. Women welcome. Play is usually on weeknight evenings. Fee $225 per season, practice time and jersey included. Equipment can be purchased at Marc's Pro Shop at the Sky Rink.

On Your Own:

The Sky Rink, above, also offers clinics and hockey instruction, Friday evenings for juniors, 5:10 P.M. to 6:30 P.M.; Friday evenings for adults, 6:30 P.M. to 7:50 P.M. The fee is $10 for children, $12 for adults.

Pickup Games:

(Adults)	Tuesday, 1:20 A.M.—$12 per session
	Thursday, noon—$12 per session
	Weekends, 7:30 A.M. to 9:00 A.M., 9:00 A.M. to 10:40 A.M.; 10:50 A.M. to 12:20 P.M.; $15 per person
(Youth)	Saturday, 6:00 A.M. to 8:00 A.M.—$10 per session

LASKER RINK ★ 106 Street, South of Lenox Avenue in Central Park

Every Saturday and Sunday between 7:30 A.M. and 9:00 A.M. ice hockey games are played and anyone can join.

ICE-SKATING

Skates to rent and lessons are available at all the locations below.

On Your Own, Outdoor:

WOLLMAN RINK ★ East Drive and 63rd Street (Central Park) ★ (212) 517-4800

33,000 square feet; October through March.

LASKER RINK ★ 106th Street, South of Lenox Avenue (Central Park) ★ (212) 722-9781

26,000 square feet; October through March.

ROCKEFELLER CENTER ★ 50th Street off Fifth Avenue ★ (212) 757-5730

7,800 square feet; October through April.

RIVERGATE ICE RINK ★ First Avenue at 34th Street ★ (212) 689-0035
9,500 square feet; October through April.

On Your Own, Indoor:
SKY RINK ★ 450 West 33rd Street, 16th Floor ★ (212) 695-6555
15,725 square feet; open year-round.

ICE STUDIO ★ 1034 Lexington Avenue, 2nd Floor ★ (212) 535-0304
30' by 50'; open year-round.

KITE FLYING

On Your Own:
Central Park in the Sheep Meadow.

Big City Kite Co. at 1201 Lexington Avenue (between 81st and 82nd Streets) has a great selection of kites.

RACEWALKING

On Your Own:
The Central Park Reservoir is 1.58 miles long.

NEW YORK WALKER CLUB ★ Engineers Gate at 90th Street and Fifth Avenue
They offer a free racewalking clinic on Saturdays at 9:00 A.M. all year round.

Clubs:
THE PARK WALKERS CLUB ★ 320 East 83rd Street, Box 18, New York, NY 10028-0013 ★ (212) 628-1317
Speak with Stella Cashman. You don't have to be a "speed setter" or even have experience to become involved. They meet twice a week on Sunday mornings and Wednesday evenings. Call for details. Fee is $10 per year, for which you will receive a T-shirt and monthly newsletter.

Walking shoes are different from running shoes. A good place to go is Super Runners located at 1337 Lexington Avenue. (369-6010) They let you walk around the block.

METROPOLITAN RACEWALKERS ★ 36 West 20th Street, New York, NY 10011 ★ (212) 675-3021
Speak with Richard Goldman. For both beginners and experienced walkers. They meet Saturday and Sunday mornings for a four- to six-mile walk. Membership fee is $10 per year and includes a T-shirt.

ROLLER SKATING, ROLLER BLADING

On Your Own:
WOLLMAN RINK ★ East Drive and 63rd Street ★ (212) 517-4800
They are open April through September, Monday, 10:00 A.M. to 5:00 P.M.; Tuesday, Wednesday, Thursday, and Sunday, until 9:30 P.M., Fri-

day and Saturday, until 11:00 P.M. Fees are $5.25 for adults, $2.50 for children, and $2.50 for the rental of skates.

Schools:

LEZLY SKATE SCHOOL ★ 622–26 Broadway (Bleecker and Lafayette) ★ (212) 777-3232
Four classes per month required at $10 per class. All levels of ability.

A good place to rent roller blades is BLADES WEST ★ 105 West 72nd Street ★ (212) 787-3911. They're open Monday through Saturday, 10:00 A.M. to 8:00 P.M., and Sunday until 6:00 P.M. Fees are $15 per two hours with a $200 deposit.

Clubs:

BIG APPLE ROAD SKATERS ASSOCIATION ★ (212) 534-7858
Membership fee is $25 per year. This is the largest club for skaters. They meet to skate recreationally as well as competitively.

RUNNING

On Your Own:

In Central Park, especially when it is closed to traffic. Also the indoor tracks in the City recreational facilities (see page 327). For those who are energetic and want to run in beautiful surroundings, you can get a seasonal pass ($5) to run in the Bronx Botanical Gardens during off hours (6:00 A.M. to 10:00 A.M.). The pass can be obtained from the security office from 10:30 A.M. to 3:30 P.M. daily except Monday when the garden is closed to everyone. For more information call (212) 220-8700.

Clubs:

THE CENTRAL PARK TRACK CLUB ★ 250 West 89th Street, New York, NY 10024 ★ (212) 619-4240
Speak to Frank Handelman, president. This is a racing club for serious runners. There are two weekly workouts, and many runs. Dues are $40 per year.

NEW YORK ROAD RUNNERS CLUB ★ 9 East 89th Street, New York, NY 10128 ★ (212) 860-4455
Club hours are Monday through Friday, 10:00 A.M. to 8:00 P.M.; Saturday until 5:00 P.M., and Sunday until 3:00 P.M. If you run at all, you should join the Road Runners. Membership dues are $25 per year for which you receive: reduced fees for Road Runners races (they hold many, including the marathon), *New York Running News Magazine* monthly, monthly newsletter, free running clinic discounts at shops around New York City, and computerized annual race results of your races.

ROBERT GLOVER ASSOCIATES ★ (212) 737-7480

They offer classes on how to improve your running style and general fitness approach. The classes convene at P.S. 6 on 81st Street and Madison Avenue in the evenings. There are six different levels of ability from beginner to expert and the classes run about seventy-five minutes. They are a combination of workouts in the school and then a jaunt in the park. A ten-week session runs $50 for members of the Road Runners Club and $60 for nonmembers.

SAILING

On Your Own:

THE NEW YORK SAILING SCHOOL ★ 560 Minnetord Avenue, City Island,
The Bronx 10464 ★ (212) 885-3103

They have Solings, Sonars, Merit 25s, and one J22 to rent. Rentals range from $70 to $185 per day. You must be ASA certified or be checked out by them at a cost of $45.

To Dock:

If you have your own boat and want to dock it call the New York Sailing School Yacht Club at (212) 885-3074 to check on their mooring availability.

Schools:

The New York Sailing School also offers a twenty-seven-hour sailing course. Twenty-four of those hours are spent on the water. The cost for the course is $395 and they teach on Sonars.

SOCCER

On Your Own:

Soccer fields in Manhattan where you may find a game:

★ In Central Park: The Great Lawn, 81st to 85th Streets; North Meadow, 97th to 103rd Streets
★ East River Park: East River at 6th and Grand Streets
★ Inwood Hill Park: Hudson River and Dyckman Street
★ Randall's Island
★ Riverside Park: Riverside Drive at West 104th and 107th Streets
★ Thomas Jefferson Park: First Avenue and 111th Street

Leagues:

THE COSMOPOLITAN SOCCER LEAGUE ★ (201) 861-6606

They represent over twenty clubs of all different levels. Call them and they will suggest a club that is appropriate for your needs.

SOFTBALL

On Your Own:

To put your own game together you will need a permit in Manhattan. The office is at 16 West 61st Street, (212) 408-0209.

Leagues:

CENTRAL PARK SOFTBALL LEAGUE ★ 435 West 23rd Street ★ (212) 956-6266

The League Commissioner is Marty Mann. Leagues play at Hecksher Ball Field (on the west side of the park between 62nd and 65th Streets). The season begins in April. Fee to join is $50 to $100 per person, $1,450 per team. They also offer an invitational league that is more informal at $25 per game per season. All abilities are welcome.

YORKVILLE SPORT ASSOCIATION ★ 530 West 23rd Street ★ (212) 645-6488

Speak with Al Moralis. They offer a co-ed men's and women's softball league. All different abilities welcome.

WOMEN ATHLETES OF NEW YORK ★ 800 Lexington Avenue ★ (212) 759-4189

Speak with Elaine Rosenberg. This is an all-women's softball league. Individuals or teams may join.

SWIMMING

There are even more pools available than the ones already mentioned at the Y's and the City recreation centers.

On Your Own:

THE MADISON AVENUE PRESBYTERIAN CHURCH ★ 921 Madison Avenue (73rd and 74th Streets) ★ (212) 288-8920

Membership is from September through May, hours are limited, and fees are $150 for a season.

MARYMOUNT MANHATTAN COLLEGE ★ 221 East 71st Street ★ (212) 517-0400

The charges are based on what type of swim you want. Lap, recreational, etc. Times are limited.

LENOX HILL NEIGHBORHOOD ASSOCIATION ★ 331 East 70th Street ★ (212) 744-5022

Membership fee is $215 for the year. Proof of living between 59th and 96th Streets, East River and Fifth Avenue in New York City is required. Pool hours are limited. (They also have a fitness room with a lot of equipment.)

Leagues:

THE RED TIDE ★ 148 West 23rd Street, Apt. 8H, New York, NY 10011 ★ (212) 989-0417

Speak with Dana Evans. Membership dues are $10 per year, $24 to pay for insurance, and additional fees for particular training packages.

You have access to pools and supervised workouts. They work out weekdays and weekends. This is a fairly serious group of swimmers who like to compete.

TENNIS

On Your Own:

In Manhattan there are 103 courts. Central Park, East River Park, Inwood Hill Park, Fort Washington Park, Frederick Johnson Playground, Riverside Park, and an indoor bubble at Randall's Island. A permit is needed. You can obtain one from the Arsenal at Central Park (near Fifth Avenue at 64th Street) or call (212) 360-8133.

Fees are: adults—$40; seniors—$20; under eighteen—$10.

Leagues:

U.S. TENNIS ASSOCIATION LEAGUE ★ (212) 302-3322

The league has about 350 people in Manhattan with about eight to twenty players per team. This is a recreational league for adults according to skill level, ranging from beginners to advanced. Season is May to July. Membership fee is $20 per person, plus $15 to $25 per match that you play. Single-gender games as well as mixed doubles.

MICHELOB PLAY TENNIS LEAGUE ★ (718) 786-7602

This league is strictly for beginners. Eight to ten per team, they have over three thousand members throughout New York City. Play is on weeknights and weekends. They hold a big championship competition at the end of the summer. Group lessons are also available.

TRIATHLON

Team:

TEAM REDLINE ★ 365 West 52nd Street, New York, NY 10019 ★ (212) 247-1250

Speak to Art Murphy, president. Membership fee is $30 per year for which you receive a T-shirt and some discounts on events. This is a serious group of people. There are swimming, biking, and running workouts as well as competitions.

VOLLEYBALL

On Your Own:

NEW YORK URBAN PROFESSIONAL LEAGUE ★ 302 West 79th Street, New York, NY 10024 ★ (212) 877-3614

Co-ed volleyball teams. There are two seasons: spring and fall. They play one evening a week, at various gyms on the Upper West Side. People are grouped by ability. Fees are individual $83, and team $830.

Leagues:

YORKVILLE SPORTS ASSOCIATION ★ (212) 645-6488

Speak with Al Moralis. Co-ed Volleyball teams based on ability. You can either join as an individual or a team. Play weekday evenings.

WOMEN ATHLETES OF NEW YORK ★ (212) 759-4189

Volleyball—individual or teams may join. Women only.

THE INTREPID PAGES

OF

ALL DRESSED UP
WITH SOME PLACE TO GO

Most people think that New York is a very expensive town to have a good time in. This is often true. But there are numerous ways to partake of all the cultural, artistic, and leisure events without going broke.

EVENTS AT LINCOLN CENTER

For a calendar of bimonthly events write to Lincoln Center Calendar of Events, 70 Lincoln Plaza, New York, NY 10023. Send a .62 cent self-addressed return envelope.

LINCOLN CENTER THEATERS ★ (212) 239-6277

There is a $25-a-year membership that entitles you to reserve any available seat for a Lincoln Center Theater production for $10. The theaters that sponsor these plays and musicals are: The Vivian Beaumont, The Mitzi Newhouse, The Barrymore, and The Brooklyn Academy of Music.

MEET THE ARTIST PROGRAMS ★ (212) 875-5365

During the summer, they offer Mostly Mozart Meet the Artist tastings. Before the concert you may have dinner and wine with the guest artist in a private room at Avery Fisher Hall. These can be booked on a one-time basis or you can take out a series. You can attend just the dinner for $30 or the dinner and the concert for $50.

THE FILM SOCIETY OF LINCOLN CENTER ★ (212) 875-5610

The membership fee is $50 a year, which entitles you to advance mailings to events as well as *Film Comment* magazine. They hold three major events: the spring gala, the new directors and new films series, and the New York Film Festival.

LINCOLN CENTER OFF STAGE ★ At Paul Hall At Juilliard ★ (212) 875-5441

These are a series of hour-long conversations that are held with a mediator, famous artist, and the audience. They usually center around a certain theme. Membership is $45 per year or $13 for each evening meeting; wine and cheese is served.

NEW YORK PHILHARMONIC AT AVERY FISHER HALL ★ (212) 875-5656

Depending on the performance, the least expensive ticket ranges from $11 to $17. For $5 you may see a rehearsal on selected mornings at 9:45. There is no standing room offered.

NEW YORK CITY BALLET AND NEW YORK CITY OPERA AT NEW YORK STATE THEATRE ★ (212) 870-5570

The least expensive seats you can purchase are $9. They do sell standing-room tickets for $6. To attend rehearsals you must become a guild member; the least expensive guild membership fee is $60, which entitles you to two rehearsal viewings as well as other benefits.

ALICE TULLY HALL CONCERTS ★ (212) 875-5050

All prices depend upon which performance is playing. There is no standing room and the cheapest seats are $5.

THE METROPOLITAN OPERA HOUSE ★ (212) 362-6000

Standing-room tickets go on sale at 10:00 A.M. Saturday mornings. The least expensive seats start at $13. You can take out a guild membership for $50, which entitles you to *Opera News*, discounted backstage tours, and more.

> Most of the Broadway and Off Broadway theaters have something called house seats. These are seats that are reserved for friends of the cast, director, producer, or others in the business. Often people do reserve these seats but do not show up for the performance. We suggest you pick three sold-out shows that you want to see and a half hour before showtime go to the theater and ask if the house seats have been used. If not, they will sell them to you. Most likely you will get into one of them. These seats are sold at normal box office prices.

> Many theaters sell standing-room-only tickets; if you buy them you might get lucky and be able to sit down in someone's seat who has not shown up.

RECITALS AT JUILLIARD SCHOOL ★ (212) 799-5000

From the beginning of September till the end of May, Juilliard holds orchestra, dance, opera, chamber music, drama, and dance recitals. Most are free, others cost about $10. Call to get an upcoming listing; usually you can get tickets the day of the performance.

EVENTS AT CITY CENTER ★ 130 West 56th Street ★ (212) 247-0430

This is the home for most of the wonderful dance troupes in New York. Martha Graham, Alvin Ailey, The Joffrey, and more. If you buy a three-or-more performance series you will receive a discount off the box office price.

MUSEUMS

All the museums in the City, both big and small, offer memberships. Most of these memberships entitle you to a variety of discounts, mailings, openings, and more. Many of the black-tie openings can be quite a lot of fun, allowing you to get dressed up and rub elbows with the rich and famous. The following list gives the minimum amount you need to contribute to be invited to the black-tie affairs.

THE METROPOLITAN MUSEUM OF ART ★ Fifth Avenue at 82nd Street ★ (212) 570-3753

$300 a year to become a sustaining member.

THE GUGGENHEIM MUSEUM ★ 1071 Fifth Avenue ★ (212) 727-6200

$125 to be a fellow associate.

THE COOPER-HEWITT MUSEUM ★ 2 East 91st Street ★ (212) 860-6872

$250 to be a sustaining member.

MUSEUM OF MODERN ART ★ 11 West 53rd Street ★ (212) 708-9480

$200 a year to be a fellow.

THE AMERICAN MUSEUM OF NATURAL HISTORY ★ Central Park West at 79th Street ★ (212) 769-5606

$250 a year to be a supporter.

THE WHITNEY MUSEUM OF AMERICAN ART ★ 945 Madison Avenue (at 75th Street) ★ (212) 570-3600

$500 to become an associate member.

THEATER

AUDIENCE EXTRAS ★ 163 West 23rd Street ★ (212) 989-9550

This is the place that sells leftover tickets to all different kinds of theater events. There is a $79 annual fee to be able to purchase these tickets very inexpensively. A recording telling you everything that is available is updated weekly.

THE HIT SHOW CLUB ★ 630 Ninth Avenue ★ (212) 581-4211

This is a free club that distributes "twofer" coupons for certain Broadway plays. If you put your name on their mailing list they will send you coupons on a regular basis. These coupons should be brought to the particular box office and then you may purchase regular seats, two for the price of one.

TKTS ★ Duffy Square at 47th Street and Broadway, TKTS Ticket Booth at Two World Trade Center (mezzanine level), The Brooklyn booth at Borough Hall Park

This is the easiest way to obtain half-price tickets to Broadway and Off Broadway shows the day/night of the performance. They sell tickets to shows that are not already sold out. For each ticket bought there is a $1.50 handling fee.

THE THEATER DEVELOPMENT FUND ★ 1501 Broadway (43rd and 44th Streets) ★ (212) 221-0885

This organization supports the arts and artists in New York. In order to join you will need to fill out their application and send $5. Each month you receive a mailing that offers you discounts to shows in New York.

FREE CULTURAL EVENTS

Many public spaces, both indoor and outdoor, offer free concerts at lunchtime throughout the year—The Citicorp Center on 53rd and Lexington, South Street Seaport, The World Trade Center, The McGraw-Hill Building, The Exxon Building, and many more.

🍒 Lincoln Center's outdoor performances occur all summer long. They are usually held in one of Lincoln Center's three open spaces. Call the Lincoln Center hotline at (212) 875-5400.

🍒 The Metropolitan Opera performs in each borough during the summer. Call (212) 362-6000.

🍒 The New York Grand Opera performs in Central Park during the summer. Call (212) 245-8837.

🍒 Joseph Papp's New York Shakespeare Festival presents free performances in Central Park at The Delacorte Theater during the summer. Call (212) 598-7100.

🍒 The New York Philharmonic gives free performances in all the boroughs during June and July. Call (212) 580-8700.

🍒 Washington Square Music Festival offers free concerts during the summer. Call (212) 431-1088.

🍒 Neighborhood concerts are sponsored by Carnegie Free To The Public. Call (212) 903-9740 to see when a concert will be performed in your neighborhood.

The following places offer numerous events and activities for free:

- The Brooklyn Arts Council; call (718) 783-3077
- The Brooklyn Public Library; call (718) 780-7722
- Queens Borough Public Library; call (718) 990-0700
- The Bronx Ethnic Heritage Festival; call (212) 590-2654
- The New York Public Library; call (212) 621-0642

RESTAURANTS

If you would like to experience many of New York's finest restaurants but feel that the dinner bill will set you back a few months in rent money, there is a solution. Go for a drink of any kind. Listed below are some examples.

THE RAINBOW ROOM ★ 30 Rockefeller Plaza ★ (212) 632-5000
You can sit at a table in the Promenade Bar and order just a drink.

WINDOWS ON THE WORLD ★ World Trade Tower ★ (212) 938-1111
You can have a drink at the bar or at a table. After 7:30 P.M. there is a cover charge of $3.50 to hear the music.

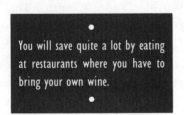

You will save quite a lot by eating at restaurants where you have to bring your own wine.

THE FOUR SEASONS ★ 99 East 52nd Street ★ (212) 754-9494
You can sit at a table in the grill room and have a drink.

LUTECE ★ 249 East 50th Street ★ (212) 752-2225
A drink can be had in the front room at their charming bar.

THE INTREPID PAGES
OF
WHERE TO VOLUNTEER IN NYC

There is more you can do than complain about what is wrong with New York City; you can actually help make it right. And in doing so we guarantee you will begin to like New York more and feel much more connected to the city in which you live and work.

TYPES OF VOLUNTEER WORK AVAILABLE

There are six general categories in which volunteers are needed. They are: culture, education, human services, recreation, public interest, and health. Within each of these categories there are numerous places you can work and many different jobs that need to be done.

Culture

Some of the places you can work:

★ museums
★ zoos
★ nursing homes
★ libraries
★ landmark preservation
★ environmental programs

Some of the work you can do:

★ serve as a docent
★ build exhibits
★ paint
★ perform
★ lead discussion groups

Education

Some of the places you can work:

★ elementary schools
★ youth programs
★ after-school programs

* community centers
* day-care centers

Some of the work you can do:

* tutor in a variety of subjects
* set up courses
* advocate
* teach résumé writing
* be a mentor

Human Services
Some of the places you can work:

* veterans groups
* AIDS organizations
* friendly visiting programs
* runaway programs
* telephone hotlines

Some of the work you can do:

* be a big brother/sister
* deliver food
* plan programs
* interpret/translate
* read to the blind

Recreation
Some of the places you can work:

* playgrounds
* settlement houses
* hobby clubs
* senior citizen centers
* parks

Some of the work you can do:

* help with animal care
* coach a team
* organize field trips
* raise funding for programs
* teach plant care

Public Interest
Some of the places you can work:

- ★ government agencies
- ★ criminal justice
- ★ school boards
- ★ community boards
- ★ tax offices

Some of the jobs you can do:

- ★ serve as a court liaison
- ★ write press releases
- ★ lobby for legislation
- ★ advise small businesses
- ★ research issues

Health

Some of the places you can work:

- ★ counseling centers
- ★ emergency disaster programs
- ★ infant/child development
- ★ rehabilitation clinics
- ★ hospice programs

Some of the work you can do:

- ★ teach parenting
- ★ keep records
- ★ drive an ambulance
- ★ entertain
- ★ feed and visit the ill and frail

HOW TO VOLUNTEER

The process can often seem forbidding but there are reasons why it can take a while to finally be placed and accepted by an agency. For one, the higher the skill level required of the job you want, the longer it will take to begin your work. In the extreme case it can take up to six months to begin.

Often the smaller, less glamorous or newer agencies are the ones that are most indebted to their volunteers.

There may be as many as five steps that you need to follow to find the right volunteer job for you.

1. Call and make an appointment with one of the six referral organizations listed below to begin your search for the specific agency that you want to volunteer for.

---

2. Once you decide on the agency, you will be asked to fill out an application.
3. After receiving your application they will ask you to come in for an interview.
4. If accepted you will have to go through a training or orientation period.
5. Then you will be ready to begin.

WHERE TO LOOK FOR A VOLUNTEER JOB

THE MAYOR'S VOLUNTARY ACTION CENTER ★ 61 Chambers Street ★ (212) 566-5950
Contact Carol Friedland, Deputy Director. The MVAC has been in existence for twenty-five years and is the largest clearinghouse for volunteers in the City of New York. They deal with over 2,000 different agencies in both the public and not-for-profit sector that offer nearly 3,000 different jobs. You need to make an appointment to go in for an interview. The good thing about the MVAC is the depth of their knowledge and the amount of agencies that deal with them. The bad thing is that it can take up to a month for them to meet with you.

NEW YORK CARES ★ 140 East 58th Street ★ (212) 753-6670
Contact Kenneth Adams, Executive Director. New York Cares was founded in 1986 to assist and organize people who wanted to volunteer but who were being discouraged by the long waiting time and the lack of any group activities. New York Cares organizes young working adults in hands-on projects with fifty not-for-profit agencies with which it is affiliated. For the most part, the volunteers work in team projects that address many of the City's most pressing social and environmental problems. They are sensitive to people's time constraints and therefore encourage people to serve whenever they can. If you want to volunteer, call and make an appointment to attend one of the two orientation meetings held each week. They field over one hundred teams a month that may be working on seventy-five different projects. Even though their emphasis is on the team approach, they do have the capability to place individuals in volunteer jobs. At present, they have over 2,000 active members.

THE VOLUNTEER REFERRAL AGENCY ★ 161 Madison Avenue ★ (212) 745-8249
This organization is associated with over 400 not-for-profit agencies throughout New York. It takes about one week to set up an appointment and, once there, they try to place you right away.

The following organizations are religious in their orientation; however, they all accept funding from the government and therefore service all people.

THE FEDERATION OF PROTESTANT WELFARE AGENCIES
★ 261 Park Avenue South ★ (212) 777-4800

Contact Peter Cavino, Program Associate. This group has connections to over 257 member agencies. They separate your volunteer interests into three different programs: (1) The Traditional Program—hands-on work, i.e., soup kitchens; (2) The Skilled Program—professional people who want to use their skills, i.e., lawyers and doctors; and (3) The Board Membership Program: people who have the talent and the expertise to sit on boards of newly emerging agencies. They do an initial screening over the phone and then set up an appointment to see you within the week.

THE UNITED JEWISH APPEAL–FEDERATION OF JEWISH PHILANTHROPIES
★ 130 East 59th Street ★ (212) 753-2288

Contact Sally Pearce, Volunteer Coordinator. The UJA is affiliated with over 130 agencies. After an initial screening over the phone, they will send you an application. The application gives them a profile of your talents, time commitments, and interests. Often, after receiving your application they can place you without coming in for an interview. The above procedure takes about two weeks.

CATHOLIC CHARITIES OF NEW YORK ★ 1011 First Avenue ★ (212) 371-1000

The Catholic Charities are connected to over one hundred different agencies that deal with the homeless, shelters, food programs, Big Brothers, and more. Sometimes they want to interview you and other times you are put into direct contact with the people for whom you want to work. Either way, the process takes about two weeks.

THE INTREPID PAGES
OF
LEISURE HOTLINES

CENTRAL PARK NUMBERS

(212) 794-6564

This number connects you to the Dairy in Central Park, which is the visitor's center. They hold a multitude of events all year long. You can get a calendar of Central Park events sent to you quarterly.

(212) 360-1333

This is a twenty-four-hour recorded hotline telling you all the park's daily events.

(800) 834-3832

If you need a live person at the Parks Department . . .

(212) 360-8133

This reaches the Arsenal, the office of permits for the park.

CITY-WIDE INFORMATION

(212) 397-8222

New York City Convention and Visitor's Bureau.

ARTS INFORMATION

(212) 956-2787

The Department of Cultural Affairs will tell you about events as well as send you printed information.

AFTERWORD: THE INTREPID PAGES OF SIMPLY THE BEST

The Intrepid New Yorker has a growing list of resources and stores that are simply the best. We couldn't find a place for many of these in the categories set up in this book. However, they certainly deserve to be listed and we think you deserve to know about them.

Milk in a bottle ★ **Ronnybrook Farm** ★ (518) 772-MILK
Lace designer ★ **Bianco** ★ (914) 762-0474
Massage studios ★ **Carapan** ★ 5 West 16th Street ★ (212) 633-6220
★ **The Stress Less Step** ★ 48 East 61st Street
★ (212) 826-6222
Women photographer ★ **Beth Green Studios** ★ (212) 580-1298
Personal poetry ★ **Carol Peck** ★ (516) 922-1031
Skin facial ★ **Elena Schell** ★ (212) 245-2170
Tennis pro ★ **Rick Meyer** ★ (212) 517-6852
Personal trainer ★ **John Claude West** ★ (212) 254-9134
Fish tackle shop ★ **Manhattan Custom Tackle** ★ (212) 964-1590
Group children
photographer ★ **Marty Hyman** ★ (516) 791-9292
Harp player for hire ★ **Wendy Kerner** ★ (203) 966-7616
Custom letter press ★ **The Petrarch Press** ★ (212) 362-7668
Calligrapher ★ **Signed, Sealed and Delivered** ★ (212) 633-0113
Private investigator ★ **Abe Berger** ★ (212) 688-4830
Children's birthday
party entertainer ★ **Wendy Gross** ★ (914) 725-6373
Waiters for hire ★ **New York Butler Service** ★ (212) 691-1798
Caterers ★ **Michael Thomas Catering** ★ (212) 966-0275
★ **Diane McConnell** ★ (212) 431-4104

Ice delivery ★ Casa Masina ★ (212) 355-3734

Party rental equipment ★ Party Rentals of New York ★ (212) 288-7384

Music D.J. company ★ Mobile Music ★ (914) 769-9056

Best salespeople at ★ Ann Taylor Stores

Manicurist ★ Jetta at Pierre Michel ★ (212) 593-1460

Children's cakes ★ Kids Kitchen ★ (212) 832-1952

Indoor fun with kids ★ Hackers, Hitters and Hoops ★ 123 West 18th Street ★ (212) 929-7482

Stew Leonard's Food Market in Norwalk, Connecticut ★ (203) 847-7213

Children's Museum ★ (212) 721-1234

F A O Schwarz ★ (212) 644-9400

Reasonably priced

fashion photographer ★ Victoria Arlak ★ (212) 879-0250

Children's magician ★ The Amazing Haroldini ★ (718) 627-3559

Outdoor fun with kids

(under $2 per child) ★ Tram ride to Roosevelt Island

South Street Seaport

Chinatown

Ferry to Staten Island

The Carousel in Central Park

The Clock Tower Building ★ 350 Broadway

Spice shop ★ Paprikas Weiss Importers ★ 1546 Second Avenue ★ (212) 288-6117

Monogramming shop ★ Hoofbeats ★ 1566 Second Avenue ★ (212) 517-2633

Gardening supplies ★ Farm and Garden Nursery ★ 2 Sixth Avenue ★ (212) 431-3577

Japanese art gallery ★ The Ronin Art Gallery ★ (212) 688-0188

Best one stop shopping ★ Bloomingdale's

Gifts that impress ★ any item from Cartier, Tiffany, or Hermes (they all have at least one item under $50)

★ Museum memberships

★ Broadway theater tickets

Music boxes ★ Rita Ford ★ 19 East 65th Street ★ (212) 535-6717

Historical research

center ★ Laura Hyland ★ (201) 333-0682

Bronze children's shoes ★ American Bronzing Company ★ P.O. Box 6504, Bexley, Ohio 43209

Reliable car repair

and body work ★ Joyson Auto Service ★ (212) 860-8888

Most practical car

for NYC ★ Honda Civic Wagon

Gift baskets ★ Finishing Touches ★ (203) 758-1449
Most accomplished
   up and coming artist ★ Rainer Gross ★ (212) 477-3859
Warhol-inspired
      portraits from
            photographs ★ Darlene Pike ★ (212) 475-8678
Humorous paintings
            of NYC life ★ Robert Lederman ★ (212) 268-3147
Best personal service
            company ★ The Intrepid New Yorker ★ (212) 534-5071

POSTSCRIPT

Hopefully you now share our belief that if you have the right attitude, knowledge, and skills, you stand a much better chance of getting what you want out of New York City. If you still need some professional assistance, The Intrepid New Yorker Company can help. As the number one personal-service business in the area, we provide the following:

Personal Services

☞ Problem solvers/ombudsmen
☞ Project expeditors
☞ Project researchers
☞ Home renovation managers
☞ Shopping specialists
☞ Resource service for the New York City area

Relocation Services
Relocation expeditors to New York area businesses. From giving neighborhood tours to getting a phone hooked up, we get the new employee settled in New York City. The idea is to make him or her more productive in the workplace—faster.

Customized Seminars
Workshops for both corporations and individuals on how to turn copping into thriving day-to-day in New York City.

Newsletter
This quarterly newsletter to subscribers provides up-to-the minute, thoroughly researched information on thematic topics essential to New Yorkers, as well as tricks, tips, and approaches to saving money and coping in all areas of a New Yorker's life.

INDEX

INDEX   •   **359**

ABOUT THE AUTHORS

KATHY MAYER BRADDOCK, a lifelong Manhattan resident, is the founder of New York City's number one personal-service business, The Intrepid New Yorker.

TORY BAKER MASTERS, veteran New Yorker and Intrepid New Yorker partner, is a former network television producer and programming executive.

INTREPID NEW YORKER MEMBERSHIP

Pamper yourself. For $75 a year, become a member of The Intrepid New Yorker and get quality customized service at even lower prices:

- ☛ 15 percent off our hourly rate whenever you use our personal service.
- ☛ Eight free phone referrals to our most current and exclusive sources. We will match you up with just the right service for your needs and give you a formal introduction to the person in charge of the respective service to insure that you are in the right hands.
- ☛ Our *Intrepid Newsletter*—free of charge.
- ☛ A monthly statement of all your transactions with our company.

For further information call or write to :

> The Intrepid New Yorker Company
> 1230 Park Avenue
> New York, NY 10128
> (212) 534-5071

WE WANT YOUR TIPS, TRICKS, AND APPROACHES TO LIVING IN NYC

New Yorkers aren't true New Yorkers if they haven't found or invented their own coping and survival techniques. We'd like to get *your* personal tips, tricks, and approaches to living here. If one of your ideas gets printed, it will appear either in a subsequent book or in an issue of our newsletter, with your byline attached. And you will also receive a $25 coupon in the mail toward the use of our personal service. Coupons are limited to two per person, per year. To send your idea(s), fill out the following form:

To: The Intrepid New Yorker Company
1230 Park Avenue
New York, NY 10128

From: _____

I want my $25 coupon sent to:

Address _____

_____

_____

Idea(s): _____

_____

_____

_____

_____

_____